Databases:
A Primer
For Retrieving
Information
By Computer

Susanne M. Humphrey
Information Scientist
National Library of Medicine
Bethesda, Maryland

Biagio John Melloni
Special Expert in Biomedical Communication (retired)
National Library of Medicine

A Reston Book
Prentice-Hall, Inc.
Englewood Cliffs, New Jersey 07632

Library of Congress Cataloging in Publication Data

Humphrey, Susanne M.
    Databases: a primer for retrieving information by
computer.

    Bibliography: p.
    Includes index.
    1. Data base management.   2. Information storage
and retrieval systems.   I. Melloni, Biagio John.
II. Title.
QA76.9.D3H85 1986   001.64′2   85-2179
ISBN 0–8359–1319–8

QA 76.9
D3
H85
1986

A Reston Book
Published by Prentice-Hall, Inc.
A Division of Simon & Schuster, Inc.
Englewood Cliffs, NJ 07632

ABSTRAX™   Information Sources, Ltd.
Auto-Cite™   Service of The Lawyer's Co-operative Publishing Company
    and its affiliate Bancroft-Whitney
BRS/Search®   BRS Information Technologies
CAS Online®   American Chemical Society
Chemical Abstracts®   American Chemical Society
Chemical Abstracts Service®   American Chemical Society
DIALOG®   DIALOG Information Services, Inc.
ENVIROLINE®   EIC/Intelligence, Inc.
ERIC®   National Institute of Education
LEXIS®   Mead Data Central
LEXPAT™   Mead Data Central
LEXTRACK™   Mead Data Central
MEDLARS®   National Library of Medicine
MeSH®   National Library of Medicine
NAARS™   Joint service of Mead Data Central and American Institute
    of Certified Public Accountants
National Newspaper Index™   Information Access Co.
NewsNet®   NewsNet, Inc.
NEXIS®   Mead Data Central
ORBIT®   SDC Information Services, Inc.
SDC®   SDC Information Services, Inc.
Shepard's®   Shepard's Division of McGraw-Hill (Shepard's/McGraw-Hill)
WILSONLINE℠   H. W. Wilson Co.

10 9 8 7 6 5 4 3 2 1

PRINTED IN THE UNITED STATES OF AMERICA

Contents

Chapter 7: Search Statement Result, Development of Search
Strategy and Formulation, 81

Chapter 8: Controlled Indexing Vocabulary for Searching
by Subject, 97

Chapter 11: Displaying Output, Offline Printout, Searching in Batch Mode, 167

Chapter 12: Saving Searches, Saving Output, 177

Chapter 13: Database Retrieval, 187

Chapter 14: Friendly Computers, Intelligent Computers, 197

Chapter 15: The Microcomputer Influence: Developments in Database Retrieval, 209

Chapter 16: Selecting a Retrieval Service, 225

Appendix A: Selected Major Computerized Retrieval Services, with Databases, 245

Preface

The National Council of Teachers of Mathematics has stated that "computer literacy is an essential outcome of contemporary education." One needs only to consider that by the time today's eighth grader is graduated from high school, 80 percent of all job opportunities will involve computers in some way. Interacting with computers, knowing how to harness the immense efficiency of this technology, is a salable skill. It translates into higher incomes for those possessing this knowledge.

According to John Naisbitt, author of the best seller *Megatrends,* schools around the nation are beginning to realize that in the "information society" in which we live, the two required languages are English and computer. At the university level there is a surge in registration for computer courses. Even in the public school system, computer use is on the increase. In the world of business, executives are enrolling in basic computer courses to get a handle on this technology. Scientists throughout the world rely on the computer for current literature searches so essential to their work. Computer learning is rapidly flouishing; the main motivational force behind the computer literacy boom throughout society is the downright necessity to get the most relevant and up-to-date information immediately and efficiently.

The purpose of this book is to help those individuals, whether students or professionals, scientists or corporate executives, in their role of information consumer, so that they can effectively interact with today's rapidly emerging computerized retrieval resources. The book is a primer, taking the reader through the fundamentals of computerized retrieval. No previous knowledge about computer science or any other discipline is assumed or required of the reader for full comprehension of the material. With a solid grasp of basic retrieval techniques, one can be assured of success in getting information at will, instantly, and with great satisfaction.

Since mid-1984, there are close to 2400 unique databases stored in the computers of about 345 retrieval services that offer online access to information to anyone with a computer terminal or personal computer and a modem that connects it to a telephone line. These databases contain information that benefit information consumers. No one should be denied access to these valuable stores of knowledge because of lack of retrieval skills.

In 1983 the Special Interest Group on User Online Interaction of the American Society for Information Science predicted:

> The area of direct "end user" access to online services is beginning. Major vendors are providing attractive combinations of low rates and popular databases to users in offices, schools, and homes. The role of the "intermediary" and "knowledge broker" will change from direct searching to user training and support. Vendors will also increase their training programs and improve online assistance features. . . .*

Yet in that same year a review of the status of user education and training in online database retrieval stated:

> . . . information education must be directed to the educator (high school teacher, college professor) as well as to the students who will become the end-user scientists of tomorrow. We hope to see more descriptions of creative and innovative user education programs in the literature, with greater detail about content and format than have appeared so far.**

Students today in junior and intermediate schools are generally still being taught library skills much as their parents were taught when they were the same age—instruction in the use of card catalogs, reference books, and published indexes. These methods are in stark contrast to the sophisticated techniques that are fast becoming standard in the research, academic, technical, and business world, not only at professional and graduate levels but also in undergraduate schools, which some of these students will be entering in less than four years.

This book is written for professionals and students of information science. However, as this is the age of the "end-user," this book is also intended for anyone who feels the need for a basic understand-

---

*"Productivity in the Information Age." Program of the 46th ASIS Annual Meeting, Washington, DC, October 2–6, 1983.

**M. Lynne Neufeld and Martha Cornog, "Secondary Information Systems and Services." *Annual Review of Information Science and Technology* 1983; 18:151–83.

ing of retrieving information by computer. Different approaches for the information science professional and the general readership are suggested in the Preface under "How to Use this Book."

In writing this book, we felt that using the conventions and formats of a particular retrieval system would be too confining since no single system exhibits all the features of computerized retrieval that we intend to discuss. Using more than one existing system would invariably lead to detailed comparisons, an approach we felt would be confusing and counterproductive for teaching the fundamentals of the subject. Except for Chapter 1, which uses examples of interactions with selected retrieval services to highlight the utility of computerized database retrieval, we preferred to forego the authenticity of "real" but rather complicated computer inputs and outputs in favor of examples that are directly to the point of the topic under discussion. The examples are nevertheless authentic since they are based on a composite of the real features and capabilities of today's computerized retrieval systems.

An advantage to this approach is that it does not necessitate having ready access to a computerized retrieval service. Furthermore, this book will provide information and a perspective that will prepare the reader for training under a formal agreement with a commercial retrieval service.

Interactive computerized retrieval of information from online databases has existed for more than ten years. It is just becoming widespread because of the new technologies, particularly in microcomputers. This book conveys the principles that are currently the basis for retrieving information from the growing number and diversity of accessible databases in a way that will prepare the reader for choosing, learning, or mastering a particular system.

Chapter 1 serves as a preview, relating the essence, value, and significance of computerized information retrieval. It cites simple but authentic examples of retrievals (using three well-known retrieval services), which highlight the advantages of computerization.

ORGANIZATION OF THE BOOK

Chapters 2 and 3 describe how information is stored and organized for retrieval. It follows an extended example of information a school might have about its students. This example is used for emphasizing the difficulties in searching and maintaining a noncomputerized information store. Chapter 4 consists of a general discussion of the organization and maintenance of information in the computer, as a contrast to the previous chapter.

Chapters 5-12 cover in detail the basic principles and practices of computerized retrieval without being specific to any existing system.

Chapter 5 introduces the model used throughout the remainder of the book—a hypothetical system for retrieving information from a file consisting of two bibliographic records. Complete coverage of logical notation used in retrieval for combining concepts one wishes to search is provided in Chapter 6. Included is a chapter on controlled indexing vocabulary (Chapter 8) for searching by subject, since many retrieval systems contain databases that are indexed in this way. The end of Chapter 7 begins the development of an actual search strategy, which is continued in Chapters 8–10; in each of these chapters, the developing strategy is based on new information covered in the respective chapters.

Chapter 13 introduces the organizational aspect of computerized retrieval, including relationships and interactions among users, retrieval services, database suppliers, and telecommunications networks that characterize "database retrieval" as opposed to the retrieval of records from files.

Chapter 14 discusses the concept of user-friendliness as applied to command languages and search formulation. The notion of intelligent computer retrieval, based on the techniques of artificial intelligence, is introduced, which, if implemented on a wide scale, could make obsolete computerized information retrieval as it presently exists. The widespread application of intelligent computer retrieval to the diversity of publicly available databases is, however, not imminent.

Chapter 15 focuses on the impact of microcomputers on retrieval. Microcomputers function as terminals that may be connected to retrieval service computers. They also use special computer programs (microcomputer software) that supplement the traditional retrieval functions by allowing retrieved information to be reformatted, repackaged, and re-used. These capabilities are affecting the form information will take, how information will be transmitted, and the organizations that will emerge for spearheading these impending changes.

Chapter 16 offers practical steps for finding out about available information retrieval services and suggests criteria for selecting a retrieval service. It is in the form of an extensive checklist, which incorporates retrieval features discussed throughout the book.

Appendix A provides information about eight major computerized database retrieval services in the United States, including their databases, with database suppliers. Appendix B cites selected sources for additional information on computerized retrieval, including organizations and various forms of written material. Appendix C cites selected readings from the recent literature that might interest the more serious students. Definitions have been placed in a glossary at the end of the book.

Readers who are students of information science may read the chapters in sequence as they appear, or take the approach recommended for the general readership.

HOW TO USE THE BOOK

For the general readership, we recommend reading the chapters in a sequence that first presents the basic principles of retrieval. The reader may then return to the remaining chapters for more detail and supplementary information. The recommended sequence is Chapters 1, 2, 5–8, 12, 13, and 16. Complete utilization of the latter part of Chapter 16, on criteria for selecting a retrieval service, will be based not only on the chapters in this sequence but also on some of the chapters that were skipped. At that point, the reader might turn to Chapters 9–11 in order to receive a fuller benefit of the selection criteria. Chapters 3 and 4 expand the reader's foundation on the organization of information in a file. Chapters 14 and 15 present a comprehensive overview of current trends and future directions in computerized database retrieval.

ACKNOWLEDGMENTS

For their encouragement, interest, and assistance, we thank Edward T. Cremmins, Donna R. Dolan, Karen Dowling, Lynn M. El-Hoshy, Andrew C. Humphrey, Andrew C. Humphrey, Jr., Amalie Kriss, F. Wilfrid Lancaster, Gary Letourneau, William F. Marovitz, Roy Rada, Roger K. Summit, and our anonymous reviewers. Throughout the preparation of this book we have enjoyed the most cordial relationship with our publisher.

Computerized Information Retrieval: A Preview

The notion of database, central to computerized information retrieval, is rather simple. A database is nothing more than an organized collection of information stored in the computer. Retrieval from this information store is basically accomplished through a matching process. You, as a customer of the information store, need certain information that you surmise can be found in the database, and you interact with the computer to locate that information. This process of matching your query against information in databases is the essence of computerized information retrieval.

DATABASES AND RETRIEVAL

Why search for information by computer? With a terminal (or microcomputer used as a terminal) and a telephone connection you can be seconds away from receiving valuable information on any imaginable topic. These rich and voluminous databases are stored in large computers that belong to information companies or agencies known as retrieval services. Once you are connected to them, much of the world's knowledge literally will be at your fingertips.

As an information source, a database may be shared by thousands of users simultaneously, and it is available whenever the retrieval service is in operation. There is no limit to the number of times a database can be searched or the number of times an item can be displayed. Unlike a library book, databases do not deteriorate physically, nor can they be misplaced, stolen, or vandalized.

DATABASE AVAILABILITY

In mid-1984 there were 2400 databases available through 345 retrieval services, and the number is growing rapidly. There is coverage in virtually all areas of knowledge: science, engineering, mathematics, medicine, agriculture, psychology, sociology, philosophy, law, business, economics, education, and more.

DATABASE COVERAGE

REFERRAL DATABASES

Databases may consist primarily of "referral" information. For example, bibliographic databases consist of references that provide information for locating full text documents, such as books and magazine articles. Many of these databases contain not only references but also abstracts of these documents, which greatly enhance one's ability to decide if there is an actual need to see the entire document. In many cases, the abstract itself may suffice.

Referral databases usually are not limited to material in a specific physical collection. You may obtain material through several sources—your local library (even if the item is not in the collection at the time), the retrieval service, or a source cited in the database reference itself.

A single database may refer to a variety of sources, including magazine articles, books, government documents, industry reports, papers at meetings, newspaper items, films, videorecordings, and computer software packages. Figure 1.1 (a–e) is a search on the topic of the Clean Water Act performed against the DIALOG® retrieval service's ENVIROLINE® (File 40) database, supplied by EIC/Intelligence, Inc., New York, NY. The five retrieved items selected for display are references to several types of sources—Senate hearing,

```
? s clean(w)water(w)act
            1    106
? t 1/7/1,3,4,7,30
1/7/1
    170863    *84-002796
    EXTENDING AND AMENDING THE CLEAN WATER ACT ,
    SEN COMM ENV PUBLIC WORKS HEARINGS 98 CON 1 98-247, APR 6, JUN 14, 83,
(1181)
    HEARING TRANSCRIPT: HEARINGS WERE CONVENED TO CONSIDER S. 431, A BILL
TO AMEND THE FEDERAL POLLUTION CONTROL ACT OF 1977 TO AUTHORIZE FUNDS
FOR FY 83-87. ALSO DISCUSSED WAS S. 432, A BILL TO AMEND THE 1977 ACT TO
EXTEND THE 1984 COMPLIANCE DATE FOR RECENTLY ESTABLISHED REQUIREMENTS.
THESE COMPLIANCE EXTENSIONS ARE DEEMED ESSENTIAL FOR THE 17 INDUSTRIAL
CATEGORIES FOR WHICH EFFLUENT GUIDELINES HAVE NOT AS OF YET BEEN ISSUED.
PROVISIONS OF THE .PROPOSED LEGISLATION ALSO ADDRESS HAZARDOUS WASTE
TREATMENT AND DISPOSAL, WATER QUALITY STANDARDS, WASTEWATER OUTFALLS IN
COASTAL WATERS, AND WATER QUALITY IN THE CHESAPEAKE AND NARRAGANSETT
BAYS. TESTIMONY WAS DELIVERED BY ROBERT ABRAMS OF THE UNIV. OF MICHIGAN,
SEN. WILLIAM PROXMIRE (D-WI), TAYLOR BANKS OF NRDC, AND OTHERS. RELATED
DOCUMENTS AND MEMORANDA ARE INCLUDED.
```
(a)

FIGURE 1.1 (a–e). A search against the ENVIROLINE® (File 40) database using DIALOG® on the topic of the Clean Water Act showing five sources: (a) Senate hearing; (b) Senate committee report; (c) article in *Sierra* magazine; (d) Library of Congress report; and (e) paper presented at the National Water Conference. *(© Copyright, EIC/Intelligence, Inc., New York, NY.)*

1/7/3
170130   *84-002063
CLEAN WATER ACT AMENDMENTS OF 1983 ,
SEN COMM ENV PUBLIC WORKS 98 CON 1 REPORT 98-233, SEP 83, (61)
   S. 431, A BILL TO AMEND THE FEDERAL WATER POLLUTION CONTROL ACT OF
1977, IS PROFILED. REAUTHORIZATION OF THE ACT IS REQUIRED TO CONTINUE
PROTECTING AND RESTORING THE QUALITY OF WATER RESOURCES. INDUSTRIAL
WASTE PRETREATMENT CRITERIA INTRODUCED IN THE ORIGINAL DRAFT OF THE BILL
HAVE BEEN DELETED. OTHER PROVISIONS MANDATE STATES TO UNDERTAKE A
PROGRESSIVE PROGRAM DIRECTED AT REDUCING TOXIC POLLUTANT LOADS WHERE
BEST AVAILABLE TECHNOLOGY IS INSUFFICIENT TO MEET STATE WATER QUALITY
STANDARDS. OTHER TOPICS COVERED IN THE BILL ARE COMPLIANCE DATES, OCEAN
DISCHARGE WAIVERS, SEWAGE SLUDGE MANAGEMENT, CIVIL AND CRIMINAL
PENALTIES, NAT'L POLLUTANT DISCHARGE ELIMINATION SYSTEM PERMITS,
NONPOINT SOURCE POLLUTION, AND STORMWATER RUNOFF FROM MINING OPERATIONS.

(b)

1/7/4
169571   *84-001504
THE CLEAN WATER ACT: NEW THREATS FROM TOXIC WASTES DEMAND A STRONGER
LAW; STRENGTHENING WETLANDS PROTECTION ,
   BRODIE, PAMELA ; ELDER, JIM
   SIERRA CLUB, DC
   SIERRA, SEP-OCT 83, V68, N5, P39, (6)
   THE FEDERAL WATER POLLUTION CONTROL ACTS OF 1972 AND 1977 WERE ENACTED
TO RESTORE AND MAINTAIN THE PHYSICAL, CHEMICAL, AND BIOLOGICAL INTEGRITY
OF U.S. WATER RESOURCES. ALTHOUGH SOME WATER BODIES HAVE BEEN RESTORED
TO PRISTINE CONDITIONS, OTHERS ARE GETTING WORSE. FUROR OVER
CONVENTIONAL POLLUTANTS IS GIVING WAY TO CONCERN OVER TOXIC SUBSTANCES
IN WATER RESOURCES. THE ACT IS DUE FOR REAUTHORIZATION, AND STRINGENT
REGULATIONS GOVERNING TOXIC POLLUTION MUST BE INCORPORATED INTO THE
STATUTE. MOST OF THE CONGRESSIONAL MEMBERS CONSIDERING THE
REAUTHORIZATION INTEND TO RESIST ATTEMPTS TO WEAKEN IT. SECTION 404 OF
THE ACT, WHICH SERVES TO PROTECT LANDS FROM HAPHAZARD DEVELOPMENT,
MUST ALSO BE RETAINED. (3 PHOTOS)

(c)

1/7/7
169408   *84-001341
WATER QUALITY: IMPLEMENTING THE CLEAN WATER ACT ,
   COPELAND, CLAUDIA
   US LIBRARY OF CONGRESS CONGRESSIONAL RESEARCH SERVICE REPORT IB83030,
JUN 28, 83, (21)
   THE 1972 CLEAN WATER ACT AND THE 1977 AMENDMENTS AUTHORIZED $49
BILLION IN MUNICIPAL WASTEWATER TREATMENT PLANT CONSTRUCTION, WITH THE
GOALS OF ZERO DISCHARGE OF POLLUTANTS BY 1985 AND WATER QUALITY THAT IS
FISHABLE AND SWIMMABLE BY MID-1983. IN ADDITION TO THE CONSTRUCTION
GRANTS, REGULATION OF INDUSTRIAL AND MUNICIPAL DISCHARGERS-INCLUDING THE
REQUIREMENT OF ''BEST AVAILABLE TECHNOLOGY''-FORMED THE SECOND MAJOR
PART OF THE ACT. FEDERAL JURISDICTION IS BROAD AND CERTAIN
RESPONSIBILITIES ARE DELEGATED TO THE STATES, SUCH AS ISSUING PERMITS TO

POINT SOURCE DISCHARGERS, ADMINISTERING PORTIONS OF THE CONSTRUCTION
GRANTS PROGRAM, AND PARTIAL REGULATION OF DREDGE OR FILL MATERIAL DUMPED
INTO U.S. WATERWAYS. PROGRESS ON THESE FRONTS IS CHRONICLED. OTHER
ISSUES DISCUSSED INCLUDE FORMULATING STANDARDS FOR TOXIC POLLUTANTS,
WATER QUALITY STANDARDS, NONPOINT SOURCE POLLUTION (URBAN AND
AGRICULTURAL RUNOFF), BUDGET PROPOSALS FOR FY 84, OCEAN DUMPING, AND
PROPOSED LEGISLATION. (NUMEROUS REFERENCES, 1 TABLE)

(d)

```
1/7/30
   161786   *83-000671
   THE CHANGING POLITICAL ECONOMY AND THE CLEAN WATER ACT ,
   LINDON, RON M.
   ASSN METROPOLITAN SEWERAGE AGENCIES
   PRESENTED AT ACADEMY OF NATURAL SCIENCES/ET AL NATL WATER CONF,
PHILADELPHIA, JAN 26-27, 82, P123, (17)
   SURVEY REPORT: UNTIL 1940, ATTENTION TO WATER POLLUTION IN THE U.S.
WAS CONFINED TO TECHNICAL RESEARCH AND ANALYSIS. ENACTMENT OF THE
FEDERAL WATER POLLUTION CONTROL ACT OF 1948 CONFIRMED THE WATER
POLLUTION ISSUE TO BE A POLITICAL AS WELL AS A SCIENTIFIC PROBLEM. A
GROWING AWARENESS IN ALL LEVELS OF GOVERNMENT OF THE POLLUTION PROBLEM
IS EVIDENT DURING 1940-60. AMENDMENTS TO THE ACT IN 1972 AND 1977
INCREASED THE NATION'S COMMITMENT TO THE WATER POLLUTION ISSUE. NUMEROUS
LAKES, RIVERS, AND STREAMS HAVE BEEN REVITALIZED BECAUSE OF THE ACT AND
ITS CONSTRUCTION GRANTS PROGRAM.
```

(e)

FIGURE 1.1 (Cont.).

Senate committee report, article in the magazine *Sierra,* Library of
Congress report, and a paper presented at the National Water Conference.

SOURCE DATABASES

The other type of database consists of "source" information. Included in this category are reference works such as handbooks and
encyclopedias. Full text documents, such as magazine articles, newsletter items, and even entire books, are beginning to comprise source
databases, a trend that is more than likely to accelerate. The older
retrieval services that started with only referral databases are starting
to add source databases, while some of the newer services are spe-
cializing in source databases from the very beginning.

A search for handbook information on dehydration was per-
formed against the BRS retrieval service's full text Comprehensive
Core Medical Library (CCML) database, supplied by BRS/Saunders,
New York, NY. The retrieved item shown in Figure 1.2 is an outline
comprising chapter six from "The Physician's Book of Lists"
(Churchill Livingstone Inc., New York, NY), one of the electronic

```
1_:      dehydration

RESULT      174

2_:      ..print 1 au,ti,so,ch,tx/doc=131
```

131
AU Margulies, David M., M.D.; Thaler, Malcolm S., M.D.
TI Fluids and Electrolytes/Dehydration.
SO Margulies, D.M., M.D.; Thaler, M.S., M.D. The Physician's Book of
   Lists. New York: Churchill Livingstone Inc., 1983.
CH 6: pp 180.
TX 1 OF 1.

DEHYDRATION
1. Signs and Symptoms
    a. Orthostatic hypotension
    b. Tachycardia
    c. Weak pulse
    d. Poor skin turgor (test over sternum or forehead)
    e. Dry mucous membranes
    f. Low jugular venous pressure
    g. Diminished axillary sweat
    h. Dry tongue with deep furrows
    i. Weight loss (often exceeding 0.2 kg/day)
    j. Apathy
    k. Weakness
2. Laboratory
    a. Increased hemoglobin and hematocrit
    b. Prerenal azotemia (elevated BUN and creatinine with BUN:
       Creatinine ratio > 15)
    c. NA+ may be low, normal, or high
    d. Diminished CVP and pulmonary wedge pressures.

FIGURE 1.2. An outline from "The Physician's Book of Lists" resulting from a search for handbook information on dehydration against
the Comprehensive Care Medical Library (CCML) database using BRS.
(*From Margulies, David M. and Thaler, Malcolm S.:* The Physician's
Book of Lists. *Copyright © 1983. Used by permission of Churchill Livingstone Inc., New York, N.Y.*)

textbooks in this database. (Most chapters are much longer and more
comprehensive than this chapter, which was selected for its brevity.)

Although some databases have corresponding publications, the computerized version may have information not available in the printed
form. In some cases there is simply no published counterpart to the
computerized form at all. The printed form is becoming an endangered species.

**NONPUBLISHED
DATABASES**

CURRENT AND SPECIFIC SUBJECT TERMS

Databases easily provide information on current topics that would be difficult to find using subject terms in published indexes. In addition, topics may be too specific to be printed subject headings (for example, specific laws such as the Clean Water Act in the sample search discussed earlier).

Topics have only to be named in portions of the database, such as in titles or abstracts, to be searchable by computer. For example, if during 1983 you had been given an assignment to report on the Contadora Group, you would have been unlikely to find it in any published reference book or as a subject heading in a published index. However, the computer search of a magazine index with abstracts would have provided valuable information in seconds (see Figure 1.3). Retrieval is from the BRS retrieval service's ABSTRAX™ 400 (A400) database, supplied by Information Sources, Ltd., Galway, Ireland (U.S. distribution/marketing by J. A. Micropublishing, Eastchester, NY). The two retrieved items selected for display are references with abstracts to magazine articles.

The items displayed include the definition of Contadora Group and the gist of the situation. Depending on the level of detail required

```
   1_:     Contadora

   RESULT        13

   2_:     ..print 1 au,ti,so,ab/doc=3,13

   3
TI TITLE: A regional solution?  (the Contadora Group's peace efforts).
SO SOURCE: World Press Review.  v30.  October, 1983.  p37(2).
AB ABSTRACT: The Contadora Group's peace making task in Central
   America is a difficult one.  At its July 1983 meeting in Cancun,
   Mexico, the Group suggested demilitarized areas, joint border
   patrol, and attempts to prevent superpower interference.  President
   Fidel Castro supports the Group.  President Reagan is less
   enthusiastic.  A regional solution is becoming less likely.
   Castro's soothing declaration raises hopes that a Reagan-Castro
   understanding could end the conflict.  Continuing tension between
   Cuba and the United States will hinder peace efforts.  Presidents of
   the Group's member countries have initiated contact with involved
   countries.  The Group faces the difficulty of persuading rebels to
   abandon violent methods for the electoral process and of encouraging
   multilateral dialogue.  E.O'D.
```

(a)

FIGURE 1.3 (a–b). References with abstracts from a search on the Contadora Group in the ABSTRAX™ 400 (A400) database using BRS. (© *Copyright, information Sources, Ltd., Galway, Ireland, U.S. distributor J.A. Micropublishing, Eastchester, NY.*)

```
     13
AU AUTHOR/S: Stone, Marvin.
TI TITLE: Next in Central America?
SO SOURCE: U.S. News and World Report.  v95.  July 11, 1983.  p76(1).
AB ABSTRACT: President Reagan is faced with a very tough decision on
     whether or not to send United States troops to prevent the spread of
     Marxism in Central America.  Either way, he will lose a lot of
     support.  Congress is against intervention but the country's
     security must be protected.  The President would not use the word
     'never' when he said that troops would not be sent there.  Since an
     agreement between the U.S. and Cuba in 1962, no Soviet missiles can
     be placed around Cuba.  The White House must find a solution by
     negotiation.  The Contadora Group which includes Mexico, Panama,
     Venezuela and Columbia may be able to negotiate first.  G.T.
```

(b)

in your assignment, they may provide sufficient information, thereby making the need to obtain the complete documents unnecessary. Note that the word "Contadora" is only in the abstract of the second item, so that even if you knew to look under Central America in a published index without abstracts, you would not have known that it referred to an article that discusses the Contadora Group.

REGULARLY UPDATED CUMULATIONS

In general, information is referenced sooner in computer indexes than in their published counterparts, where it takes at least six months before information is referenced. Most databases represent several years of accumulated information. They remain cumulative with the addition of regularly scheduled updates. In contrast, published indexes may be produced in several volumes during the year. For example, manually finding the references retrieved in the Contadora search, the first published in July and the second in October, may well have required a search through two quarterly volumes of a published index.

SEARCH OF NONTOPICAL CATEGORIES

Databases allow you to limit your retrieval by nontopical aspects, also not usually indexed in printed indexes—publication date, type of document, language, author addresses, sponsoring organizations, geographic locations, etc. In this type of search, sometimes merely the number of items retrieved can be an answer to your query.

The search in Figure 1.4 was performed against the DIALOG® retrieval service's American Men and Women of Science (File 236) database, a biographical registry of 130,000 eminent, active American and Canadian scientists, supplied by R. R. Bowker, New York, NY. A display of only the counts of items in the database is used for answering the queries "How many scientists in this registry have degrees

```
? s ed=BROWN(w)ed=UNIV or ed=COLUMBIA(w)ed=UNIV or ed=CORNELL or
ed=DARTMOUTH or ed=HARVARD or ed=UNIV(w)ed=PA or ed=PRINCETON or
ed=YALE
                    1287  ED=BROWN(W)ED=UNIV
                    4027  ED=COLUMBIA(W)ED=UNIV
                    5094  ED=CORNELL
                     653  ED=DARTMOUTH
                    5452  ED=HARVARD
                    2384  ED=UNIV(W)ED=PA
                    2393  ED=PRINCETON
                    3096  ED=YALE
            1 22218
? s ed=UNIV(w)ed=ILL or ed=IND(w)ed=UNIV or ed=UNIV(w)ed=IOWA or
ed=UNIV(w)ed=MICH or ed=MICH(w)ed=STATE or ed=UNIV(w)ed=MINN or
ed=NORTHWESTERN(w)ed=UNIV or ed=OHIO(w)ed=STATE or ed=PURDUE or
ed=UNIV(w)ed=WIS
                    6451  ED=UNIV(W)ED=ILL
                    1489  ED=IND(W)ED=UNIV
                    1616  ED=UNIV(W)ED=IOWA
                    4768  ED=UNIV(W)ED=MICH
                    2445  ED=MICH(W)ED=STATE
                    3946  ED=UNIV(W)ED=MINN
                    1999  ED=NORTHWESTERN(W)ED=UNIV
                    3539  ED=OHIO(W)ED=STATE
                    3882  ED=PURDUE
                    5774  ED=UNIV(W)ED=WIS
            2 32952
```

FIGURE 1.4. A search on educational background of scientists against R.R. Bowker's American Men and Women of Science (File 236) database using DIALOG® illustrating counts of items for answering queries and the OR operator.

from Ivy League universities? How many have degrees from the Big Ten universities of the Midwest?'' The search statements for Ivy League and for Big Ten each illustrate the OR operator, which allows you to search topics in parallel without regard for whether or not the topics intersect; in this instance, each university is a topic.

HUMAN-COMPUTER INTERACTION

Let's discuss the advantages of computerized retrieval from the standpoint of the process itself. The computer allows you to be in control. The computer gives you customized service. Interacting with the computer allows a freshness of thought, enabling you to pursue ideas immediately without outside interference, without even leaving your chair. Knowing how to search by computer will make you more independent in your quest for information than you even thought possible. The computer is patient and will never think less of you when you make a mistake or appear unfamiliar with commands. The computer will help you by displaying guides. In time, a bond will develop between you and the computer that will have a positive effect on your retrieval abilities.

The computer respects your schedule. It is available for hours at a time. When it is not available for direct interaction, or when you are busy doing other things, you can instruct the computer to search without your presence and then send the results to you the following day. You can even arrange for the computer to search specific topics automatically against newly added information whenever a database is updated, thereby providing you with a customized current awareness service.

COMPUTER PROCESSING AVAILABILITY

Just three words—AND, OR, NOT—account for the immense power of computerized retrieval. An entire chapter in this book is devoted to covering these logical operators, or special computer words used for combining search terms. The AND operator enables you to cross-sect topics, each of which would by itself retrieve a large number of items, in order to retrieve the relatively few items that are exactly on your topic.

COMBINING SEARCH TERMS

For example, to research the topic "effect of television on public elections," the search in Figure 1.5 was performed against the DIALOG® retrieval service's National Newspaper Index™ (File 111)

```
? s television and elections
             14456 TELEVISION
              8480 ELECTIONS
        1      87
? t 1/3/8,9,11
1/3/8
0839959   DATABASE: NNI File 111
  Letter asks networks to  withhold projections.  (California Democrats'
letter)
  New York Times   v133   Section 1  p20(N) p26(L)  May 13  1984
  CODEN: NYTIA
  col 6   002 col in.
  EDITION: Sun
  GEOGRAPHIC LOCATION: California
  GEOGRAPHIC CODE: NNUSWCA
  DESCRIPTORS:  public opinion  polls-television  use;  Democratic Party
(California)-political activity; California-elections
```
(a)

FIGURE 1.5 (a–c). References to *The New York Times* from a search on the effect of television on public elections performed against the National Newspaper Index™ (File 111) database using DIALOG® illustrating the AND operator. (© *Copyright, Information Access Company, Belmont CA.*)

```
1/3/9
 0837294   DATABASE: NNI File 111
  Polls near voting places banned in Minnesota.
  New York Times   v133  pA12(L)  April 30  1984
  CODEN: NYTIA
  col 6   002 col in.
  EDITION: Mon
  GEOGRAPHIC LOCATION: Minnesota
  GEOGRAPHIC CODE: NNUSCMN
  DESCRIPTORS: public opinion polls-television use; Minnesota-elections
```

(b)

```
1/3/11
 0821259   DATABASE: NNI File 111
  Democracy  enlarged; also polluted; cheating the voters on the evening
news. (TV network abuse of exit polls) (editorial)
  New York Times   v133  p26(N)  pA22(L)  April 5  1984
  CODEN: NYTIA
  col 1   010 col in.
  EDITION: Thu
  ARTICLE TYPE: editorial
  GEOGRAPHIC LOCATION: New York (State)
  GEOGRAPHIC CODE: NNUSLNY
  DESCRIPTORS:  television  broadcasting  of  news-political  aspects;
election forecasting-television use; New York (State)-elections
```

(c)

FIGURE 1.5 (Cont.)

database, supplied by Information Access Company, Belmont, CA. The database provides front-page to back-page indexing of *The New York Times, The Wall Street Journal, The Los Angeles Times, The Washington Post,* and *The Christian Science Monitor.* The three retrieved items selected for display are references to articles in *The New York Times.*

You will note that the database contains 14,456 items posted to the topic "television," and 8480 items posted to the topic "elections." The AND operator caused the computer to perform an intersection between these two sets of items and resulted in 87 items common to both sets. In an instant, the computer eliminated 14,369 items about "television" that do not relate to "elections," and 8393 items about "elections" that do not relate to "television."

FEEDBACK FOR LOCATING SUBJECT TERMS

As you search by computer, the computer immediately notifies you if you are on the right track by responding with counts of retrieved items and allowing you to sample items by displaying them. Based on this instantaneous feedback, you can make adjustments by either broadening or narrowing your search strategy.

This type of interaction is illustrated in Figure 1.6 with a search on the topic of "knee joint replacement" performed against the MEDLINE database of the National Library of Medicine (NLM) retrieval service. The retrieved item is a reference to a medical journal article.

The search shows how you can use words that you know express the topic and that you hope also express your topic in the database, particularly in titles and abstracts, for the purpose of improving your search. After retrieving some items in this way, you may then display them in order to examine the relevant ones for additional terminology

```
SS 1 /C?
USER:
(tw) knee and replacement
PROG:
SS (1) PSTG (138)

SS 2 /C?
USER:
prt compr abstr,mh,1
PROG:

1
AU  - Besser MI
TI  - Bilateral Attenborough total knee replacement as a single
      procedure.
AB  - A series of 19 cases of simultaneous bilateral Attenborough Total
      Knee Replacement is presented. This semi-constrained prosthesis
      is ideal for this procedure as early mobilization is possible. In
      comparison to the available series of unilateral replacement,
      there has been no indication of an increase in any of the usual
      complications met in this type of surgery. This procedure is
      recommended for severe bilateral knee arthritis as it not only
      saves a second anaesthetic, but it helps rehabilitation and
      reduces the total hospital stay.
MH  - Aged ; Female ; Human ; *Knee Prosthesis/ADVERSE EFFECTS ; Length
      of Stay ; Male ; Middle Age ; Postoperative Complications
SO  - Arch Orthop Trauma Surg 1983;101(4):271-2

SS 2 /C?
USER:
knee prosthesis
PROG:
SS (2) PSTG (233)
```

FIGURE 1.6. A reference to a medical journal article from a search on knee joint replacement performed against the National Library of Medicine's MEDLINE database using the NLM retrieval service illustrating use of a search term from an official vocabulary, NLM's *Medical Subject Headings (MeSH®)*.

that when used in a revised search will result in retrieval of a greater number of relevant items.

In this example, the additional term "Knee Prosthesis" is not from the title or abstract, but from subject terms assigned from a special vocabulary, NLM's *Medical Subject Headings* (*MeSH®*), designed to cover material in the MEDLINE database. This term represents the search topic and was uniformly assigned to items in the database on that subject, including the item retrieved by the original search. When it replaces the words in the original search, the revised search retrieves a dramatically increased number of relevant items.

COMPUTER PRINTOUTS

In response to your instruction, the computer will display the items retrieved from the database. You may obtain this information in printed form, either directly from the terminal or by mail, which is certainly considerably more convenient than photocopying or having to take notes by hand.

COMPUTERIZED RETRIEVAL AND DISCOVERY

Searching by computer is a concentrated process. You will rarely come away from it without learning something new. You will frequently have the experience of acquiring new information in response to questions you hadn't even thought of asking when you started. The computer promotes immediate and continual discovery.

Retrieving by computer is fun. In playing a video game, success is often measured in terms of hits. Likewise, "hit" is the term frequently used for a relevant item you retrieve by computer. Even as you begin the process of learning computerized retrieval, you will soon be scoring hits. As you gain confidence, you may feel challenged to try for a greater proportion of hits in your retrievals.

Computerized searching is like playing—but the reward does not end when the game is over. Computerized searching is an intellectual exercise that can bring lasting benefits. It promotes mental discipline and places a wealth of knowledge at your fingertips just for the asking.

COMPUTERS AND LIBRARIES

Let us consider, for a moment, the university as a microcosm of an information-based society and the role of the computerized university library in that world. Computerized catalogs are being installed at a rapid rate as replacements for card catalogs in most major universities throughout the United States, to enable students and faculty to use campus libraries more effectively.

The computer unifies the library branches on a campus; it unifies the libraries on all the campuses of a university. The computer furnishes the current status of a library item (which branch has it, how many copies, its shelf location, catalog number, and loan status). It records and issues requests for transfers of items among branches. The computer recalls books that are overdue or placed on hold because of high demand. The computer anticipates patrons' needs by notifying them of new items.

The computer provides a retrieval function to locate library items by the usual access points (author, title, and subject). The great majority of noncomputerized searching of card catalogs is by author and title. With computerization, it is expected that nearly half of all library searches will be by subject.

Figure 1.7 is based on a computerized library system purchased from GEAC Computers International, Milford, CT, by the University of Maryland for its Library Information Management System (LIMS). The system uses visual display terminals that offer choices from

```
SCREEN #1
 GEAC LIBRARY SYSTEM   08-22-84  Function: Main Selection Menu
Enter a number corresponding to the list below, then press 'SEND'.

          1 - Look for a book.

          2 - Place a hold on a book.

          3 - Display Borrower information.

          4 - Show Borrower Library activity.

ENTER: 1
```

```
SCREEN #2
 GEAC LIBRARY SYSTEM   08-22-84  Function: Look up a Book
Enter a letter corresponding to the list below, then press 'SEND'.

          T - Look for a book using a TITLE.

          A - Look for a book using an AUTHOR.

          C - Look for a book using a CALL NUMBER.

          X - Go back to Main selection menu.

ENTER: A
```

FIGURE 1.7. An author search for a particular item in the online public access catalog of the University of Maryland's Library Information Management System (LIMS) illustrating the use of menus.

```
SCREEN #3
 GEAC LIBRARY SYSTEM    08-22-84   Function: Get an Author
Enter Author:   SHORTLIFFE

Enter the text for the Alphabetic search above, OR
Enter 'E' and press 'SEND' to go back to Search Type choice, OR
Enter 'X' and press 'SEND' to go back to Main selection menu.


SCREEN #4:
 GEAC LIBRARY SYSTEM    08-22-84   Function: Find an Author
Enter Author:   SHORTLIFFE

1. (reference)

2. (reference)

3. AUTHOR: Clancy, William J.  Shortliffe, Edward H.
   TITLE:  Readings in medical artificial intelligence:  the
           first decade
   CALL #: R585.A2R4 1984

4. (reference)

5. (reference)

Choose from this list, enter here:
   The number of the item above that you wish to display.
   F - to browse Forwards in the index.      B - to browse Backwards.
   E - to get a new Search Type for a book.  S - get a new Author.
   X - to go back to Main selection menu.
```

FIGURE 1.7 (Cont.).

menus, a format that is particularly "friendly" for novice users. However, as these computerized functions become increasingly familiar, formats will need to be developed that are better suited to experienced patrons, such as the direct commands described in the next paragraph.

The same result might be achieved without menus, using a command language. A command in a hypothetical command language that would be equivalent to the preceding menus might be SHORTLIFFE (AUTHOR) PRINT AUTHOR, TITLE, CALL NUMBER, or a more abbreviated form SHORTLIFFE (AU) P AU TI CA.

Because of computerization, the university library can become a focal point of the educational process. Reliance on the library by faculty will increase. Assignments given to students will require them to use the library more extensively. Students who are facile in using the library will learn more, perform better, and achieve greater success.

Learning computerized retrieval will prepare you for today's world. Whether or not you choose to learn it, computerized retrieval is, as they say, "what's happening now." The increasing availability and ease of obtaining information by computer will make it more important than ever to be well informed. Computerized retrieval will soon be the norm for obtaining information in practically every profession, academic field, or walk of life. Its impact on learning thrusts us into a new era of enlightenment. As we move from an industrialized society to one based on the creation and distribution of information, computerized retrieval holds the key to achievements; it offers us a framework of knowledge to better understand the world we live in and the people we share it with.

THE INFORMATION AGE

1. Recall an occasion when you needed to locate information manually, using reference books, indexes, catalogs, or the like. Given a similar task, if the materials to be searched were now stored in a database, how might computerized retrieval enhance the location of information in comparison with your earlier experience? Consider both the process and the outcome. Identify as well any limitations of computerized retrieval that you would foresee.

2. Imagine that you have access to a database containing information about colleges and universities. In addition to the name and location of the school, categories of information would include:

EXERCISES

- description of the setting
- enrollment figures
- number of faculty
- grading system
- admission requirements
- undergraduate profile
- expenses
- financial aid
- special programs
- career services
- housing
- campus life
- athletics
- major subjects

Compare computerized retrieval from this database with manual
searching of a publication containing this information. Include in
your assessment examples of specific queries that would highlight
the points of comparison.

Records, Fields, Files 2

RECORDS

A record is a basic unit of information. In order to develop a definition that more fully characterizes a record, we will describe, as an example, a record about you when you were a youngster.

When you were first registered at an elementary school your parents were asked to furnish information about you. That information constituted a record (see Figure 2.1). The type of information in your school record included your name, address, telephone number, entering grade level, date of birth, names of your parents, date of registration, any health condition that would require emergency care, whom to contact in case of an emergency, and so forth. Your school record might be characterized as consisting of a collection of information.

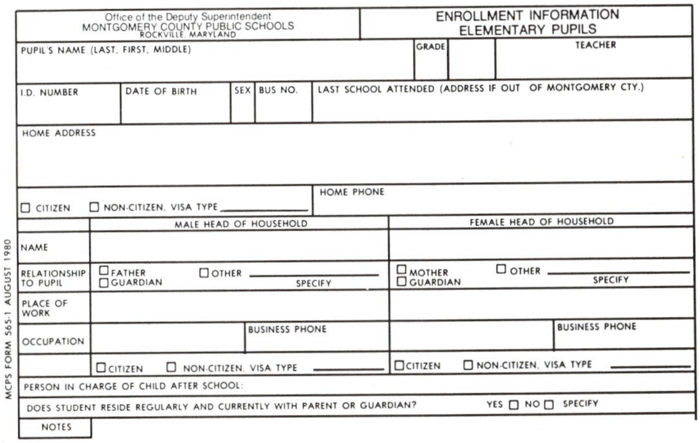
Office of the Deputy Superintendent
MONTGOMERY COUNTY PUBLIC SCHOOLS
ROCKVILLE, MARYLAND
ENROLLMENT INFORMATION
ELEMENTARY PUPILS
PUPIL'S NAME (LAST, FIRST, MIDDLE)
GRADE
TEACHER
I.D. NUMBER
DATE OF BIRTH
SEX
BUS NO.
LAST SCHOOL ATTENDED (ADDRESS IF OUT OF MONTGOMERY CTY.)
HOME ADDRESS
☐ CITIZEN ☐ NON-CITIZEN, VISA TYPE
HOME PHONE
MALE HEAD OF HOUSEHOLD
FEMALE HEAD OF HOUSEHOLD
NAME
RELATIONSHIP TO PUPIL
☐ FATHER ☐ GUARDIAN ☐ OTHER SPECIFY
☐ MOTHER ☐ GUARDIAN ☐ OTHER SPECIFY
PLACE OF WORK
OCCUPATION
BUSINESS PHONE
BUSINESS PHONE
☐ CITIZEN ☐ NON-CITIZEN, VISA TYPE
☐ CITIZEN ☐ NON-CITIZEN, VISA TYPE
PERSON IN CHARGE OF CHILD AFTER SCHOOL:
DOES STUDENT RESIDE REGULARLY AND CURRENTLY WITH PARENT OR GUARDIAN? YES ☐ NO ☐ SPECIFY
NOTES
MCPS FORM 565-1 AUGUST 1980

FIGURE 2.1. School registration form is a record about the student.

Another characteristic of your school record was that it contained information about you that was requested by the school. We now can generalize that a record is a collection of information related to a specific purpose. A third characteristic of your school record was that it contained information only if it related to you. In other words, the record was treating you as a unit.

YOUR RECORD HAS INFORMATION ONLY ABOUT YOU --- IT TREATS **YOU** AS A UNIT

We have now developed a definition of your school record: a collection of information about you requested by the school. We may broaden our definition of school record by taking into consideration that the school also requested a record for each of your schoolmates as well. The unit is not only you, but any student that attended your school. The new definition of a school record: a collection of information about a student requested by the school.

We can set up a fill-in-the-blanks definition for a record, as follows: A _____ record is a collection of information _____

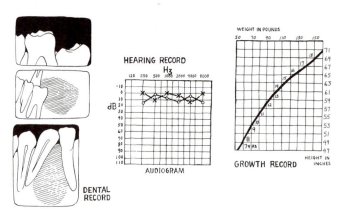

DENTAL RECORD

HEARING RECORD

AUDIOGRAM

GROWTH RECORD

wants to know about _____. Using this form, we can define other types of records. A dental record is a collection of information the dentist wants to know about a patient. Growth chart record, eyesight record, hearing record, and mental skills record are other important collections of information about you that someone may want to know.

A record could have another name. For example, a baseball card is a collection of information a baseball fan wants to know about a baseball player. A record can be about a thing. For example, a library catalog card is a collection of information that library patrons want to know about a book in the library. A record can be about how to do something, and it does not need to be on a separate piece of paper from other records. For example, a recipe in a cookbook is a collection of information a chef wants to know about preparing a dish.

To summarize, the characteristics of a record are:

- Collection of information.

- Information related to a purpose.

- Information about a unit, such as a person, an object, a place, an event, a method or procedure, or an idea.

A record could be broadly defined as a collection of information related to a purpose, where the information is about a unit, such as a person, an object, a place, an event, a procedure, or an idea. A shorter definition is: a record is a collection of related information, treated as a unit.

FIELDS AND SUBFIELDS

There are different kinds, or categories, of information in a record. Categories in the school record were student name, address, telephone number, date of birth, and so on. A category of information in a record is called a *field*. A field does not give us specific information. It only tells us the kind of information. A field may be divided into *subfields*. For example, the subfields for the student name field could be first name, middle initial, and last name.

FIELD AND SUBFIELD VALUES

A specific piece of information in the name field of a school record would be "John J. Doe," or any other specific name. Specific information that belongs in a field is called a *field value*. Another example of a field value in a school record would be "(617) 496–9000," a field value of a telephone number field. Specific information that belongs in a subfield is called a *subfield value*.

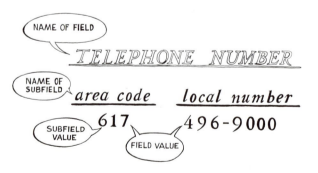

FILES

We will continue with the school record example to develop the definition of a *file*. If a school has a record for each student registered, it then has a file, or a collection of school records. Another characteristic of a file of school records is that it contains information about students requested by the school.

Just as a school record is a collection of information about a student requested by the school, a file of school records is a collection of information requested by the school about many students.

As we did for the school record earlier, we can generalize about the school's file as follows: a file is a collection of information related to a specific purpose. A third characteristic of a file of school records is that it contains records only for the students that attend the school. In other words, the file treats the body of students attending the school as a unit.

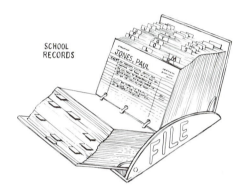

We have now developed a definition of a file of school records: a collection of information requested by the school about its students. The definition of a file of school records looks almost like the definition of a school record, which, if you recall, is a collection of information requested by the school about a student. The difference between a school record and a file of school records is that a school record is about one student, taken as a unit, and a file of school records is a collection of school records about all the students in attendance, taken as a unit.

To summarize, the characteristics of a file are:

• Collection of records.

• Records related to a purpose.

• Records about a unit. The unit is a collection of the units in the definition of the record.

A file could be broadly defined as a collection of records related to a purpose, where the collection is about a unit that is a collection of the units in the definition of the record. A shorter definition is: a file is a collection of related records, treated as a unit.

EXERCISES

Design the following records:

1. Personnel record for employees in a company.
2. Inventory record that would be maintained by a parts distributor.
3. Record of a library patron.
4. Birth certificate.
5. Certificate of title for a motor vehicle.

Conventional (Noncomputerized) Files

3

Suppose that the records in the school file, discussed in the previous chapter, were in a file box, and the records in the file were in random order. To find the record of a student named Laura Brown, you could start with the first record and search forward one record at a time until you located the one with her name as the value in the student name field. At the other end of the alphabet, you could search for the record of Robert Williams in the same way, by starting with the first record and searching forward one record at a time until you found the one with his name as the field value. In either case, it wouldn't matter whether you started with the first record or the last because the records, being in random order, are not organized in a way that helps you search.

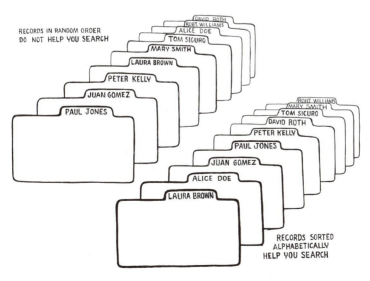

RECORDS IN RANDOM ORDER
DO NOT HELP YOU SEARCH

DAVID ROTH
ROBT. WILLIAMS
ALICE DOE
TOM SICURO
MARY SMITH
LAURA BROWN
PETER KELLY
JUAN GOMEZ
PAUL JONES

ROBT WILLIAMS
MARY SMITH
TOM SICURO
DAVID ROTH
PETER KELLY
PAUL JONES
JUAN GOMEZ
ALICE DOE
LAURA BROWN

RECORDS SORTED
ALPHABETICALLY
HELP YOU SEARCH

SORTED SEQUENTIAL (ALPHABETIC) FILE

Let's say the records are now sorted alphabetically from A to Z by student last name. You could easily find Laura Brown's record by searching forward starting at the beginning of the file. On the other hand, it would make more sense to search backward starting at the end of the file in order to find Robert Williams' record. For locating Jennifer Johnson's record in an ordered file, you could start somewhere in the middle, and then continue your search in either direction depending on the student's last name on the first record you see.

SORT KEYS

When searching the ordered file for a student's last name, the last name subfield of the student name field would be the *sort key*. Suppose, however, when you search for Jennifer Johnson's record, there are five records having Johnson as the last name. You could locate the record faster if the Johnson record were sorted by student first name. In that case, student last name would be the primary sort, and student first name the secondary sort. Student last name is considered to be the primary sort key, and student first name would be the secondary sort key.

SEARCH KEYS AND SEARCH KEY VALUES

The fields or subfields by which a file is searched are *search keys*. Let's begin a definition of search key that applies to the preceding examples: a search key is a field or subfield whose exact value, called a search key value, is used in locating a record. We will soon modify the definition somewhat.

So far, we have been discussing a sorted sequential file, a file in which records are arranged in ascending (forward) or descending (backward) order according to a designated field or subfield, known as the sort key. In locating a specific record, knowing that the sort is alphabetic assisted us in guessing the best place in the file to start.

PRIMARY SORT KEYS
FORM THE INDEX
TO THE FILE

Dividers with alphabetic tabs are commonly used in file boxes to determine more precisely the best place to start searching. When searching for Jennifer Johnson's record, we could go immediately to the records located after the "J" divider, which is used for locating all records in which the student last name subfield value begins with the letter "J." In a file that uses these dividers, the set of alphabetic characters A–Z is a search key.

However, the alphabetic tab is not a field or subfield value in a record but merely the first character in the last name subfield. Since we nevertheless use it as a search key, we can conclude that a search key value need not equal a field or subfield value as in our original definition of search key. An improved definition for search key would therefore be: a category of information standing for information in a record, and whose value, called a search key value, is used for locating the record.

The set of alphabetic tabs has a specific function. It indexes the file. In fact, alphabetic tabs are sometimes called index tabs. An *index* may be defined as follows: a collection of search key values that point to the location of records in the file for each search key value.

INDEXES

The comparison between fields and field values (including subfields and subfield values) on the one hand and search keys and search key values on the other may be summarized as follows: a field value is a specific piece of information that is an instance of a field, and a search key value is a specific piece of information that is an instance of a search key. Therefore, the relationship between search key and search key value is the same as the relationship between field and field value. The difference between these two sets of concepts is that fields and field values pertain to records directly, while search keys and search key values pertain to the index to the records.

FIELDS/FIELD VALUES AND SEARCH KEYS/SEARCH KEY VALUES

We now have a filing system that is a file of indexed records searchable by search key values (index points) that are specific alphabetic characters on index tabs. However, for the index tabs to be effective, the file must still be sorted sequentially. Therefore, a new

A NEW RECORD MUST BE PUT IN THE RIGHT ORDER IN THE FILE

record must be inserted into the proper place in the file, and a temporarily removed record must be returned to its proper place.

INDEXING AND MECHANICAL INDEXING ERRORS: A CASE STUDY

Suppose the file has a field for the grade in which the student entered school (K = kindergarten, 1 = first grade, 2 = second grade, and so on). To find the records of all students who transferred from another school, you could search the grade field for any value except K or 1. But would this search strategy really work? No, it would exclude records for the following transfer students: students who were repeating first grade and had been in first grade at another school, first graders who had been in kindergarten at another school, and first graders who had had formal schooling in a foreign country at any grade level.

Perhaps it would be better if the file contained a transfer status field with two possible values, "transfer" and "nontransfer." You could then search the file for records of transfer students by searching the file sequentially for records with the value "transfer." You would have to examine every record in the file, since any record could have that value. This is in contrast to looking for a specific student name in a random file where you can stop searching once you locate the record.

You could avoid this exhaustive search by duplicating each record and sorting the duplicate file using transfer status as the primary sort and student last name as the secondary sort. The problem with this approach is that if you followed it for all the search keys you might need, you would have multiple copies of each record, and you might

CHANGING THE ADDRESS IN A SCHOOL RECORD
IN MULTIPLE FILES OF COMPLETE RECORDS

NAME - PETER KELLY
ADDRESS - 25 ELM ST.
GRADE - 2
TRANSFER STATUS -
NON-TRANSFER

NAME - PETER KELLY
ADDRESS - 25 ELM ST.
GRADE - 2
TRANSFER STATUS -
NON-TRANSFER

NAME - PETER KELLY
ADDRESS - 25 ELM ST.
GRADE - 2
TRANSFER STATUS -
NON-TRANSFER

THE ADDRESS NEEDS TO BE CHANGED 3 TIMES IN EACH COMPLETE RECORD IN THE MULTIPLE FILES

NAME - PETER KELLY

NAME - PETER KELLY

NAME - PETER KELLY

FILE SORTED BY STUDENT LAST NAME

FILE SORTED BY TRANSFER STATUS

FILE SORTED BY GRADE

soon run out of space in your file box. In addition, the problem of keeping these files current would be overwhelming. For example, suppose one of the students changed his or her home address. You would need to locate and correct all multiple copies of the record.

A file may be indexed by physically marking records; for example, by attaching paper clips, you could tag the records of transfer students. One problem with this method of indexing is that clips have a tendency to come off or become attached to more than one record. Also, if you use clips for other search keys, you would need differently shaped or colored clips to distinguish among the search keys. Records on paper that is color-coded for search keys is an alternate method of physical marking. However, a record might need to be coded for multiple search keys, so that you would need to code for combinations of search keys as well. The restriction in the number of possible search keys makes physical marking a limited approach for indexing a file.

You could create a list consisting only of student names and their transfer status, with transfer status as the primary sort and student last name as the secondary sort. Since there are only two transfer statuses, your list actually consists of two sublists: a list of names of transfer students sorted by student last name, and a list of names of nontransfer students sorted by student last name.

The student name list sorted primarily by transfer status is an index to student names in the school file. Transfer status is the search key, and "transfer" and "nontransfer" are the possible search key values. The index shows which student names are associated with either

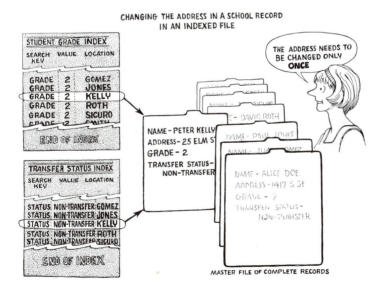

CHANGING THE ADDRESS IN A SCHOOL RECORD
IN AN INDEXED FILE

MASTER FILE OF COMPLETE RECORDS

the value "transfer" or the value "nontransfer." In addition, the student name in the index is used for locating the student's complete record in the school file. Compared with the multiple file system discussed earlier, if a student moved to a different address, this type of index would require changing only the complete student record in the master file.

How could the transfer status index just described, with each student name assigned to one of the two search key values "transfer" and "nontransfer," be made simpler? The transfer status index could have consisted of only the transfer students, and if a student's name is not on the list, then the student is not a transfer student. If, however, a student's name is not on the list of transfer students, you could not be sure that the student is not a transfer student. Other possibilities are that the transfer status was never entered into the record, or the transfer status and index are both incorrect, or the transfer status was "transfer" but this information was erased from the record, or the transfer status in the record is "transfer" but the student's name was still not placed in the index.

However, in an index that has both transfer statuses as search key values, if a student's name is not in the index, the only possibilities are that the transfer status of the student was never entered into the record, or that the transfer status entered in the record was erased. However, if the transfer status is both in the record and in the index, there are two more possible mistakes: (1) the transfer status could be correct in the record, but it could have been put in the index incorrectly, or (2) the transfer status could be wrong in the record, and wrong information could have been put in the index.

If the codes T (for transfer) and NT (for nontransfer) were designated field values, the record could not be indexed if the transfer status field had an unrecognized code, such as "N."

In the next chapter, we'll see how the computer can eliminate the problems caused by many of the possible omissions and errors in the preceding discussion. Essentially the only type of problem remaining in a computerized index would stem from the presence of information in a record that does not correspond to the true situation.

DESIGNING AND MODIFYING INDEXES

In any system, sooner or later an index will need to be changed. For example, you would need to change the transfer status index for the following reasons:

1. If the name of the student changes.

2. If someone discovers a mistake in the student's name.

3. If the transfer status, previously not known, becomes known.

4. If someone discovers a mistake in the student's transfer status.

5. When a new student registers at the school.

6. When a student who attended the school leaves.

Each of the changes to the index would be preceded by a change to the master file of complete student records, as follows:

REASON FOR CHANGE	CHANGE TO THE MASTER FILE
1. student name change	student name field updated
2. student name error	student name field corrected
3. transfer status now known	transfer status field updated
4. transfer status error	transfer status field corrected
5. student new to school	new record created
6. student leaving school	record deleted

Steps for designing and modifying separate indexes to a master file may be summarized as follows:

1. Identify the information in a record that needs to be indexed; that is, determine what information would be the basis on which someone would want to search the file.

2. Organize the information as fields and subfields, which will be represented as search key values.

3. Determine the values in these fields and subfields that will be the source of the search key values. Usually a search key value is identical to a field or subfield value.

4. Identify the field or subfield that determines the address that should be used in the index in order to locate the record in the master file. For example, if the master file is sorted by the name field, addresses would consist of name field values.

5. Build an index for each search key, and enter the search key values and addresses. Entries in an index would be sorted by search key value.

6. Establish procedures for modifying the index according to modifications or additions to the master file.

Modifying the contents of a file to keep the information accurate and current is known as *file maintenance. File updating* is merging recently created records, reflecting new information, with a master file. Maintaining and updating an indexed file require the index to be modified to reflect the revised or new version.

FILE MAINTENANCE AND FILE UPDATING

EXERCISES

1. Using a record you designed in the exercises for Chapter 2, determine which fields or subfields might be useful as search keys for indexing a file of these records.

2. a. Based on the eight school records shown, construct an index to transfer students by listing the appropriate student names under the heading "Index to Transfer Students."

   b. Using the same records, construct an erroneous "Index to Transfer Students" by assuming all of the following errors:

      • Transfer status value in the records of Laura Brown and Robert Williams is missing.

      • Transfer status value in the records of Alice Doe and Peter Kelly is incorrect.

      • Transfer status value in the records of Juan Gomez and Paul Jones has been transferred to the index incorrectly.

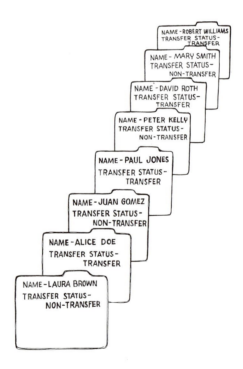

   Which records are indexed correctly? Which of these was indexed correctly even though it was erroneous? Explain your answer.

3. a. Using the same records shown previously, complete the following index to nontransfer students by listing the appropriate stu-

dent names under the heading "Index to Nontransfer Students." This index, and the "Index to Transfer Students," comprise a "transfer status" index to the file of records.

b. Using these records, and assuming the same errors as described, construct an erroneous "Index to Nontransfer Students." According to the two-value transfer status index (consisting of both the index to transfer and the index to nontransfer students), which records are indexed correctly? Which record is indexed erroneously that was indexed correctly using only a single-value index as the transfer status index? Explain your answer.

Records in a Computer

4

From now on, we will be discussing records in the computer. Before we go further, you should know what a computer program is. A computer program is a set of steps that instruct the computer to perform specific tasks in order to solve a problem. When we say that the computer knows or does something, we are really saying that a person wrote a program that gives the computer that knowledge or ability.

COMPUTER PROGRAM

Records listed from a computerized file may be sorted automatically in a specific way. For example, they could be sorted in the order that they were accepted by the computer, with the most recently accepted

SORTING OF RECORDS

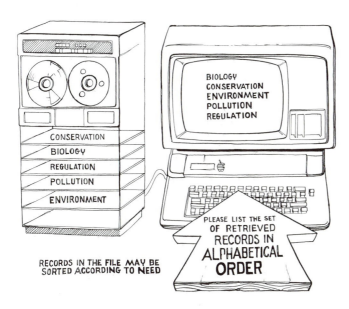

RECORDS IN THE FILE MAY BE
SORTED ACCORDING TO NEED

PLEASE LIST THE SET OF RETRIEVED RECORDS IN ALPHABETICAL ORDER

record coming first. In this type of sort, each new record that is accepted by the computer becomes the first record in the file.

However, the computer may permit you to specify some other order. For example, you may want the listing to be sorted according to the last name in a name field in the record. Sorting of resulting records, or output, is discussed in Chapter 11. In any case, the computer will never require human intervention for sorting records as they are added or returned to the file.

CREATION OF INDEXES

The computer creates indexes according to a set of specified search keys. As in noncomputer indexes discussed in the previous chapter, search keys are categories of information that stand for information in a record. In creating an index, the computer is able to provide as many search keys as needed.

RECORD ADDRESSES

A record in the computer is stored in a numbered location. After a record is input, that is, first entered into and accepted by the computer, it is automatically assigned a number in the computer, which is called the *address* of that record.

In the noncomputerized index to the school file developed in Chapters 2 and 3, search key values were associated with student names indicating the location of a record in the school file, which was sorted alphabetically by student name. In computerized indexes, the computer-assigned number is used as the address of records in the computer. As long as the record exists, that address will not change. In fact, you never have to know what the address is. It is the computer's job to locate records using these addresses. You will never need to specify addresses for locating records in a file. Once a record is located by the index, you can immediately tell the computer to display it and not be concerned with its physical location in the computer.

SORTING OF INDEXES

Indexes are sorted by the computer to make it easier to look through a display of the index. For example, the computerized sort of an index consisting of alphabetic search key values could be alphabetic from A to Z, as follows:

LEMON

LEMON PIE

LEMONADE

In this sort, the space between words comes before the letter A, and the sort is called ''word-by-word.'' If the space were ignored, the sort would be called ''letter-by-letter,'' as follows:

LEMON

LEMONADE

LEMON PIE

The computer can be programmed to help prevent errors in the record using rules about values the computer should accept in a particular field. Checking values against these rules is called "validation." If a value is against the rule, the computer can be programmed to reject the value and generate an error message.

VALIDATION

One type of rule is that a specific field must always have a value. This would be a good rule to apply to the student name field. Another rule could be that a date field must consist of numeric characters, such as 19700922 (for September 22, 1970), as its value. The rule could also state that the number must be within a certain range; for example, not less than 19700101 and not greater than 19781231. There could also be a rule for how many separate values, or occurrences, a field may have. For example, the student name field in a school record should have only one occurrence, but a field containing information about whom to contact if the student has an emergency could be set for two occurrences.

VALIDATION RULES

THE COMPUTER CAN BE PROGRAMMED TO REJECT A VALUE AGAINST THE RULE

Validation rules could be used for cross-checking values between fields. A rule could make sure that if a school record has a field for the school from which a student was transferred, and that field has no value, then the transfer status field must show "nontransfer" as its value, but if this "school transferred-from" field does have a value, the transfer status field must show "transfer" as its value.

TABLES FOR OFFICIAL FORMS

The computer may contain tables for automatically changing various forms of information into a single official form. For example, there may be a table that contains the full name and abbreviations of each state in the United States. Entries in this table for the state of California would be as follows:

UNOFFICIAL FORM	OFFICIAL FORM
CAL	CA
CALIF	CA
CALIFORNIA	CA

This table would be used for establishing CA as the official form for the state subfield in an address field. The computer could accept a record in which either the official or an unofficial form from the table had been entered. If an unofficial form is entered, the computer would automatically change it to the official form, according to the table, before accepting the record into the file. The official form as the only acceptable form assures a person searching for a state that using this form will locate all records with addresses to that state.

UPDATING AND MAINTAINING RECORDS

We know, from the example of the noncomputerized index (described in the previous chapter) that new records are added to and deleted from files, and that values in records can be changed. The computer is programmed to receive instructions for performing these operations.

Modifications to files also affect their indexes. The most obvious advantage of updating and maintaining indexes to computerized files is that the computer will do all the mechanical work of indexing. That is, if information is present in an indexed field, that information will automatically generate all appropriate search key values in the index, with associated addresses. If the information in an indexed field is changed, the computer can automatically modify the index or regenerate it (generate a totally new index) so that the record can be located by the new set of search key values.

When search key values are maintained (added, deleted, or changed), addresses must be associated with new or replacing search key values, but no longer be associated with deleted or replaced search key values. Whenever a new record is added to the file, the computer must make sure that its search key values are in the index, and that they point to the address of the new record. When a record is deleted from the file, its address must be deleted from all the indexes. The search key values themselves are not necessarily removed since they may still be needed for indexing other records.

UPDATING AND MAINTAINING INDEXES

The problem of missing or incorrect information is common to both computerized and noncomputerized files, although validation rules cut down on some types of errors in computerized files. Since the creation and maintenance of indexes in the computer is automatic, errors in indexed fields in a record will carry over as errors in the index as well. Carryover of errors from a record to its indexes is also likely to occur in noncomputerized files.

On the other hand, in noncomputerized files, the index could have an error even though the information it comes from in the record is correct. In computerized files, errors in the index, when the record is correct, are usually due to an error in the program that generates the index and would affect the indexing of many records. Fortunately, such system errors are rare, and generally speaking the index will always be correct according to the information in the record. Since the index is not generated automatically in noncomputerized files, individual indexing errors, when the record is correct, occur more frequently in noncomputerized than in computerized files.

ERRORS IN COMPUTER INDEXING

Creating records in the computer and file maintaining them involve computerized functions that can be performed in *real time* or *batch* or a combination. Real time processing means that these functions are performed at the same time as instructions for performing them are entered into the computer. During real time processing, the computer is in *interactive mode*, also called *conversational mode*, which is a

REAL TIME (INTERACTIVE MODE) AND BATCH PROCESSING

method of operation in which the user is in direct communication with the computer and receives an immediate response from the computer after entering each message. In contrast, batch processing means that, even though instructions are entered into the computer now, the computer performs these functions later.

For example, in creating a record totally in real time processing, the computer would process the record as it is being entered; if accepted, the record will immediately be in the computerized file. In total batch processing, the computer would not process the record immediately; even though it has been entered, the record is not considered for acceptance by the computer until later.

Sometimes a combination of real time and batch processing is used, where information is entered into the computer, and the computer does some of the processing in real time, but finishes the processing in batch. The computer might perform simple validations (number of occurrences, character set, number within a range) in real time, but save more complex validations (matching against tables, conversion to official forms, cross-field checking) for batch.

EXERCISES

1. List the advantages of computerization for creating, maintaining, and updating records, compared with manual methods.

2. In Chapter 3, three types of errors in manual indexing were identified. These were due to:

   • Information missing in the record.

   • Information in the record incorrect.

   • Record indexed incorrectly by the computer.

   How well does computerization prevent these types of errors? Explain your answer.

3. If validation were performed in real time, show how the computer might respond to the following errors:

- ALIC4 DOE
- 840241 (date in form YearMonthDay)
- 830229 (date in form YearMonthDay)
- White Plains, NY 10406 (zip code should be 10604)

Basic Concepts
of Retrieval

5

Beginning with this chapter, we will describe retrieval from a file consisting of just two records. We will employ a composite of existing publicly available retrieval systems to explain and illustrate the principles and practice of computerized retrieval.

Our illustrative file consists of two bibliographic records (references to books). The fields of these records follow. The upper case characters (AU, TI, PU, PL, PY) are the field abbreviations.

AUthor

TItle

PUblisher

PLace of publication

Publication Year

The following are the records, including field abbreviations, comprising our file:

37.
AU - Smith, John
TI - Guide to enjoying the teenage years.
PL - Chicago, Illinois
PU - Atlas Publishing Company
PY - 1983

24.
AU - Jones, Mary
TI - Guide to enjoying yourself on a rainy afternoon.
PL - Dallas, Texas

PU - Tops Publishing Company
PY - 1983

COMPUTER ADDRESS

The numbers 37 and 24 are computer addresses; that is, the first record (AU - Smith, John, etc.) is stored in the computer in location #37, and the second (AU - Jones, Mary, etc.) in location #24. Computer addresses are usually not part of a display of records but are needed for the following explanation of index searching.

SEARCH STATEMENTS AND SEARCH TERMS

Searching a file by computer involves two operations: your input and subsequent processing of that input by the computer. The computer starts to process when you signal the end of your input by striking a key on your terminal generally designated ENTER or RETURN. The human input operation is the entering of messages to the computer, known as search statements, at a computer terminal. A search statement prompts the computer to locate records in the file that match the search terms (usually words or phrases) in these statements. Most of the time the computer will be searching the index to a file rather than the records in the file directly.

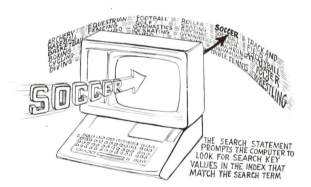

THE SEARCH STATEMENT PROMPTS THE COMPUTER TO LOOK FOR SEARCH KEY VALUES IN THE INDEX THAT MATCH THE SEARCH TERM

INDEX TO FILE

The best way to begin understanding how a computer index to a file is searched is to see what an index looks like. The following is an index to our bibliographic file, preceded by another display of the records being indexed. As in the display of records, computer addresses are usually not part of a display of the index, but are needed for further explanation.

37.
AU - Smith, John
TI - Guide to enjoying the teenage years.
PL - Chicago, Illinois

PU - Atlas Publishing Company
PY - 1983

24.
AU - Jones, Mary
TI - Guide to enjoying yourself on a rainy afternoon.
PL - Dallas, Texas
PU - Tops Publishing Company
PY - 1983

SEARCH KEY VALUE	SEARCH KEY	ADDRESS OF RECORD	NUMBER OF RECORDS
A	TW	24	1
AFTERNOON	TW	24	1
ATLAS PUBLISHING COMPANY	PU	37	1
CHICAGO, ILLINOIS	PL	37	1
DALLAS, TEXAS	PL	24	1
ENJOYING	TW	24,37	2
GUIDE	TW	24,37	2
GUI/T/E/T	TF	37	1
GUI/T/E/Y	TF	24	1
GUIDE TO ENJOYING THE TEENAGE YEARS	TI	37	1
GUIDE TO ENJOYING YOURSELF ON A RAINY AFTERNOON	TI	24	1
JONES, MARY	AU	24	1
ON	TW	24	1
RAINY	TW	24	1
SMITH, JOHN	AU	37	1
TEENAGE	TW	37	1
THE	TW	37	1
TO	TW	24,37	2
TOPS PUBLISHING COMPANY	PU	24	1
YEARS	TW	37	1
YOURSELF	TW	24	1
1983	PY	24,37	2

Before examining this index, let's review the definition of search key and search key value. A search key is a category of information in the index that stands for information in the record and whose value (the search key value) is used for locating records by association with addresses of records in the computer. The following are the search key abbreviations in the preceding index, with their full-length equivalents:

SEARCH KEY AND SEARCH KEY VALUE

AU = AUTHOR

TI   = TITLE

TF = FORMULA-DERIVED TITLE

TW = TITLE TEXTWORD

PU = PUBLISHER

PL = PLACE OF PUBLICATION

PY = PUBLICATION YEAR

Notice that a number of search keys in the index correspond directly to fields in the record. (For the present, don't be concerned about the remaining search keys.) The values of these search keys in the index came directly from their corresponding field values in the record. These field values are known as *keywords*.

KEYWORD

A keyword is a value in the record that becomes a search key value in the index when the record is indexed by the computer. According to the search keys in this index, the following field values in the record are keywords: author, title, publisher, place of publication, and publication year. Note that a keyword is not necessarily a "word." In fact, the only single word of the five keywords just mentioned is 1983, the value of the publication year [PY] field.

COMPUTER INDEXING, LOCATION OF RECORD, AND RECORD COUNT

The matching search key values in the index locate records by naming their addresses. For example, when the record in location #37 was indexed by the computer, the computer was programmed to know that the value in the place of publication [PL] field is a keyword, and that it should be copied to the index as a value for the place of publication [PL] search key. This is the process whereby CHICAGO, ILLINOIS became a search key value in the index. When the computer copied this keyword from the record to the index, it added address #37 to the index as an ADDRESS OF RECORD so that CHICAGO, ILLINOIS could locate the record it came from.

The index also keeps count of the number of records located by each search key value. For example, when the first record was indexed, and the search key value 1983 was established (in the same manner just described), the computer set the NUMBER OF RECORDS count to "1." When the second record was indexed, 1983 was processed as a keyword in that record as well. Since the search key value was already there from indexing of the previous record, the computer had only to add the address of the second record as an AD-DRESS OF RECORD so that 1983 would locate this record as well, and increase the NUMBER OF RECORDS count to ''2.''

In searching the index, you would enter search statements containing search terms, which are then matched against search key values in the index. For example, when you enter a search statement containing DALLAS, TEXAS [PL], the computer matches this search term to DALLAS, TEXAS, the [PL] search key value in the index, and locates the record in address #24. The computer has thereby located a record that is associated with a particular search term. This process is the essence of searching the index.

INDEX SEARCHING

The terminology pertaining to keywords, search key values, and search terms is summarized in the following table:

SUMMARY: SEARCH KEY, SEARCH KEY VALUE, KEYWORD

Nomenclature for Words or Phrases Used for Searching the Index

NAME	LOCATION	FUNCTION
keywords	record	are values that are transformed into search key values when records are indexed by the computer
search key values	index	stand for information in records and, after being matched against search terms, locate records by their association with addresses of records in the computer
search terms	search statement	stand for information in search queries, and are matched against search key values during computer processing of search statements against the index

Until now, we have described only one type of keyword, namely, key-words that are complete field values taken directly from the item being indexed. The computer may be programmed to derive or extract ad-ditional search key values from these, or other, fields. Derived or ex-tracted search key values are particularly useful as alternatives to long search key values such as titles.

    A formula-derived search key value from the title might be de-rived as follows: first three letters of the first word/first letter of the second word/first letter of the third word/first letter of the fourth word. Examples of complete titles with formula-derived titles accord-ing to this formula follow.

FORMULA-DERIVED SEARCH KEY VALUE FROM TITLE

COMPLETE TITLE	FORMULA-DERIVED TITLE
Guide to enjoying the teenage years.	GUI/T/E/T
Guide to enjoying yourself on a rainy afternoon.	GUI/T/E/Y

The formula-derived title [TF] search key is useful as shorthand for locating a particular bibliographic record when you know the title of the book. It is possible for more than one record to be located by the same formula-derived title. For example, all titles starting with ''Guide to enjoying yourself'' would be located by GUI/T/E/Y. In general, however, the likelihood of locating a large number of records by formula-derived search keys would be small. The main disadvantage of using a formula-derived title as a search term is that even though you need not know the complete title, it may still require more information about the title than you may have.

TITLE TEXTWORD

Individual words in a compound keyword, such as most titles, may be extracted by the computer as values for a title textword [TW] search key. In the index, each word in a title is a search key value and can be used for locating its respective record. For example, GUIDE would locate both records, as would ENJOYING; TEENAGE and YEARS would each locate only the record in address #37, and RAINY and AFTERNOON would each locate only the record in address #24.

The advantage of title textwords locating a particular record is the requirement of minimal knowledge about the title, with respect to the number of words you must know and their relative positions. The disadvantage is that some textwords occur in titles rather frequently. For example, in a normal-size file, ''guide'' as a search term might locate a substantial number of records, among which would be the specific record you wanted to locate. Textwords from titles are extremely valuable, however, as search terms for subject searching.

STOPWORDS

Certain common words are usually omitted as textwords in an index. The computer contains a list of these words, called *stopwords,* and ensures that they are not extracted as search key values. The reason for having stopwords is that they are usually not helpful in searching because they occur frequently and contribute little meaning. For example, compare the following sets of titles.

Complete titles:

Guide to enjoying the teenage years.

Guide to enjoying yourself on a rainy afternoon.

Versions of the same titles without the words "to," "the," "on," and "a":

Guide enjoying teenage years.

Guide enjoying yourself rainy afternoon.

If there were no stopwords, these common words as search key values would use up quite a bit of room in the index. In most indexes to titles, search key values such as THE, AN, A, TO, IN, OF, AND, OR, would be associated with a huge number of addresses. If stopwords were included as search key values, it would take the computer considerably more time to create and maintain indexes and to process search statements.

Let's regenerate the index without the stopwords TO, THE, ON, and A.

SEARCH KEY VALUE	SEARCH KEY	ADDRESS OF RECORD	NUMBER OF RECORDS
AFTERNOON	TW	24	1
ATLAS PUBLISHING COMPANY	PU	37	1
CHICAGO, ILLINOIS	PL	37	1
DALLAS, TEXAS	PL	24	1
ENJOYING	TW	24,37	2
GUIDE	TW	24,37	2
GUI/T/E/T	TF	37	1
GUI/T/E/Y	TF	24	1
GUIDE TO ENJOYING THE TEENAGE YEARS	TI	37	1
GUIDE TO ENJOYING YOURSELF ON A RAINY AFTERNOON	TI	24	1
JONES, MARY	AU	24	1
RAINY	TW	24	1
SMITH, JOHN	AU	37	1
TEENAGE	TW	37	1
TOPS PUBLISHING COMPANY	PU	24	1
YEARS	TW	37	1
YOURSELF	TW	24	1
1983	PY	24,37	2

Two search keys, not shown, come from keywords that are added to the record as a result of intellectual subject indexing, which is the assigning of subject terms to a record for the purpose of augmenting the information provided directly by the item being indexed. Subject terms are usually selected from an official vocabulary, a set of predetermined words and phrases intended to represent the subject

INTELLECTUAL INDEXING: CONTROLLED AND FREE TERMS

content of the file. (Subject term search key and controlled indexing vocabulary for subject searching are the topics of Chapter 8.) Free indexing terms may be assigned to records in the same way as controlled indexing terms, but there is no official source for these terms.

SEARCH COMMAND

Search statements for searching the index may need to be introduced by a search command, such as FIND, SELECT, or S, but since index searching is usually the norm, the computer may consider "search" to be a default command and thereby permit you to omit any search command and simply begin the search statement with a search term. You may restrict search terms and search statements to specified search keys (as described in Chapter 9).

Most search statements do not consist of single search terms but specify logical relationships between search terms for locating records that have corresponding terms in the same relationship. Logical operators, for connecting search terms, are the subject of the next chapter, although the operators AND and OR were introduced in Chapter 1.

SEQUENTIAL SEARCHING

Searching the index is not the only method of searching by computer. The computer may examine a set of records sequentially by matching search terms in search statements directly against sequences of characters in the records, known as character strings. In a large file, sequential searching of the complete file would be too time-consuming; sequential searching would therefore be permitted only for searching a portion of the file. Sequential searching in computerized retrieval is known as stringsearching (discussed in Chapter 10). The computer would recognize a stringsearch statement that would be introduced by a special command. You may restrict search terms and search statements to specified fields.

SEARCH STATEMENT AND SEARCH QUERY

We will avoid from now on using "search" as an unqualified noun because of the various meanings it may have. A search may refer to one of four entities: statement, query, formulation, or strategy. A *search statement* is a computer-readable message containing search terms and logical operators for combining them. A *search query,* in contrast, is a statement of an information need that is usually not yet expressed in terms directly understood by the computer.

SEARCH FORMULATION AND SEARCH STRATEGY

When translated into computer-readable form, a search query may correspond to any number of search statements. These comprise a *search formulation,* defined as a set of search statements translated from a search query. A *search strategy* is an intermediate form between search query and search formulation; that is, it is more structured than a search query in terms of computer readability, but not as structured as a search formulation. The following table summarizes the four meanings of "search."

CLASSIFICATION OF "SEARCH"

NOT NECESSARILY (USUALLY NOT) COMPUTER-READABLE:

Search Queries, original expressions of information need,
less structured than:

Search Strategies, translated into forms that:

MUST BE COMPUTER-READABLE:

Search Formulations, consisting of sets of:

Search Statements

In a broad sense, searching by computer includes not only human input at the terminal, and subsequent computer locating of records, but also the translation of search queries into search strategies and ultimately into search formulations that comprise the direct input to the computer, as well as the subsequent revision of any version of the search, from query to formulation. *Retrieval* (retrieving) is a process that includes searching a file, storage by the computer of addresses to records located by search statements, display of search statement results as counts (described below), and display of records located by the stored addresses.

**SEARCHING
AND RETRIEVAL**

RETRIEVAL SET AND SEARCH STATEMENT RESULT

The term "retrieval" is sometimes used for referring to records located and available for display as the output of the retrieval process, but we will refer to these records as the *retrieval set*. The computer signals that it is finished processing a search statement by displaying a count of the total number of records in the retrieval set, referred to as the *search statement result* (discussed in Chapter 7). Some computers also display counts for each search term in the search statement. After viewing the search statement result, you can then decide whether to revise or disregard the search statement or display records in the retrieval set.

FEEDBACK DURING INTERACTIVE RETRIEVAL

You may decide to revise a search statement based on viewing the records. An example was presented in Chapter 1 where searching for "knee joint replacement" in titles of articles resulted in the display of a record containing the keyword "Knee Prosthesis," suggesting its use as a search term for retrieving additional relevant records. This type of feedback is used frequently during interactive retrieval, namely, searching for terms that originate from the document being indexed, such as the title, for displaying relevant records in order to discover additional search terms. In this example, the additional term had been assigned to the record from a controlled indexing vocabulary.

PRECISION AND RECALL RATIOS

A retrieval set resulting from a search query on a particular topic usually contains records of varying relevant to the topic. Two measures of effectiveness of retrieval are *precision ratio* and *recall ratio,* defined as follows:

$$precision = \frac{number\ of\ relevant\ records\ in\ the\ retrieval\ set}{number\ of\ records\ in\ the\ retrieval\ set}$$

$$recall = \frac{number\ of\ relevant\ records\ in\ the\ retrieval\ set}{number\ of\ relevant\ records\ in\ the\ file}$$

These measures are sometimes expressed as percentages. In general, precision and recall are considered inversely related. The purpose of revising search formulations is to improve precision without drastically lowering recall or to improve recall without drastically lowering precision.

In Chapter 7, after logical operators and search statement results have been covered, we will describe and illustrate the techniques of developing search strategies and formulations.

EXERCISES

1. Select two or three actual textbooks that are on the same subject (with some title words in common), and do the following:

   a. Create bibliographic records on paper for these books, with at least the same fields as the bibliographic records in this chapter, and assign them to hypothetical computer addresses.

   b. Construct an index to these records, patterned after the index in this chapter.

   c. Describe how at least one search key value was placed in the index.

   d. Identify at least one search term for each search key value, and specify which bibliographic record(s) the search term would locate.

2. Distinguish among the following in terms of their location and function:

   • search key values

   • search terms

   • keywords

3. Describe three types of search key values that may come from a title field. Include examples of each, based on a specific title. Rank these for effectiveness as search terms for retrieving a particular record, and explain. Rank them again, this time for effectiveness as search terms for subject searching.

4. Would textwords using the author field as a keyword source be useful? Explain your answer.

5. Cross out words in the following passage that a computer might identify as stopwords. Read the passage omitting the stopwords.

The immune system, which equals in complexity the intricacies of the brain and nervous system, displays several remarkable characteristics. It is able to distinguish between "self" and "nonself." It is able to remember previous experiences and react accordingly: once you have had the mumps, your immune system will prevent you from getting it again. The immune system displays both enormous diversity and extraordinary specificity: not only is it able to recognize many millions of "nonself" molecules, it can produce molecules to match up with and counteract each one of them. And it has at its command a sophisticated array of weapons.

The success of this system in defending the body depends on an incredibly elaborate and dynamic regulatory communications network. Millions and millions of cells, organized into sets and subsets, pass information back and forth like clouds of bees swarming around a hive. The result is a sensitive system of checks and balances that produces an immune response that is prompt, appropriate, effective, and self-limiting.*

6. Name and briefly characterize the two basic types of computer searching introduced in this chapter.

7. Distinguish among the four meanings of the word "search."

8. Compare the processes of searching and retrieval.

9. Describe the use of feedback for discovering additional search terms. Give an example of using feedback to find additional search terms for searching titles of articles.

10. Based on a given search statement result and corresponding retrieval set, describe how you would proceed to determine the precision ratio and the recall ratio. Which measure is harder to determine? Why?

Understanding the Immune System. NIH Publication No. 84–529, October 1983.

Logical Operators
Used in Searching

6

In Chapter 1 you read about the two logical operators AND (operator for intersection) and OR (operator for union). AND was used in the search statement TELEVISION AND ELECTIONS for retrieving a set of records resulting from intersection of the set of TELEVISION records with the set of ELECTIONS records. OR was used for searching in parallel sets of records, each of which pertained to a university: ED = CORNELL OR ED = DARTMOUTH OR ED = PRINCETON OR . . . (ED is the abbreviation for the education search key).

We learned in the preceding chapter that in searching an index, the computer locates records by matching search terms in the search statement against search key values in the index. Based on the use of logical operators in search statements, we can define the condition for a successful match. When logical operators are used in search statements processed against the index, a successful match means not only that search terms in the search statement are identical to search key values in the index, but also that the same relationship between search terms, as specified by these logical operators, also applies to the matching search key values. In the case of the search statement TELEVISION AND ELECTIONS, the two search terms are being intersected in order to identify, by computer address, and retrieve only those records that are located by both TELEVISION and ELECTIONS as search key values.

The logical operators will be defined and illustrated systematically in this chapter. At the end of the chapter, we will describe and illustrate the logical operations specifically in terms of searching the index. For now, we will be concerned with understanding relationships between search terms as defined by logical operators.

BOOLEAN LOGIC COMBINING SETS OF SEARCH TERMS

Logical operators are words that represent logical relationships between terms in a search statement, and they are used in a system known as *Boolean logic,* named after the mathematician George Boole. It is a combinational system for representing logical relationships between sets. Computerized searching is normally concerned with combining sets of search terms. A set of search terms represents a concept in a search query. During searching, a set of search terms is matched against terms in the retrieval file, either indirectly by searching the index or by searching records directly.

In order to define logical operators as simply as possible, most sets in this chapter will be a single word from the title of one of the two bibliographic records introduced in the previous chapter. (Constructing search strategies and formulations—identifying concepts from search queries, building sets of search terms for those concepts, and combining them using logical operators—will be described and fully illustrated in the next chapter.)

A computer might not permit all the logical operators described in this chapter. The rules that govern the order of precedence of logical operators in a search statement might not be the same for all computers. Therefore, a computer that you use may have different rules of precedence from those used in this discussion.

VENN DIAGRAMS

In order to illustrate sets of records that would be retrieved, or not retrieved, by a search statement, it is helpful to have a visual representation of the universal set, which is the set of all records in a file. A diagram of a rectangle labeled U for universe may be used for this purpose (see Figure 6.1).

Labels, such as A and B, may be used for representing subsets of U, which are subsets of the universal set of records in a file. In Figure 6.2, A and B are subsets of the universal set. The area that would contain records in common (i.e., where A and B intersect) is labeled A∩B.

U = universe of all
    records in a file

FIGURE 6.1. Visual representation of a universal set.

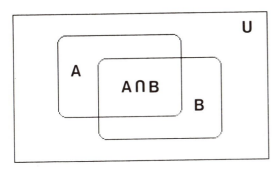

U = universe of all
    records in a file

A = subset of the
    universal set

B = subset of the
    universal set

FIGURE 6.2. Visual representation of subsets of a universal set.

A graphic representation showing the universal set and intersecting subsets is known as a *Venn diagram*.

The universes in the remaining Venn diagrams in this chapter will
represent all bibliographic records in a library, and the labeled subsets
will stand for sets of these records having particular words, namely
title words from our two-record bibliographic file, as mentioned previously. The universe excluding these subsets stands for the set of rec-

ords not having any of those words. The ∩ will be used for denoting intersection as in the previous example.

We will use these diagrams for identifying sets of records that would be retrieved according to a particular search statement. The shaded area in the diagram represents a set of records retrieved by a particular search statement containing search terms that the computer has matched against certain words. Although you have learned in the previous chapter that matching during retrieval normally occurs between search terms and search key values in the index, in order to simplify the discussion we will speak in terms of direct matching between search terms and words in titles of bibliographic records.

In this chapter, we have employed a format that immediately tests your understanding of each logical operator after the explanation by asking you to apply a search statement using the logical operator to a bibliographic file of two records. The same file is used in each question, and the answer provided directly after it. Other types of questions, immediately followed by answers, appear as well. There are two ways you might approach a question:

1. Answer the question as you read the chapter.

2. As you read the chapter, regard the question with its answer as illustrative. You may return to the question later, and answer it as a way of reviewing the material.

SINGLE-TERM SEARCH STATEMENT

Let's first examine a single-term search statement, that is, a search statement that does not contain a logical operator. To illustrate, let's use the Venn diagram in Figure 6.3 for the single-term search statement GUIDE. The search statement GUIDE would retrieve only records having the word GUIDE in the title, represented by G in the diagram.

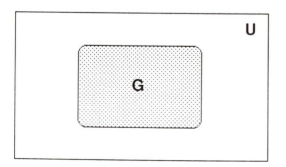

U = universe of all records in a bibliographic file

G = records having the word GUIDE in the title

FIGURE 6.3. Venn diagram of the search statement GUIDE.

Which of the records having the following titles would be retrieved using the search statement GUIDE?

1. Guide to enjoying the teenage years.

2. Guide to enjoying yourself on a rainy afternoon.

Since both records are in set G, both records would be retrieved.

You could increase your chances of finding a particular record by employing a search statement that has two search terms and requires that both words matching these terms be in the title. For example, a search statement requiring both "guide" and "rainy" as words in the title could be used for retrieving only the second record, titled "Guide to enjoying yourself on a rainy afternoon." This type of search statement uses the AND operator:

LOGICAL OPERATOR FOR INTERSECTION: AND

GUIDE AND RAINY

AND is the logical operator for intersection. Figure 6.4 is a Venn diagram illustrating this search statement. The search statement GUIDE AND RAINY would retrieve only records having as words in the title both GUIDE and RAINY, represented by the intersection of G and R in the diagram.

Which of the records having the following titles would be retrieved using the search statement GUIDE AND RAINY?

1. Guide to enjoying the teenage years.

2. Guide to enjoying yourself on a rainy afternoon.

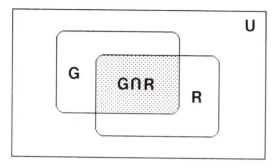

U = universe of all records in a bibliographic file

G = records having the word GUIDE in the title

R = records having the word RAINY in the title

FIGURE 6.4. Venn diagram of the search statement GUIDE AND RAINY.

Since the first record is not in the intersection of sets G and R, and the second record is in the intersection of sets G and R, only the second record would be retrieved.

An extension of intersection searches for records having words that co-occur in a record, but that furthermore occur in specific positions in relation to one another in the record. This capability uses positional operators (discussed in Chapter 10).

LOGICAL OPERATOR FOR UNION: OR

Another operator is OR. Suppose you want to retrieve only records having as words in the title either GUIDE or RAINY or both. This type of search statement uses the OR operator:

GUIDE OR RAINY

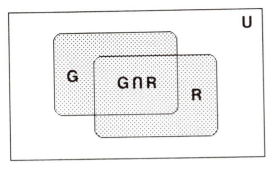

U = universe of all records in a bibliographic file

G = records having the word GUIDE in the title

R = records having the word RAINY in the title

FIGURE 6.5. Venn diagram of the search statement GUIDE OR RAINY.

OR is the logical operator for union. Figure 6.5 is a Venn diagram illustrating this search statement. The search statement GUIDE OR RAINY would retrieve only records having as words in the title either GUIDE, represented by G, or RAINY, represented by R, or both, represented by the intersection of G and R.

Which of the records having the following titles would be retrieved using the search statement GUIDE OR RAINY?

1. Guide to enjoying the teenage years.

2. Guide to enjoying yourself on a rainy afternoon.

Since the first record is in set G, and the second record is in set R, both records would be retrieved. It does not matter that the first record is not in the intersection of sets G and R, and the second record is in the intersection of sets G and R.

LOGICAL OPERATOR FOR COMPLEMENT: NOT

The operator NOT is the logical operator for complement. When a universe of records U, which is not empty, is divided into two sets, the two sets are complementary, or each set is the complement of the other. If U contains a set of records A, the complement of A would be a set of records excluding A, or NOT A. Suppose you want to retrieve all records not having the word GUIDE in the title. You would enter the search statement:

NOT GUIDE

Figure 6.6 is a Venn diagram illustrating this search statement. The search statement NOT GUIDE would retrieve only records not having GUIDE as a word in the title, represented by U excluding G. U excluding G is the complement of G.

Which of the records having the following titles would be retrieved using the search statement NOT GUIDE?

1. Guide to enjoying the teenage years.

2. Guide to enjoying yourself on a rainy afternoon.

Since neither record is in the universal set excluding set G, neither record would be retrieved.

The difference between NOT and the two operators AND and OR is that rather than relating one nonuniversal subset to another, the NOT operator, as the operator for complement, relates a subset to the universe by representing the universe excluding the subset.

BASIC LOGICAL OPERATORS: AND, OR, NOT

AND, OR, and NOT are the basic logical operators since they cannot be further broken down into other operators. In other words, a basic

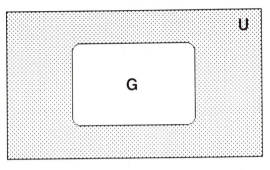

U = universe of all records in a bibliographic file

G = records having the word GUIDE in the title

FIGURE 6.6. Venn diagram of the search statement NOT GUIDE.

operator is not made up of combinations of other operators. Basic operators may, however, be combined with each other into more complex operators for logically relating search terms to each other.

The logical operators AND and NOT may be used together. Figure 6.7 is the Venn diagram for the search statement:

GUIDE AND NOT RAINY

The search statement GUIDE AND NOT RAINY would retrieve only records having the word GUIDE in the title that do not also have the word RAINY in the title, represented by G excluding the intersection of G and R.

Which of the records having the following titles would be retrieved using the search statement GUIDE AND NOT RAINY?

1. Guide to enjoying the teenage years.

2. Guide to enjoying yourself on a rainy afternoon.

COMBINED LOGICAL OPERATORS: AND NOT

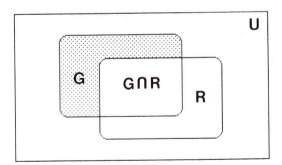

U = universe of all records in a bibliographic file

G = records having the word GUIDE in the title

R = records having the word RAINY in the title

FIGURE 6.7. Venn diagram of the search statement GUIDE AND NOT RAINY.

Since only the first record is in the portion of set G excluding the intersection of sets G and R, the first word would be retrieved, and the second record would not be retrieved.

Some computers accept NOT instead of the combination AND NOT, so that, for example, GUIDE NOT RAINY is equivalent to, and used in place of, the search statement GUIDE AND NOT RAINY.

COMBINED LOGICAL OPERATORS: OR NOT

The logical operators OR and NOT may be used together. Figure 6.8 is the Venn diagram for the search statement:

RAINY OR NOT GUIDE

The search statement RAINY OR NOT GUIDE would retrieve all records in the universe except for those having the word GUIDE in the title that do not also have the word RAINY in the title, represented by U, including all of R, and excluding the part of G that does not intersect with R. In other words, the only records not retrieved would be those having GUIDE and not also RAINY, represented by the part of G not intersecting with R.

Comparing the area in Figure 6.8 representing retrieval for RAINY OR NOT GUIDE with the area in Figure 6.7 representing retrieval for GUIDE AND NOT RAINY, how could you show the relationship RAINY OR NOT GUIDE using complement?

Comparing the two diagrams shows that RAINY OR NOT GUIDE and GUIDE AND NOT RAINY are complementary. Since the area in the diagram representing retrieval for RAINY OR NOT GUIDE is the complement of GUIDE AND NOT RAINY (the part of G not intersecting with R), you can show the relationship GUIDE OR NOT RAINY using the following search statement:

NOT (GUIDE AND NOT RAINY)

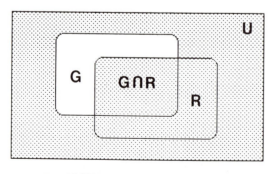

U = universe of all records in a bibliographic file

G = records having the word GUIDE in the title

R = records having the word RAINY in the title

FIGURE 6.8. Venn diagram of the search statement RAINY OR NOT GUIDE.

As described later in this chapter, parentheses are used for clarifying the order of operations, in this case ensuring that the enclosed operation GUIDE AND NOT RAINY is done first, and that the initial NOT is applied to the result of that operation.

Similarly, the following two search statements are equivalent:

RAINY OR NOT RAINY

NOT (RAINY AND NOT RAINY)

Since no record could simultaneously have and not have the word RAINY in the title, in the latter search statement RAINY AND NOT RAINY is an operation that retrieves the empty set, which is the complement of the universe. Since this search statement is applying NOT to the empty set, its result is the complement of the empty set, which is the universe. Therefore, both of these search statements would retrieve all records in the universe. If X stands for any search term, how could you use OR NOT in a search statement to retrieve all records in the universe?

If X stands for any search term, the following search statement would retrieve all records in the universe:

X OR NOT X

Which of the records having the following titles would be retrieved using the search statement RAINY OR NOT GUIDE?

1. Guide to enjoying the teenage years.

2. Guide to enjoying yourself on a rainy afternoon.

Since the first record is in the part of set G that does not intersect with set R, and the second record is in set R, the first record would not be retrieved, and the second record would be retrieved.

Another operator is XOR, the exclusive OR logical operator. Suppose you want to retrieve only records having as words in the title either GUIDE or RAINY, but not both. You would enter the search statement:

NONBASIC LOGICAL OPERATOR: XOR

GUIDE XOR RAINY

Figure 6.9 is a Venn diagram illustrating this search statement. The search statement GUIDE XOR RAINY would retrieve only records having as words in the title GUIDE or RAINY, but not both, represented by the union G OR R except for the intersection G AND

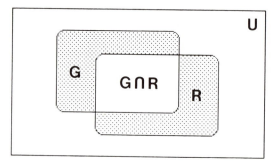

U = universe of all records in a bibliographic file

G = records having the word GUIDE in the title

R = records having the word RAINY in the title

FIGURE 6.9. Venn diagram of the search statement GUIDE XOR RAINY.

R. How could you show this relationship without the logical operator XOR?

Instead of GUIDE XOR RAINY, you can use the following search statement:

GUIDE AND NOT RAINY OR RAINY AND NOT GUIDE

Since we intend this search statement to return records having either (1) GUIDE and not RAINY, or (2) RAINY and not GUIDE, we want the AND to be done before the OR. We can put parentheses in the search statement for clarity, as follows:

(GUIDE AND NOT RAINY) OR (RAINY AND NOT GUIDE)

Operations in parentheses are performed first. This use of parentheses is similar to the use of parentheses in clarifying the following arithmetic calculation:

$9 + 4 \times 2$

The rule is that multiplication is done before addition, and everyone who knows the rule would know that:

$9 + 4 \times 2 = 9 + (4 \times 2) = 9 + 8 = 17$

Let's rewrite the calculation so that the order of operations from left to right is according to the rule, as follows:

$4 \times 2 + 9$

If you intend for the addition to be done first, you would have to clarify the order using parentheses, since the order you want is against the rule. This other calculation, with its solution, would be written as follows:

$(9 + 4) \times 2 = 26$

or:

$2 \times (9 + 4) = 26$

If the logical operators AND and OR are both used in a single search statement, the rule is that AND (in this case, combined with NOT) is done first, and OR is done second. Everyone understanding that rule would know that:

GUIDE AND NOT RAINY OR RAINY AND NOT GUIDE

is the same as:

(GUIDE AND NOT RAINY) OR (RAINY AND NOT GUIDE)

Using the preceding diagram for XOR, which of the records having the following titles would be retrieved by the search statement GUIDE XOR RAINY?

1. Guide to enjoying the teenage years.
2. Guide to enjoying yourself on a rainy afternoon.

Since the first record is in the part of set G that does not intersect with set R, and the second record is in the intersection of sets G and R, the first record would be retrieved, and the second record would not be retrieved. XOR is not a basic operator since, as shown previously, the XOR relationship can also be expressed using AND, OR, and NOT.

In the alternative search statement for GUIDE XOR RAINY,

(GUIDE AND NOT RAINY) OR (RAINY AND NOT GUIDE)

what is wrong with saying that the search statement would retrieve records having either (1) GUIDE and not RAINY, or (2) RAINY and not GUIDE, or (3) both of these relationships?

It is wrong since only the first two choices could apply. Choice 3, "both of these relationships," cannot occur. If you'll look at the XOR Venn diagram, you can see that it is impossible for a record to be in G AND NOT R and R AND NOT G simultaneously.

NONBASIC LOGICAL OPERATOR: NOR

NOR is another logical operator that is not basic. Suppose you want to retrieve only records having neither the word GUIDE nor the word RAINY in the title. You would enter the search statement:

GUIDE NOR RAINY

Figure 6.10 is a Venn diagram illustrating NOR. The search statement GUIDE NOR RAINY would retrieve only records not having as words in the title either GUIDE or RAINY or both, in other words the complement of the union GUIDE OR RAINY, represented by U excluding the union G OR R. How could you show this relationship using NOT and OR instead of NOR?

Instead of NOR, you can use the following:

NOT (GUIDE OR RAINY)

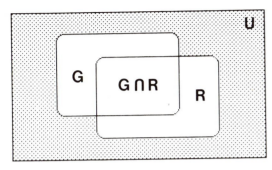

U = universe of all records in a bibliographic file

G = records having the word GUIDE in the title

R = records having the word RAINY in the title

FIGURE 6.10. Venn diagram of the search statement GUIDE NOR RAINY.

The parentheses in the preceding search statement are necessary since we want OR to be done first, contrary to the rule that NOT is done before OR. How else could you show this relationship, this time using NOT and AND instead of NOR?

Instead of NOR, you can use the following:

(NOT GUIDE) AND (NOT RAINY)

Since the rule is that NOT is done before AND, we could, in this case, leave out the parentheses, as follows:

NOT GUIDE AND NOT RAINY

Using the diagram for NOR (Figure 6.10), which of the records having the following titles would be retrieved by the search statement GUIDE NOR RAINY?

1. Guide to enjoying the teenage years.

2. Guide to enjoying yourself on a rainy afternoon.

Since both records are in set G, neither record would be retrieved.

The final logical operator, also not basic, is NAND. Suppose you want to retrieve only records not having both GUIDE and RAINY as words in the title, whether or not they had either. You would enter the search statement:

GUIDE NAND RAINY

Figure 6.11 is a Venn diagram illustrating NAND. The search statement GUIDE NAND RAINY would retrieve only records not having as words in the title both GUIDE and RAINY whether or not they had either GUIDE or RAINY; in other words, the complement of the intersection of GUIDE and RAINY, represented by U excluding the intersection G AND R. How could you show this relationship using NOT and AND instead of NAND?

Instead of NAND, you can use the following:

NOT (GUIDE AND RAINY)

The parentheses in the preceding search statement are necessary since we want AND to be done first, contrary to the rule that NOT is done before AND.

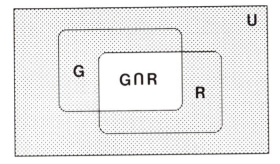

U = universe of all records in a bibliographic file

G = records having the word GUIDE in the title

R = records having the word RAINY in the title

FIGURE 6.11. Venn diagram of the search statement GUIDE NAND RAINY.

Comparing the Venn diagrams for XOR, NOR, and NAND, how could you show this NAND relationship using XOR, NOR, and OR?

Instead of this NAND relationship we can use the following:

(GUIDE XOR RAINY) OR (GUIDE NOR RAINY)

How could you show this relationship using only the basic logical operators? (Hint: Transform XOR and NOR into basic operators, as shown earlier.)

You can show this relationship using only the basic operators in either of the two following ways:

(GUIDE AND NOT RAINY) OR (RAINY AND NOT GUIDE) OR (NOT (GUIDE OR RAINY))

(GUIDE AND NOT RAINY) OR (RAINY AND NOT GUIDE) OR (NOT GUIDE AND NOT RAINY)

Using the preceding Venn diagram illustrating NAND (Figure 6.11), which of the records having the following titles would be retrieved by the search statement GUIDE NAND RAINY?

1. Guide to enjoying the teenage years.

2. Guide to enjoying yourself on a rainy afternoon.

Since only the second record is in the intersection of sets G and R, the first record would be retrieved, and the second record would not be retrieved.

SUMMARY: ORDER OF BASIC LOGICAL OPERATIONS

Let's summarize the order of the three basic logical operations when parentheses are not needed. The order we will use is NOT, AND, OR; when identical operators appear in sequence, their order of operation will proceed from left to right. Again using a comparison with arithmetic operations, the NOT, AND, OR rule may be viewed as similar to the rule for processing negation, multiplication, and addition in the following arithmetic calculation:

$$9 + -4 \times 2$$

(The "−" is the negation sign, not the minus sign.)

The rule requires that negation is done first, multiplication is done second, and addition is done last. Complying with that rule results in the following:

$$9 + -4 \times 2 = 9 + ((-4) \times 2) = 9 + (-8) = 1$$

The order of calculation from left to right can be rewritten according to the rule, and would appear as follows:

$$-4 \times 2 + 9$$

UNION AND INTERSECTION: COMBINING THREE SUBSETS

If we had three subsets, A, B, and C, how would you write a search statement for the following expression: the union of set A and the intersection of sets B and C?

The following is a search statement for the union of set A and the intersection of sets B and C:

A OR B AND C

Adding parentheses to show the order of operations according to the rule would result in the following:

A OR (B AND C)

The search statement A OR B AND C is represented by the Venn diagram in Figure 6.12.

What could you do to clarify the search statement A AND B OR C if you want it to mean the following English expression: the intersection of set A and the union of sets B and C?

Since the order you want is against the rule, you would need to clarify the order using parentheses, as follows:

A AND (B OR C)

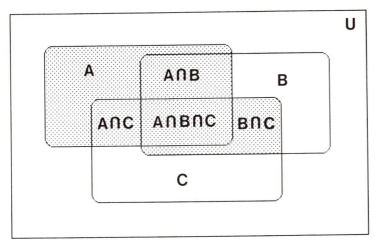

FIGURE 6.12. Venn diagram of the search statement A OR B AND C.

This search statement A AND (B OR C) is represented by the Venn diagram in Figure 6.13. Some computers do not allow the use of parentheses in search statements. If parentheses are not permitted, the search statement A AND (B OR C) would need to be written another way. How could it be rewritten without parentheses and still have the same meaning?

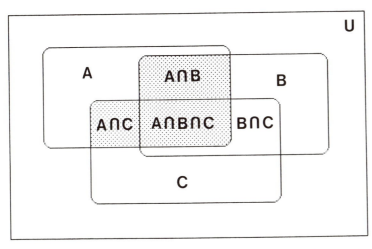

FIGURE 6.13. Venn Diagram of the search statement A AND (B OR C).

The search statement A AND (B OR C) could be written without parentheses as follows:

A AND B OR A AND C

You may want to check that this alternate version is represented by the same Venn diagram as the original version with parentheses.

EXERCISE: INTERSECTION OF FOUR SUBSETS

The Venn diagram in Figure 6.14 intersects four subsets and uses the numbers of the titles, 1 and 2, to show in which areas you would find records having the following titles:

1. Guide to enjoying the teenage years.

2. Guide to enjoying yourself on a rainy afternoon.

As a final exercise, determine which of the two preceding records represented by title would be retrieved using each of the search statements (SSs) that follow. You should attempt the exercise without referring to the Venn diagram.

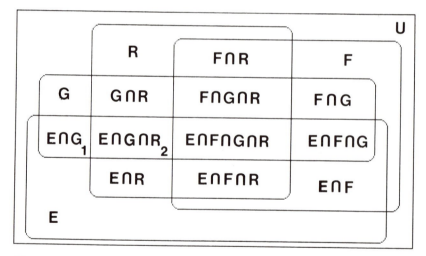

U = universe of all records in a bibliographic file

G = records having GUIDE in the title

R = records having RAINY in the title

E = records having ENJOYING in the title

F = records having FOOTBALL in the title

FIGURE 6.14. Venn diagram intersecting four subsets.

Before checking the answers against those given at the end of the exercise, you may check them using the diagram in Figure 6.14, as follows: Locate the area defined by the search statement. If E∩G (i.e., the area containing the number 1) is a subset of that area, then the first record would be retrieved. If E∩G∩R (i.e., the area containing the number 2) is a subset of that area, then the second record would be retrieved. Note that a set is considered a subset of itself.

As an example, let's consider the search statement GUIDE AND RAINY. The area in the diagram defined by this search statement is G∩R. Since E∩G (i.e., the area containing the number 1) is not a subset of G∩R, the search statement would not retrieve the first record. However, E∩G∩R (i.e., the area containing the number 2) is a subset of G∩R. Therefore the search statement would retrieve the second record.

SS1 RAINY
SS2 FOOTBALL
SS3 GUIDE AND ENJOYING
SS4 GUIDE AND FOOTBALL
SS5 GUIDE OR ENJOYING
SS6 RAINY OR FOOTBALL
SS7 NOT RAINY
SS8 NOT FOOTBALL
SS9 GUIDE AND NOT ENJOYING
SS10 GUIDE AND NOT FOOTBALL
SS11 GUIDE OR NOT ENJOYING
SS12 GUIDE OR NOT GUIDE
SS13 FOOTBALL OR NOT RAINY
SS14 FOOTBALL OR NOT GUIDE
SS15 GUIDE XOR ENJOYING
SS16 GUIDE XOR FOOTBALL
SS17 GUIDE NOR ENJOYING
SS18 FOOTBALL NOR RAINY
SS19 GUIDE NAND ENJOYING
SS20 GUIDE NAND FOOTBALL

Answers:

SS1-#2 only; SS2-neither; SS3-both; SS4-neither;
SS5-both; SS6-#2 only; SS7-#1 only; SS8-both;
SS9-neither; SS10-both; SS11-both; SS12-both;
SS13-#1 only; SS14-neither; SS15-neither; SS16-both;
SS17-neither; SS18-#1 only; SS19-neither; SS20-both

**LOGICAL
OPERATORS
AND INDEX
SEARCHING**

We have shown in the previous chapter how the computer searches the index in processing single-term search statements. We will now describe how the computer searches the index to process search statements that contain logical operators. To illustrate, we will use a portion of an index, similar to the one developed in the preceding chapter, but we will assume that two new records have been added to the file. The titles of the records indexed, and their addresses, are as follows:

address #37: GUIDE TO ENJOYING THE TEENAGE YEARS
address #24: GUIDE TO ENJOYING YOURSELF ON A RAINY
            AFTERNOON
address #55: RAINY DAYS
address #19: SUNNY DAYS

In the index, the words GUIDE, RAINY, and SUNNY are indexed as title textwords. The following is the portion of the index showing these words as search key values:

SEARCH KEY VALUE	SEARCH KEY	ADDRESS OF RECORD	NUMBER OF RECORDS
GUIDE	TW	24,37	2
RAINY	TW	24,55	2
SUNNY	TW	19	1

In the following explanations, addresses of records located by a search statement will be in bold type.

In processing GUIDE AND RAINY, the AND causes the computer to search the index and locate records as follows:

SEARCH KEY VALUE	SEARCH KEY	ADDRESS OF RECORD	NUMBER OF RECORDS
GUIDE	TW	**24**,37	2
RAINY	TW	**24**,55	2
SUNNY	TW	19	1

This search statement will thereby locate the record with the following title:

GUIDE TO ENJOYING YOURSELF ON A RAINY AFTERNOON

In processing GUIDE OR RAINY, the OR operator causes the computer to search the index and locate records as follows:

SEARCH KEY VALUE	SEARCH KEY	ADDRESS OF RECORD	NUMBER OF RECORDS
GUIDE	TW	24,37	2
RAINY	TW	24,55	2
SUNNY	TW	19	1

This search statement will thereby locate records with the following titles:

GUIDE TO ENJOYING THE TEENAGE YEARS
GUIDE TO ENJOYING YOURSELF ON A RAINY AFTERNOON
RAINY DAYS

In processing NOT GUIDE, the NOT operator causes the computer to search the index and locate records as follows:

SEARCH KEY VALUE	SEARCH KEY	ADDRESS OF RECORD	NUMBER OF RECORDS
GUIDE	TW	24,37	2
RAINY	TW	24,55	2
SUNNY	TW	19	1

This search statement will thereby locate records with the following titles:

RAINY DAYS
SUNNY DAYS

In processing GUIDE AND NOT RAINY, the AND NOT operator causes the computer to search the index and locate records as follows:

SEARCH KEY VALUE	SEARCH KEY	ADDRESS OF RECORD	NUMBER OF RECORDS
GUIDE	TW	24,37	2
RAINY	TW	24,55	2
SUNNY	TW	19	1

This search statement will thereby locate the record with the following title:

GUIDE TO ENJOYING THE TEENAGE YEARS

In processing GUIDE OR NOT RAINY, the OR NOT operator causes the computer to search the index and locate records as follows:

SEARCH KEY VALUE	SEARCH KEY	ADDRESS OF RECORD	NUMBER OF RECORDS
GUIDE	TW	24,37	2
RAINY	TW	24,55	2
SUNNY	TW	19	1

This search statement will thereby locate records with the following titles:

GUIDE TO ENJOYING THE TEENAGE YEARS
GUIDE TO ENJOYING YOURSELF ON A RAINY AFTERNOON
SUNNY DAYS

In processing GUIDE XOR RAINY, the XOR operator causes the computer to search the index and locate records as follows:

SEARCH KEY VALUE	SEARCH KEY	ADDRESS OF RECORD	NUMBER OF RECORDS
GUIDE	TW	24,37	2
RAINY	TW	24,55	2
SUNNY	TW	19	1

This search statement will thereby locate records with the following titles:

GUIDE TO ENJOYING THE TEENAGE YEARS
RAINY DAYS

In processing GUIDE NOR RAINY, the NOR operator causes the computer to search the index and locate records as follows:

SEARCH KEY VALUE	SEARCH KEY	ADDRESS OF RECORD	NUMBER OF RECORDS
GUIDE	TW	24,37	2
RAINY	TW	24,55	2
SUNNY	TW	19	1

This search statement will thereby locate the record with the following title:

SUNNY DAYS

In processing GUIDE NAND RAINY, the NAND operator causes the computer to search the index and locate records as follows:

SEARCH KEY VALUE	SEARCH KEY	ADDRESS OF RECORD	NUMBER OF RECORDS
GUIDE	TW	24,37	2
RAINY	TW	24,55	2
SUNNY	TW	19	1

This search statement will thereby locate records with the following titles:

GUIDE TO ENJOYING THE TEENAGE YEARS
RAINY DAYS
SUNNY DAYS

After locating and storing addresses of records in response to a search statement, the computer returns a result, which is the topic of the next chapter.

Exercises for this chapter are based on the following passage. Each sentence should be considered a separate record. Assume that words in the passage, except stopwords, are search key values that locate the sentence a word is in. Your answers should identify sentences by number, and a set of sentences as numbers in curly brackets, e.g. {1 2 3 4}.

EXERCISES

(1) The immune system, which equals in complexity the intricacies of the brain and nervous system, displays several remarkable characteristics. (2) It is able to distinguish between "self" and "nonself." (3) It is able to remember previous experiences and react accordingly: once you have had the mumps, your immune system will prevent you from getting it again. (4) The immune system displays both enormous diversity and extraordinary specificity: not only is it able to recognize many millions of "nonself" molecules, it can produce molecules to match up with and counteract each one of them. (5) And it has at its command a sophisticated array of weapons.
(6) The success of this system in defending the body depends on an incredibly elaborate and dynamic regulatory communications network. (7) Millions and millions of cells, organized into sets and subsets, pass information back and forth like clouds of bees swarming around a hive. (8) The result is a sensitive system of checks and balances that

produces an immune response that is prompt, appropriate, effective, and self-limiting.*

1. Identify the set of sentences, by number, from the preceding passage that would be retrieved by the following search statements. The first answer is given.

    a. SYSTEM   {1 3 4 6 8}

    b. IMMUNE

    c. NOT SYSTEM

    d. NOT IMMUNE

    e. IMMUNE AND SYSTEM

    f. IMMUNE OR SYSTEM

    g. IMMUNE AND NOT SYSTEM

    h. SYSTEM AND NOT IMMUNE

    i. IMMUNE OR NOT SYSTEM

    j. SYSTEM OR NOT IMMUNE

    k. IMMUNE XOR SYSTEM

    l. IMMUNE NOR SYSTEM

    m. NOT IMMUNE AND NOT SYSTEM

    n. IMMUNE NAND SYSTEM

    o. MOLECULES AND MOLECULES

    p. SYSTEM AND SYSTEM

    q. MILLIONS AND MILLIONS

2. a. Construct Venn diagrams for:

    SYSTEM AND NOT IMMUNE
    IMMUNE AND NOT SYSTEM
    SYSTEM XOR IMMUNE

    b. Are the first two search statements complementary? Write a statement showing that the union of two of these search statements is equivalent to the remaining search statement.

*Understanding the Immune System System. NIH Publication No. 84–529, October 1983.

A AND NOT B
B AND NOT A
A XOR B

3. a. Construct Venn diagrams for:

IMMUNE AND SYSTEM
IMMUNE NAND SYSTEM

b. What is the relationship between retrieval sets resulting from the following search statements?

A AND B
A NAND B

4. Insert parentheses for clarification in search statements a − d. Identify the set of sentences, by number, from the passage that would be retrieved by these search statements.

a. BRAIN AND NOT IMMUNE AND NOT SYSTEM

b. BRAIN AND NOT IMMUNE OR NOT SYSTEM

c. BRAIN OR NOT IMMUNE AND NOT SYSTEM

d. BRAIN OR NOT IMMUNE OR NOT SYSTEM

5. a. Using the search term CLOUDS, devise a search statement that would result in the retrieval set {7}.

b. Using the search term CLOUDS, devise a search statement that would result in the retrieval set {1 2 3 4 5 6 8}.

c. Using only the union operator, devise a search statement, using the fewest search terms possible, that would result in the retrieval set {1 2 3 4 5 6 7 8}.

d. Using the search terms in 5c, devise a search statement that would retrieve none of the sentences.

e. Devise a search statement containing only one search term and only one logical operator that would result in the same retrieval set as 5c.

f. Devise a search statement containing only one search term connected by a combination of two logical operators that would result in the same retrieval set as 5c.

g. Using the search terms IMMUNE and SYSTEM, devise a search statement that would result in the retrieval set {2 5 7}.

h. Assuming that the computer ignores double quote marks (""), and treats hyphens as blank characters, using only the search terms SELF and NONSELF, devise a search statement that would result in the retrieval set {4 8} but not {2}.

Search Statement Result, Development of Search Strategy and Formulation

7

After processing a search statement, the computer displays a count of the number of records in the retrieval set. This search statement result provides immediate feedback for judging the appropriateness of the search statement. If the count is not in accordance with your expectation, you will want to revise your search statement. At the end of this chapter, we will explain how search statement results were used in developing and revising a search formulation.

SEARCH STATEMENT RESULT FOR FEEDBACK

Searching may be enhanced by knowing search term results (counts of the number of records retrieved by individual search terms). A search term result may be obtained simply by entering the search term as a search statement, as follows:

SEARCH TERM RESULT

SEARCH STATEMENT

      GUIDE [TW]

RESULT   2 RECORDS

     The computer may automatically display search term results for each term in a search statement, as follows:

SEARCH STATEMENT

    [TW] GUIDE AND RAINY

RESULT   GUIDE [TW] - 2 RECORDS
              RAINY [TW] - 1 RECORD
              GUIDE [TW] AND RAINY [TW] - 1 RECORD

     Search term results may be known in advance of entering a search statement by requesting and then examining displays of the index to the retrieval file (as discussed in Chapter 10). These displays are similar to the index display in Chapter 5. For example, the following display from the index shows you that the search term result for GUIDE [TW] would be 2.

SEARCH KEY VALUE	SEARCH KEY	NUMBER OF RECORDS
GUIDE	TW	2

A search term missing from the index would result in no records retrieved (a zero count) if you entered it as a search statement.

NEGATIVE RESULT

The computer notifies you if the result of a search statement you have entered is zero. A zero count means that no record matched the search statement, or, in other words, no record qualified to be included in the retrieval set. In this case, we may say that the retrieval set is empty. A zero count message does not give you any information about why the count is zero. However, the computer would also send you a message indicating that a specific search term in your search statement was not found in the index.

To summarize, there are two kinds of negative search statement results. One kind would occur if a search term is not found in the index. The other would occur if the retrieval set is empty. A search statement could have both kinds of results, or one without the other.

VENN DIAGRAMS AND COMPUTER MESSAGES SHOWING RESULTS

In this chapter we will use Venn diagrams to visualize negative search statement results in response to specific search statements. Nonuniversal subset labels will appear outside the subsets. Within sets, the number of records in a region will be indicated by x = (number). If there are no records in a region or, in other words, the region is empty, x = 0 will be used. In addition, we will show the actual search statements followed by messages from the computer giving search statement results.

This chapter uses questions and answers in the same way as the previous chapter. The same approaches to this format, suggested there, also apply here. For example, let's assume that the following title is the only information in the record and that there are no other records in the file:

Guide to enjoying yourself on a rainy afternoon.

In searching this file, the search statement DAY could be diagrammed as in Figure 7.1. What search statement result would you receive from the computer?

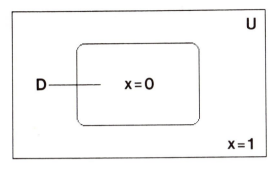

FIGURE 7.1. Venn diagram of the search term DAY.

The computer would send you two messages, one that the search term DAY (represented by D, which is empty) was not successfully matched, and the other that the retrieval set resulting from the search statement DAY (also represented by D) is empty. The following is the search statement and its result:

SEARCH STATEMENT

      DAY

RESULT   NO MATCH (DAY)
              0 RECORDS

For the same file, if the search statement is DAY AND RAINY, the diagram in Figure 7.2 would apply. What search statement result would you receive from the computer?

The computer would send you two messages, one that the search term DAY (represented by D, which is empty) was not successfully matched, and the other that the retrieval set resulting from the search

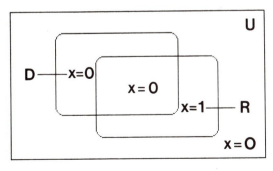

FIGURE 7.2. Venn diagram of the search terms DAY and RAINY.

statement DAY AND RAINY (represented by the intersection D AND R) is empty. The following is the search statement and its result:

SEARCH STATEMENT

   DAY AND RAINY

RESULT   NO MATCH (DAY)
           0 RECORDS

Again for this file, if the search statement is DAY OR RAINY, what search statement result would you receive from the computer?

The computer would send you two messages, one that the search term DAY (represented by D, which is empty) was not successfully matched, and the other that the retrieval set resulting from the search statement DAY OR RAINY (represented by the union D OR R) contains one record. The following is the search statement and its result:

SEARCH STATEMENT

   DAY OR RAINY

RESULT   NO MATCH (DAY)
           1 RECORD

Suppose you add another record to the file, thereby resulting in a file consisting of the following two records:

1. Guide to enjoying yourself on a rainy afternoon.

2. Spending the day at the museum.

If the search statement is DAY AND RAINY, the diagram in Figure 7.3 would apply. What search statement result would you receive from the computer?

There would be no message about not matching a search term since the search term DAY (represented by D, which is not empty) and the search term RAINY (represented by R, which is not empty) were both successfully matched. But since they were not found in the same record, as required by the logical operator AND, the computer would send you a message that the retrieval set resulting from the search statement DAY AND RAINY (represented by the intersection D AND R) is empty. The following is the search statement and its result:

SEARCH STATEMENT

   DAY AND RAINY

RESULT   0 RECORDS

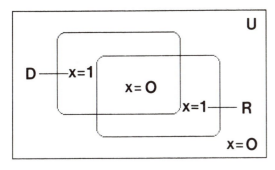

FIGURE 7.3. Venn diagram of the search terms DAY and RAINY.

For the same file, if the search statement is DAYS AND SUNNY, the diagram in Figure 7.4 would apply. What search statement result would you receive from the computer?

The computer would send you three messages: first, that the search term DAYS (represented by DS, which is empty) was not successfully matched; second, that the search term SUNNY (represented by S, which is empty) was not successfully matched; and third, that the retrieval set resulting from the search statement DAYS AND SUNNY (represented by the intersection DS AND S) is empty. The following is the search statement and its result:

SEARCH STATEMENT

      DAYS AND RAINY

RESULT   NO MATCH (DAYS)
              NO MATCH (SUNNY)
              0 RECORDS

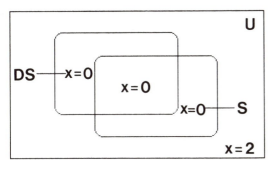

FIGURE 7.4. Venn diagram of the search terms DAYS and SUNNY.

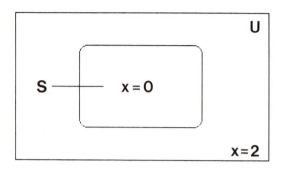

U = universe of all records in a bibliographic file

S = records having the word SUNNY in the title

FIGURE 7.5. Venn diagram of the search term SUNNY.

Again for this file, if the search statement is NOT SUNNY, the diagram in Figure 7.5 would apply. What search statement result would you receive from the computer?

The computer would send you two messages, one that the search term SUNNY (represented by S, which is empty) was not successfully matched, and the other that the retrieval set resulting from the search statement NOT SUNNY (the complement of S, which is not empty, as represented by the complement expression NOT S) contains two records. The following is the search statement and its result:

SEARCH STATEMENT

   NOT SUNNY

RESULT   NO MATCH (SUNNY)
              2 RECORDS

DEVELOPING SEARCH STRATEGY AND FORMULATION (I)

The following topics, covered in Chapters 5, 6, and in the beginning of this chapter, have prepared you for the task of developing a search formulation:

• searching the index

• logical operators

• search statement result

We will begin now to develop a search formulation, based on knowledge of these topics, and continue to develop the formulation at the conclusion of Chapters 8, 9, and 10. In each of these chapters, we will modify the formulation based on topics covered by that chapter. Development of a search formulation is usually an interactive process that depends, in part, on the viewing of retrieved records. In this chapter, we will use displays of titles to assist in developing the search formulation.

The search query under consideration is APPROACHES TO SOLVING THE SHORTAGE OF MATHEMATICS AND SCIENCE TEACHERS IN THE SCHOOLS. We will assume that the file being searched contains records that are references to journal articles, and that the file covers the subject of education. We will base the developing search strategy and formulation on retrieval from the ERIC® database, supplied by the Educational Resources Information Center (ERIC®), National Institute of Education, Washington, DC. In this chapter, we will be searching the index for title textwords. In the following chapter, we will make use of official subject terms from the thesaurus for this database (Thesaurus of ERIC® Descriptors, 9th Edition—1982, Oryx Press, Phoenix, AZ).

The first step is to identify the concepts in the search query. These concepts will correspond to sets that will be combined using logical operators (discussed in the previous chapter). Concepts (also called facets, aspects, or concept groups) should not be confused with words in the query. If we were to categorize the query by significant word, we would have seven parts to the query, as follows:

APPROACHES
SOLVING
SHORTAGE
MATHEMATICS
SCIENCE
TEACHERS
SCHOOLS

These words do not, however, directly represent the concepts in the query. APPROACHES and SOLVING signify too fine a breakdown, and actually represent a single concept, which we might call SOLVING, and thereby eliminate APPROACHES as a separate concept. We will assume that teachers are always "school teachers," and thereby eliminate SCHOOLS as a separate concept. (If this were someone else's query, we might need clarification in order to be sure that SCHOOLS did not refer to elementary and secondary schools only.) The remaining words now represent the concepts of the query, which are as follows:

SOLVING
SHORTAGE
MATHEMATICS

SCIENCE
TEACHERS

We will begin with the straightforward approach of combining all the concepts using the logical operators AND and OR. (The stated query does not require the remaining basic logical operator, NOT. However, AND NOT will be used for a special purpose later in the formulation.) In deciding how to apply logical operators, let's consider which concepts are necessary to express the meaning of the query. SOLVING, SHORTAGE, and TEACHERS are each necessary concepts. Neither MATHEMATICS nor SCIENCE is, by itself, necessary, but the query requires either the concept MATHEMATICS or the concept SCIENCE. Despite "MATHEMATICS AND SCIENCE TEACHERS" in the query statement, this is a union relationship, which uses the OR operator for forming the combination MATHEMATICS OR SCIENCE. We now have four necessary concepts, as follows:

SOLVING
SHORTAGE
MATHEMATICS OR SCIENCE
TEACHERS

The necessary concepts of a search query are intersected using the AND operator, since the query requires that each concept be represented in a record in order for the record to be considered relevant to the query. Our final search strategy could be represented as the following logical combination of concepts:

SOLVING AND SHORTAGE AND (MATHEMATICS OR SCIENCE) AND TEACHERS

In order to translate the above strategy into a formulation, we must assign search terms to each of these concepts. The search terms for each concept will be in a union relationship since they will be alternate terms for expressing the concept. In this chapter, we will identify, as search terms representing a concept, words that might be title textwords in the index, which, in turn, come from titles of articles that are indexed.

The first concept listed, SOLVING, happens to be the most difficult concept to translate into words. There are many ways of expressing this concept, so we will skip it for the time being and proceed to the other concepts. Search terms for the remaining concepts might be as follows:

CONCEPTS:	SHORTAGE	MATHEMATICS OR SCIENCE	TEACHERS
SEARCH TERMS:	shortage shortages scarcity	mathematics math science biology chemistry physics	teacher teachers

The following is the formulation resulting from this translation of concepts into search terms for matching title textwords in the index. We will use all lower case for these search terms.

(shortage OR shortages OR scarcity) AND (mathematics OR math OR science OR biology OR chemistry OR physics) AND (teacher OR teachers)

Since we anticipate difficulty in assigning search terms to the concept SOLVING, we will display titles of records retrieved by the above formulation, and see if those titles can help us in identifying search terms for this difficult concept. The following are the titles of the ten records in the retrieval set produced by the preceding search formulation:

1. Solving the math and science teacher shortage: one district's initiative.

2. The science teacher shortage in North Carolina: facts and myths.

3. Crisis in our high schools: the math and science teacher shortage.

4. A shortage of mathematics teachers in New York City.

5. The shortage of science teachers.

6. Use technology to cope with the scarcity of math and science teachers.

7. The shortage of chemistry teachers—a national crisis.

8. Beneath the surface of the mathematics teacher shortage.

9. The mathematics teacher shortage—some solutions.

10. Critical shortages of mathematics and science teachers in Iowa.

Although we can identify some SOLVING terms, namely "solving," "cope," and "solutions," we probably would not have wanted to limit the retrieval set to titles containing those terms; that is, an article with a general title, such as title #5, might discuss SOLVING. In fact, an article with a title that seems to refer to some other aspect, such as title #8, might nevertheless discuss SOLVING as well.

Assuming that we are not satisfied with the few records retrieved so far, we will attempt to find new search terms to assign to the concepts in the search strategy. We would do this by intersecting pairs of these concepts in order to find new terms for the omitted concept. For example, we might omit the SHORTAGE terms, and enter the following search formulation:

(mathematics OR math OR science OR biology OR chemistry OR physics) AND (teacher OR teachers)

The search statement result for this formulation is 961, which is clearly too many titles to scan for finding additional SHORTAGE terms. We might next intersect SHORTAGE with MATHEMATICS OR SCIENCE in order to find additional TEACHERS terms, as follows:

(shortage OR shortages OR scarcity) AND (mathematics OR math OR science OR biology OR chemistry OR physics)

The result was 11 records, but ten of these overlapped with the set of ten records retrieved previously. In order to retrieve only new records, we might have "negated" the third concept, TEACHERS, in the formulation, as follows:

(shortage OR shortages OR scarcity) AND (mathematics OR math OR science OR biology OR chemistry OR physics) AND NOT (teacher OR teachers)

This formulation resulted in the single new record, with the following title, which does not appear relevant to the query:

Social science research under siege: scarcity or conspiracy.

Let's now intersect SHORTAGE with TEACHERS, negating MATHEMATICS OR SCIENCE, in order to find additional MATHEMATICS OR SCIENCE terms, as follows:

(shortage OR shortages OR scarcity) AND (teacher OR teachers) AND NOT (mathematics OR math OR science OR biology OR chemistry OR physics)

This formulation resulted in 15 new records, with the following titles:

1. Recruiting shortage area teachers: is there a more effective way.

2. Corrective measures in the teacher shortage: consequences and conclusions.

3. But U.S. teachers oppose scarcity bonuses.

4. Teacher surplus and shortage: getting ready to accept responsibilities.

5. Teacher shortages—some proposed solutions.

6. Perceptions of teaching that may be influencing current shortage of teachers.

7. This bold incentive pay plan pits capitalism against teacher shortages.

8. The nature of teacher shortages in secondary schools.

9. Teacher shortage: fact or fiction.

10. Teacher supply: shortage or surplus.

11. Teacher shortage in U.S. vocational education: WHY.

12. The critical shortage of qualified Latin teachers.

13. Solving the teacher shortage in bilingual education.

14. Teacher shortage: big problems for small schools.

15. Midwest schools face shortages of good teachers.

These titles contain no new MATHEMATICS OR SCIENCE terms, but it is difficult to assess the relevance of some of them by title alone. We will see in the next chapter how official subject indexing terms provide additional clues to assessing relevance.

These new titles suggest additional SOLVING terms, namely, "corrective," "bonuses," and "incentive," to add to those found in titles in the first retrieval set. It still appears, however, that there is a good possibility that articles may be relevant to the query even when their titles do not contain any SOLVING term. In assuming that articles discussing the shortage of mathematics and science teachers might propose solutions to this problem, without the SOLVING concept appearing in the title, we are confirming our original strategy of excluding the SOLVING concept.

Our strategy of pairing concepts has not yielded additional terms, but if we take another look at the original set of ten titles, we notice that two of these also contain the word "crisis." In the second set, one title contains the word "supply." We might assign these as new search terms to SHORTAGE, as shown:

CONCEPTS:	SHORTAGE	MATHEMATICS OR SCIENCE	TEACHERS
SEARCH TERMS:	shortage shortages scarcity crisis supply	mathematics math science biology chemistry physics	teacher teachers

The following would be our revised formulation:

(shortage OR shortages OR scarcity OR crisis OR supply) AND (mathematics OR math OR science OR biology OR chemistry OR physics) AND (teacher OR teachers)

The revised formulation resulted in four new records, with the following titles:

1. The teacher crisis in secondary school science and mathematics.

2. The "crisis" in mathematics instruction and a new teacher education at grammar school level.

3. What research says—science teacher supply and demand.

4. Teacher supply and demand in mathematics and science.

Titles #1, #3, and #4 might be relevant. Based on the revised formulation, if we now repeat our strategy of intersecting concept pairs, specifically SHORTAGE and MATHEMATICS OR SCIENCE and negating the third concept, TEACHERS, we will retrieve additional possibly relevant titles, as follows:

1. The crisis in mathematics education.

2. The crisis in high-school and college physics education.

3. The crisis in high-school physics teaching.

4. The uneven crisis in science education.

5. Classroom crisis in science and math.

The last two sets of titles suggest additional terms to be assigned to the concepts ("demand," "teaching," "education," "classroom"). Note that three of these are new TEACHERS terms, found by intentionally negating this concept in the most recent strategy.

CONCEPTS:	SHORTAGE	MATHEMATICS OR SCIENCE	TEACHERS
SEARCH TERMS:	shortage	mathematics	teacher
	shortages	math	teachers
	scarcity	science	teaching
	crisis	biology	education
	supply	chemistry	classroom
	demand	physics	

If we now enter a final revised formulation to include all search terms, the result will be 29 records. This retrieval set will be "noisier" than the original one; that is, only 14 of the titles will appear relevant. The remaining 15 will either not be informative enough to evaluate or will appear not to be relevant. For example, titles may refer to a crisis that is clearly not the teacher shortage, such as:

The energy crisis as a theme in physical science education.

Others may refer to an educational crisis that appears not be the teacher shortage, for example:

Let kids experience science, and watch the crisis in science education subside.

Tolerating noise, such as that caused by introducing "crisis" into the search formulation, in order to retrieve additional relevant titles, and, conversely, not tolerating noise but thereby retrieving fewer relevant titles, illustrate the trade-off between precision and recall. Factors influencing your degree of tolerance include the purpose of the information you are seeking, your schedule, and your patience.

We have seen, in developing a search formulation, how the logical operator AND NOT might be used to avoid redisplaying records. The danger of using NOT for negating a concept, particularly at the outset, can be illustrated as follows. Suppose the search query has been restricted to elementary and secondary schools; in effect, excluding the shortage of mathematics and science teachers in college. It may seem easier, rather than building a list of search terms for ELEMENTARY SCHOOL OR SECONDARY SCHOOL, to use NOT

COLLEGE for the complement of COLLEGE, as seen in the following strategy:

SHORTAGE AND (MATHEMATICS OR SCIENCE) AND TEACHERS AND NOT COLLEGE

This strategy would, however, eliminate one of the relevant titles, namely:

The crisis in high-school and college physics education.

USING SEARCH STATEMENT RESULT

In developing our search formulation, we used techniques based on assessment of search statement results. They influenced our decisions to:

• not limit the retrieval set at the outset

• expand the retrieval set

• limit the retrieval set

The decision to initially omit SOLVING from the strategy was related not only to the difficulty of assigning search terms to this concept but also to the small initial retrieval set, even without this concept.

If this retrieval set had been much larger, for example if the result had been greater than 50, we might have attempted to include the intersection with SOLVING in the initial search strategy in order to produce a smaller, more precise retrieval set.

Efforts to discover alternate search terms and thereby expand the retrieval set were continued based on the modest initial retrieval set. Intermediate results were used in decisions to restrict the retrieval set. For example, intersecting SHORTAGE and TEACHERS, in order to find additional MATHEMATICS OR SCIENCE search terms, resulted in 61 records. Had this result been smaller, we might have elected to omit MATHEMATICS OR SCIENCE from our final strategy.

When we continue developing this search formulation at the end of Chapter 8, we will show how the use of a controlled indexing vocabulary simplifies searching, compared with searching textwords from natural language text.

EXERCISES

1. The following exercises are based on the passage in the Exercises for Chapter 6. What search statement result message would you receive from the computer based on the following search state-

ments? Use a number from 1–8 for the count of sentences that would be retrieved. Use NONE if no sentence would be retrieved. Use NO MATCH if a search term is not successfully matched.

   a. CLOUDS

   b. CLOUDY

   c. NOT CLOUDS

   d. NOT CLOUDY

   e. SUNNY AND CLOUDS

   f. SUNNY AND CLOUDY

   g. SUNNY OR CLOUDS

   h. SUNNY OR CLOUDY

2. Develop a search strategy and formulation for a query of your choice. The strategy you develop should contain at least three concepts. Assign possible search terms to the concepts based on expected title textwords. Indicate how you would discover additional search terms. Show how search statement results and your tolerance (or intolerance) for noise might affect the outcome.

3. Explain the use of search statement results in decisions to:

- limit retrieval
- not limit retrieval
- expand retrieval

Include examples (other than those given in this chapter) as part of the explanations.

Controlled Indexing Vocabulary for Searching by Subject

8

How do you locate information on a particular subject in a book without actually reading the book? The following are methods to use:

SUBJECT INDEX FOR LOCATING INFORMATION

- skimming through the body of the book

- reading chapter titles in the table of contents

- locating the topic in the index at the back of the book

The following are criteria for assessing these methods:

- Does the source cover all the topics you want to locate?

- Does the method require looking through too much information?

- Are the topics in the source sorted in a useful way? For example, are they in alphabetic order? Are they subdivided?

- Is each topic in the source in a single place?

- Does the source give cross references? Cross references tell you where else in the source to look for information.

- Does the source give all locations for each topic?

Let's compare these methods by ranking them, where a rank of 1 is the best rank.

METHOD	SKIM BOOK	READ TABLE OF CONTENTS	LOCATE IN INDEX
Number of topics	1	3	2
Least amount of unnecessary information	3	2	1
Useful sorting of topics	2 (a tie)	2 (a tie)	1
Each topic in one place	3	2	1
Cross references between topics	2	3	1
All locations for each topic	1 (a tie)	2	1 (a tie)

It appears that using the index is the best overall method for locating information on a particular subject in a book. A computerized controlled vocabulary index (explained in this chapter) has the same advantages for locating information on a particular subject in a file.

SUBJECT TERMS AND SUBJECT INDEX

We will build a subject index to our continuing bibliographic file and place the subject terms in a subject field in each record, using SU as the field abbreviation.

37.
AU- Smith, John
TI - Guide to enjoying the teenage years.
PL - Chicago, Illinois
PU- Atlas Publishing Company
PY - 1983
SU - Adolescents
     Family Relationships
     Hygiene
     Peer Relationship
     Recreational Activities
     Student School Relationship

24.
AU- Jones, Mary
TI - Guide to enjoying yourself on a rainy afternoon.
PL - Dallas, Texas
PU- Tops Publishing Company
PY - 1983
SU - Adolescents
     Arts Activities
     Children
     Games

Hobbies
Recreational Activities
Recreational Reading

The subject index, with each subject term a search key value, would appear as follows:

SEARCH KEY VALUE	SEARCH KEY	ADDRESS OF RECORD	NUMBER OF RECORDS
ADOLESCENTS	SU	24,37	2
ARTS ACTIVITIES	SU	24	1
CHILDREN	SU	24	1
FAMILY RELATIONSHIPS	SU	37	1
GAMES	SU	24	1
HOBBIES	SU	24	1
HYGIENE	SU	37	1
PEER RELATIONSHIP	SU	37	1
RECREATIONAL ACTIVITIES	SU	24,37	2
RECREATIONAL READING	SU	24	1
STUDENT SCHOOL RELATIONSHIP	SU	37	1

The subject terms were assigned from a controlled vocabulary, which is a set of predetermined words or phrases created and maintained specifically for representing the subject content of a file. Indexing using a controlled vocabulary is an intellectual effort whereby a trained indexer assigns to records terms from the vocabulary that best characterize the item being indexed. Assigned subject terms are keywords that are transformed into subject search key values in the index.

In indexing with a controlled vocabulary, a subject term for a topic is always used for indexing that topic. Therefore, controlled sub-

CONTROLLED VOCABULARY AND SUBJECT INDEXING

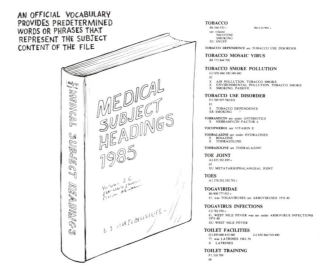

AN OFFICIAL VOCABULARY
PROVIDES PREDETERMINED
WORDS OR PHRASES THAT
REPRESENT THE SUBJECT
CONTENT OF THE FILE

ject terms, when transformed into search key values, facilitate searching based on meaning; that is, they provide a unique location for information on a specific subject regardless of what words and phrases express that subject in the physical item. Indexers frequently choose the appropriate subject terms from alphabetized displays of subject terms. Later in the chapter, we will discuss other formats that facilitate selection of terms.

WHY ARE CONTROLLED SUBJECT TERMS
TRANSFORMED TO SEARCH KEY VALUES?

TO FACILITATE SEARCHING
BASED ON MEANING

CONTROLLED NONSUBJECT AUTHORITIES

The controlled indexing vocabulary is a convenient place for terms that are descriptive in ways other than subject content, such as the physical form of the item being indexed (e.g., hard cover, soft cover, videocassette), its literary form (e.g., essay, novel, technical report), or the language in which it is written or spoken.

Other controlled authorities may be used in indexing, such as authority lists of names of individuals or organizations. These authorities are used primarily for standardizing certain information that already exists in the item being indexed, such as names of authors, publishers, or serials (magazines, journals, regularly held conferences, etc.). An overlap between the controlled indexing vocabulary and a name authority list would occur when a person or organization whose name is in a name authority list is also a subject.

In this book, the focus will be on the controlled indexing vocabulary for subject indexing, but the principles discussed are applicable to controlled vocabularies for descriptive indexing as well as other types of authority lists.

The computer usually applies validation rules to the indexing process for ensuring that subject terms in the record exactly match official subject terms in the controlled indexing vocabulary file. Validation rules thereby enhance the reliability of the controlled indexing vocabulary for retrieval. Subject terms from controlled indexing vocabularies are useless if the computer allows unofficial forms to become search key values in the index.

VALIDATION OF SUBJECT TERMS

Controlled indexing vocabularies do not, however, remain static. Therefore, deleting or changing subject terms from controlled indexing vocabularies would result in previously indexed records that still contain deleted terms or former versions of changed terms, respectively. These unofficial forms also would remain in the index as subject term search key values. The implications of this situation for retrieval, and actions taken as a result, are discussed in Chapter 13.

The controlled vocabulary is usually a file in the computer, just as the file of bibliographic records indexed by subject terms from that vocabulary is a file. Therefore, in addition to being in published form, the vocabulary may be searchable by computer.

VOCABULARY FILE AND VOCABULARY RECORD

In the controlled vocabulary file, there is a separate record for each official term; that is, the controlled vocabulary file consists of records each of which represents a unique subject term. Along with the official (or preferred) version of the term, which would be a field value in a subject term [SU] field, the vocabulary file record would probably have other fields for additional information about the term, such as fields for entry date [ED], scope note [SN], entry term [ET] (for synonyms of the official form), broader term [BT], narrower term [NT], and related term [RT].

The value of the scope note [SN] field is characteristically a brief statement of the intended usage of the subject term. It usually includes a definition, but may also be used for clarifying the term or restricting its usage. The value of the entry date [ED] field is the date the record entered the computer. The remaining parts of the vocabulary record will be described later in this chapter.

The following is an example of a vocabulary record for the subject term PEER RELATIONSHIP:

COMPUTER-ASSIGNED ADDRESS:	275
FILE NAME [FN]:	VOCABULARY
SUBJECT TERM [SU]:	PEER RELATIONSHIP
ENTRY DATE [ED]:	19720101
SCOPE NOTE [SN]:	Relationship between persons in the same social group.
ENTRY TERM [ET]:	(NONE)
BROADER TERM [BT]:	RELATIONSHIPS
NARROWER TERM [NT]:	(NONE)
RELATED TERM [RT]:	FRIENDSHIP

INDEX TO VOCABULARY FILE

Just as there is an index for searching a bibliographic file, there is also an index to the controlled vocabulary file. Differences between the index to the vocabulary file and the subject index to a bibliographic file may be summarized as follows:

1. The index to the controlled vocabulary file contains all official subject terms, but the subject index to the bibliographic file only contains subject terms that have been used at least once in indexing.

2. Even if every subject term had been used at least once in indexing, the index to the vocabulary file would not be identical to the subject index of the bibliographic file because each index locates records in a different file. The vocabulary file index locates vocabulary records, and the index to the bibliographic file locates bibliographic records.

3. The number of records located by a value corresponding to a subject search key value in the index to the bibliographic file records could be 1 or greater, depending on how many items are indexed to that term. However, the number of records located by this value in the controlled vocabulary index is always 1 since this value is unique in the controlled vocabulary file; that is, each controlled vocabulary record has a single-occurrence field for the official version of a subject term, and no two records have the same value in that field.

Let's show an example of the vocabulary file index that locates the PEER RELATIONSHIP record (repeated here). The complete value for each field is indexed as well as textwords extracted from each nonnumeric field. Notice that textword search key values each locate the PEER RELATIONSHIP record, but also locate other vocabulary records. However, the subject term search key value, which is PEER RELATIONSHIP, locates only the PEER RELATIONSHIP record.

COMPUTER-ASSIGNED ADDRESS:	275
FILE NAME [FN]:	VOCABULARY
SUBJECT TERM [SU]:	PEER RELATIONSHIP
ENTRY DATE [ED]:	19720101
SCOPE NOTE [SN]:	Relationship between persons in the same social group.
ENTRY TERM [ET]:	(NONE)
BROADER TERM [BT]:	RELATIONSHIPS
NARROWER TERM [NT]:	(NONE)
RELATED TERM [RT]:	FRIENDSHIP

SEARCH KEY VALUE	SEARCH KEY	ADDRESS OF RECORD	NUMBER OF RECORDS
FRIENDSHIP	RT	23,275	2
FRIENDSHIP	TW	23,275	2
GROUP	TW	109, 143, 275,318	4
PEER	TW	275,380	2
PEER RELATIONSHIP	SU	275	1
PERSONS	TW	22,43,78, 134,143, 275,289	7
RELATIONSHIP	TW	57,66, 134,275, 351,400	6
RELATIONSHIPS	BT	57,134, 275,351	4
RELATIONSHIPS	TW	57,66, 81,134, 275,306, 351,400	8
SOCIAL	TW	23,109, 275	3
VOCABULARY	FN	22,23,43, 57,66,78, 81,109,134, 143,275, 289,306,318, 351,380, 400, . . .	750
19720101	ED	22,109, 134,275, 380, . . .	62

SUBJECT TERMS ALPHABETI- CALLY DISPLAYED

The remaining vocabulary displays in this chapter are intended to be published displays. The following is a list of official subject terms in a controlled indexing vocabulary. An alphabetic display normally contains other information from the vocabulary record. An example of a full alphabetic display of the subject terms GAMES, RECREA- TIONAL ACTIVITIES, and TOYS is shown later in this chapter.

ACTIVITIES
ADOLESCENTS
ARTS ACTIVITIES
CHILDREN
FAMILY RELATIONSHIPS
FRIENDSHIP
GAMES
HOBBIES
HYGIENE
PEER RELATIONSHIP
RECREATIONAL ACTIVITIES
RECREATIONAL READING
RELATIONSHIPS
STUDENT SCHOOL RELATIONSHIP
TOYS

ENTRY TERMS

A controlled indexing vocabulary may include an entry vocabulary consisting of entry terms. An entry term is not an official subject term, but a term that sends the indexer to the official subject term. Entry terms may appear in an alphabetic display of the vocabulary as "see" (or "use") cross references. For example:

LEISURE ACTIVITIES see RECREATIONAL ACTIVITIES
PERSONAL GROOMING see HYGIENE
PERSONAL HEALTH see HYGIENE
TEENAGERS see ADOLESCENTS

There would also be corresponding backward cross references, as follows:

ADOLESCENTS
X   TEENAGERS

HYGIENE
X   PERSONAL GROOMING
X   PERSONAL HEALTH

RECREATIONAL ACTIVITIES
X   LEISURE ACTIVITIES

The above backward cross references tell you that the term following "X" is a "see" cross reference to the official subject term directly above it.

The computer may permit indexers to use entry terms, but then automatically convert them to their corresponding official subject terms. For example, an indexer may use the entry term TEENAGERS with the full assurance that it will automatically be converted to the official subject term ADOLESCENTS. Automatic conversion of entry vocabulary to official indexing terms benefits retrieval in two ways. First, it facilitates indexing and thereby results in a more timely retrieval file. Second, the same automatic conversion may be applied during searching, thereby allowing entry terms to be used in search statements as direct alternatives to their official subject term equivalents.

The alphabetic display may show relatedness of subject terms. This relationship may appear in the vocabulary as "see related" cross references. For example:

RELATED TERMS

PEER RELATIONSHIP see related FRIENDSHIP
RECREATIONAL ACTIVITIES see related HOBBIES

There would also be corresponding backward cross references, as follows:

FRIENDSHIP
XR PEER RELATIONSHIP

HOBBIES
XR RECREATIONAL ACTIVITIES

The above backward cross references tell you that the term following "XR" is a "see related" cross reference to the official search term directly above it. Relatedness cross references may be mutual, as:

GAMES see related TOYS
XR TOYS

TOYS see related GAMES
XR GAMES

HIERARCHICAL CLASSIFICATION AND DISPLAY

A controlled indexing vocabulary may be displayed in a hierarchical classification, which is a conceptual arrangement of terms according to a specified system of rankings, usually tree-like segments, that is, with more general concepts at the top branching down to more specific concepts. The term AGE GROUPS [NONINDEXING TERM] has been added only for the purpose of occupying a node of a tree segment to group the subordinate terms ADOLESCENTS and CHILDREN; AGE GROUPS would be rejected by the computer if assigned to a document.

The following is a hierarchical display of the controlled indexing vocabulary:

ACTIVITIES
    ARTS ACTIVITIES
    GAMES
    RECREATIONAL ACTIVITIES
        HOBBIES
        RECREATIONAL READING
AGE GROUPS [NONINDEXING TERM]
    ADOLESCENTS
    CHILDREN
HYGIENE

RELATIONSHIPS
    FAMILY RELATIONSHIPS
    FRIENDSHIP
    PEER RELATIONSHIP
    STUDENT SCHOOL RELATIONSHIP
TOYS

Hierarchical classifications may be shown in an alphabetic display, as follows:

ACTIVITIES
    Narrower Term: ART ACTIVITIES
                   GAMES
                   RECREATIONAL ACTIVITIES

ARTS ACTIVITIES
    Broader Term: ACTIVITIES

GAMES
    Broader Term: ACTIVITIES

HOBBIES
    Broader Term: RECREATIONAL ACTIVITIES

RECREATIONAL ACTIVITIES
    Narrower Term: HOBBIES
                   RECREATIONAL READING
    Broader Term: ACTIVITIES

RECREATIONAL READING
    Broader Term: RECREATIONAL ACTIVITIES

The advantage of the tree display over the alphabetic display is that the tree display shows more than two levels at one time in either direction. The alphabetic display shows only one level at a time in either direction. For example, in the alphabetic display you cannot tell by looking only at ACTIVITIES that HOBBIES is a narrower concept. You must follow through, starting with ACTIVITIES, by looking at the narrower term RECREATIONAL ACTIVITIES, and then the narrower term under that, which is HOBBIES.

The disadvantage of the tree display is that it may be hard to locate a term if you don't know what tree it is in to begin with. For example, in the tree display, to locate the RECREATIONAL ACTIVITIES tree, you must know that it is in the ACTIVITIES tree.

Two-level hierarchical classifications, relatedness, entry terms, and entry dates may all be shown in the alphabetic display, as follows:

GAMES
Entry Date: 19760101
Broader Term: ACTIVITIES
Related Term: GAMES
TOYS

LEISURE ACTIVITIES
Use: RECREATIONAL ACTIVITIES

RECREATIONAL ACTIVITIES
Entry Date: 19780101
Used For: LEISURE ACTIVITIES
Narrower Term: HOBBIES
RECREATIONAL READING
Broader Term: ACTIVITIES
Related Term: GAMES

TOYS
Entry Date: 19760101
Related Term: GAMES

**PERMUTERM
DISPLAY: KWIC
AND KWOC
INDEXES**

How else, other than alphabetically, can a controlled indexing vocabulary be displayed to help indexers locate the appropriate term? Each word in an official subject term can be made a keyword for this display, and the list of terms can be sorted by keyword. This type of display is known as a *permuted index* to the vocabulary. Keywords in this display are also known as *permuterms*. Permuted indexes may also include "see" cross references.

When an entry in this list consists of the complete subject term, the index is a KeyWord In Context (KWIC) index. The following is a KWIC index to a controlled indexing vocabulary:

ACTIVITIES
ARTS ACTIVITIES
LEISURE ACTIVITIES see
RECREATIONAL ACTIVITIES
RECREATIONAL ACTIVITIES
ADOLESCENTS
ARTS ACTIVITIES
CHILDREN
FAMILY RELATIONSHIPS
FRIENDSHIP
GAMES
HOBBIES
HYGIENE

PERSONAL GROOMING see HYGIENE
PERSONAL HEALTH see HYGIENE
                        LEISURE ACTIVITIES see
                            RECREATIONAL
                            ACTIVITIES
                        PEER RELATIONSHIP
                        PERSONAL GROOMING see
                            HYGIENE
                        PERSONAL HEALTH see
                            HYGIENE
            RECREATIONAL READING
                        RECREATIONAL ACTIVITIES
                        RECREATIONAL READING
                PEER RELATIONSHIP
    STUDENT SCHOOL RELATIONSHIP
                        RELATIONSHIPS
            FAMILY RELATIONSHIPS
            STUDENT SCHOOL RELATIONSHIP
                        STUDENT SCHOOL
                            RELATIONSHIP
                        TEENAGERS see ADOLESCENTS
                        TOYS

When an entry consists of the keyword as a heading followed by
the complete subject terms containing that word, the index is a
KeyWord Out of Context (KWOC) index. The following is a KWOC
index to the same controlled indexing vocabulary:

ACTIVITIES
    ACTIVITIES
    ARTS ACTIVITIES
    LEISURE ACTIVITIES see RECREATIONAL ACTIVITIES
    RECREATIONAL ACTIVITIES

ADOLESCENTS
    ADOLESCENTS

ARTS
    ARTS ACTIVITIES

CHILDREN
    CHILDREN

FAMILY
    FAMILY RELATIONSHIPS

FRIENDSHIP
  FRIENDSHIP

GAMES
  GAMES

GROOMING
  PERSONAL GROOMING see HYGIENE

HEALTH
  PERSONAL HEALTH see HYGIENE

HOBBIES
  HOBBIES

HYGIENE
  HYGIENE

LEISURE
  LEISURE ACTIVITIES see RECREATIONAL ACTIVITIES

PEER
  PEER RELATIONSHIP

PERSONAL
  PERSONAL GROOMING see HYGIENE
  PERSONAL HEALTH see HYGIENE

READING
  RECREATIONAL READING

RECREATIONAL
  RECREATIONAL ACTIVITIES
  RECREATIONAL READING

RELATIONSHIP
  PEER RELATIONSHIP
  STUDENT SCHOOL RELATIONSHIP

RELATIONSHIPS
  FAMILY RELATIONSHIPS
  RELATIONSHIPS

SCHOOL
  STUDENT SCHOOL RELATIONSHIP

STUDENT
  STUDENT SCHOOL RELATIONSHIP

TEENAGERS
  TEENAGERS see ADOLESCENTS

TOYS
   TOYS

Some subject terms may be used as required tags. For example, you may have a rule in indexing that if a book is about a person or a group of people, the record should be indexed under an age group term that identifies the age level of the person or group. In the subject index to our bibliographic file ADOLESCENTS and CHILDREN are subject terms used as required tags in indexing the "rainy afternoon" book; however, ADOLESCENTS represents more the topic of the "teenage years" book.

SUBJECT TERMS AS REQUIRED TAGS

Some controlled indexing vocabularies include a small set of special subject terms used for subdividing other terms. For example, instead of having age group terms as required tags, they could be subdividers, as in the combination HOBBIES/CHILDREN, where CHILDREN is used for subdividing HOBBIES. Validation rules would outlaw indexing with illegal (nonsensical) combinations; for example, HOBBIES/NEWBORN INFANTS. If used as search terms, these would produce a "no match" search term result.

SUBDIVIDING SUBJECT TERMS

We will continue the development of a search formulation for the query APPROACHES TO SOLVING THE SHORTAGE OF MATHEMATICS AND SCIENCE TEACHERS IN THE SCHOOLS initiated in Chapter 7. A controlled indexing vocabulary for this file could be used for selecting official subject terms relating to the concepts in the query. We will again concentrate on the following concepts previously identified from the query:

DEVELOPING SEARCH STRATEGY AND FORMULATION (II)

SHORTAGE
MATHEMATICS OR SCIENCE
TEACHERS

    Using the permuterm index to the controlled vocabulary for indexing this education file (Thesaurus of ERIC® Descriptors, mentioned in the previous chapter), we can locate the following subject terms related to the listed concepts:

Teacher Shortage
Mathematics Teachers
Science Teachers

    The subject terms are precoordinate search terms that combine TEACHERS with SHORTAGE, and TEACHERS with MATHEMATICS OR SCIENCE, as follows:

CONCEPTS:	SHORTAGE	TEACHERS	MATHEMATICS OR SCIENCE
SEARCH TERMS:	Teacher Shortage	Mathematics Teachers Science Teachers	

The following is a new search strategy of coordinate concepts with the search terms assigned to them:

CONCEPTS:	SHORTAGE AND TEACHERS	MATHEMATICS AND TEACHERS OR SCIENCE AND TEACHERS
SEARCH TERMS:	Teacher Shortage	Mathematics Teachers Science Teachers

The following is the corresponding search formulation for matching subject terms in the index. We will use upper/lower case for these search terms, in contrast to completely lower case for search terms that search textwords.

Teacher Shortage AND (Mathematics Teachers OR Science Teachers)

The following is a display of the 23 titles of records retrieved by this formulation, along with selected subject terms used for indexing them. Note that in the previous chapter displaying subject terms, along with the titles, would have provided clues for assessing relevance of retrieval, as well as revealed the pertinent search terms (Teacher Shortage, Mathematics Teachers, Science Teachers) that we located in the permuterm index.

1. What research says—science teacher supply and demand.
   Science Education; Science Teachers; Secondary School Science; Teacher Shortage; Teacher Supply and Demand

2. Corrective measures in the teacher shortage: consequences and conclusions.
   Mathematics Teachers; Science Teachers; Teacher Shortage

3. The crisis in mathematics education.
   Mathematics Teachers; Teacher Shortage

4. The crisis in high-school and college physics education.
   College Science; Secondary School Science; Teacher Shortage

5. The science teacher shortage in North Carolina: facts and myths.
   Science Teachers; Secondary School Science; Teacher Shortage

6. Crisis in our high schools: the math and science teacher shortage.
   Mathematics Teachers; Science Teachers; Teacher Shortage

7. Mathematics teachers—we need you.
   Mathematics Instruction; Mathematics Teachers; Teacher Shortage

8. North Carolina's efforts to strengthen science and mathematics.
   Mathematics Education; Mathematics Teachers; Science Education; Science Teachers; Teacher Shortage

9. A shortage of mathematics teachers in New York City.
   Mathematics Education; Mathematics Teachers; Teacher Shortage

10. Quality of math, science teaching—Federal Commission studies problem.
    Mathematics Instruction; Mathematics Teachers; Science Instruction; Science Teachers; Teacher Shortage

11. The shortage of science teachers.
    Science Teachers; Secondary School Mathematics; Secondary School Science; Teacher Shortage

12. Teacher supply and demand in mathematics and science.
    Mathematics Teachers; Science Teachers; Teacher Shortage

13. Use technology to cope with the scarcity of math and science teachers.
    Mathematics Teachers; Teacher Shortage

14. What to do when your science and math teachers abandon their classrooms.
    Mathematics Teachers; Science Teachers; Teacher Shortage

15. Classroom crisis in science and math.
    Science Teachers; Secondary School Mathematics; Secondary School Science; Teacher Shortage

16. The shortage of chemistry teachers—a national crisis.
    Science Teachers; Secondary School Science; Teacher Shortage

17. Beneath the surface of the mathematics teacher shortage.
    Mathematics Education; Mathematics Teachers; Teacher Shortage

18. The mathematics teacher shortage—some solutions.
    Mathematics Education; Mathematics Teachers; Teacher Shortage

19. Physicists: an endangered species.
    Science Teachers; Teacher Shortage

20. Critical shortages of mathematics and science teachers in Iowa.
    Mathematics Teachers; Science Teachers; Teacher Shortage

21. Science teaching in transition.
    Science Teachers; Teacher Shortage

22. A national problem.
Science Teachers; Teacher Shortage

23. Editorial: Lo, the vanishing physics teacher.
Science Education; Science Teachers; Teacher Shortage

Inspecting the subject terms in the records in order to discover new search terms, we can assign the following new terms to MATHEMATICS AND TEACHERS OR SCIENCE AND TEACHERS:

Science Education
Secondary School Science
College Science
Mathematics Instruction
Mathematics Education
Science Instruction
Secondary School Mathematics
Mathematics Education

We can then insert them into the search formulation, as follows:

Teacher Shortage AND (Mathematics Teachers OR Science Teachers OR Science Education OR Secondary School Science OR College Science OR Mathematics Instruction OR Mathematics Education OR Science Instruction OR Secondary School Mathematics OR Mathematics Education)

The revised formulation will retrieve the following five new records, showing their titles and selected subject terms:

1. Federal policy for education in mathematics and science.
Mathematics Education; Science Education; Teacher Shortage

2. National Council of Teachers of Mathematics: President's report: courage to change.
Mathematics Education; Mathematics Instruction; Teacher Shortage

3. The uneven crisis in science education.
Mathematics Education; Science Education; Teacher Shortage

4. The teacher crisis in secondary school science and mathematics.
Secondary School Mathematics; Secondary School Science; Teacher Shortage

5. Association affairs.
Science Education; Teacher Shortage

The initial formulation, based entirely on subject terms, retrieved more than twice as many relevant-looking titles as the original formulation based on title textwords in the previous chapter. The first revision of the subject term formulation, for inserting new search terms, retrieved five additional titles, for a total of 28 relevant titles, based solely on controlled subject terms assigned to concepts in the search strategy. This may be compared to a total of 29 titles retrieved by the title textword formulation in the previous chapter, which entailed at least two revisions for inserting new search terms; however, only 14 of these titles appeared relevant to the query.

The following 12 titles, duplicated from the 28 records retrieved by the subject term formulation, were not retrieved by the title textword formulation:

1. Corrective measures in the teacher shortage: consequences and conclusions.

2. Federal policy for education in mathematics and science.

3. National Council of Teachers of Mathematics: President's report: courage to change.

4. Mathematics teachers—we need you.

5. North Carolina's efforts to strengthen science and mathematics.

6. Quality of math, science teaching—Federal Commission studies problem.

7. What to do when your science and math teachers abandon their classrooms.

8. Association affairs.

9. Physicists: an endangered species.

10. Science teaching in transition.

11. A national problem.

12. Editorial: Lo, the vanishing physics teacher.

Were there any relevant-looking titles retrieved by the title textword formulation that were missed by the initial and revised subject term formulation? Yes, the title textword formulation retrieved a record with the following title and selected subject terms that was not retrieved by the subject term formulation:

Solving the math and science teacher shortage: one district's initiative. Mathematics Instruction; Science Instruction; Teacher Supply and Demand

This record may have been retrieved had we expanded SHORTAGE to include the search term "Teacher Supply and Demand," which was used as a subject term to index six of the records retrieved by the initial subject term formulation. We might also have noted the following cross reference in the controlled indexing vocabulary:

Teacher Shortage
     Broader Term: Teacher Supply and Demand

     A search strategy that serves as a type of "insurance" against missing records that are obviously relevant, by title, but would possibly not be retrieved by the subject term formulation alone, is to perform as comprehensive a subject term formulation as possible, but supplement it with a first-effort title textword formulation. In this case the supplementary search formulation might be as follows:

(shortage or shortages or scarcity) AND (mathematics OR math OR science OR biology OR chemistry OR physics) AND (teacher OR teachers)

     Let's return to the concept in the query of SOLVING, which had been characterized as a difficult concept for assigning search terms in developing a title textword search formulation. New titles resulting from the subject term formulation contain additional SOLVING terms, such as "policy" and "strengthen."

     Furthermore, subject terms displayed as part of the record are a source of controlled terminology for this concept. These include: Teacher Recruitment, Retraining, Merit Pay, Cooperative Programs, Federal Aid, Financial Support, Premium Pay, Inservice Teacher Education, Master Teachers, School-Business Relationship, Federal Programs, Research Needs, Policy Formation, and Government Role. If enough subject terms for SOLVING can be identified, they, plus SOLVING terms from titles, can be used for distinguishing records that are more likely to be relevant to this concept, and therefore more relevant to the query, since SOLVING was expressed as a necessary concept. Perhaps the union of these search terms can be intersected with the final search formulation in order to display them first, and the remaining records reserved for a second display.

     Rather than rely on discovering new terms by viewing search terms that index previously retrieved records, we might use the controlled indexing vocabulary by assigning subject terms directly from displays of the vocabulary to the concepts in the search strategy. The vocab-

ulary (Thesaurus of ERIC® Descriptors) contains the following hierarchically classified subject terms relevant to the query:

Mathematics Curriculum
    Narrower Term: College Mathematics
                    Elementary School Mathematics
                    Modern Mathematics
                    Secondary School Mathematics

Science Curriculum
    Narrower Term: College Science
                    Elementary School Science
                    General Science
                    Secondary School Science

Education
    Narrower Term: Engineering Education
                    Mathematics Education
                    Science Education

Instruction
    Narrower Term: Mathematics Instruction
                    Science Instruction

Teachers
    Narrower Term: Mathematics Teachers
                    Science Teachers

Teacher Supply and Demand
    Narrower Term: Teacher Shortage

    In addition, there is an extensive network of related-term cross
references, for example:

Science Teachers
    Related Term: Science Education
                   Science Instruction

Science Education
    Related Term: College Science
                   Elementary School Science
                   Engineering Education
                   Science
                   Secondary School Science

Science Instruction
Related Term: College Science
Elementary School Science
Science Curriculum
Science Education
Science Teachers
Secondary School Science

Elementary School Science
Related Term: College Science
Science Departments
Science Education
Science Instruction
Secondary School Science

Secondary School Science
Related Term: College Science
Elementary School Science
Science Departments
Science Education
Science Instruction

College Science
Related Term: Elementary School Science
Science Departments
Science Education
Science Instruction
Secondary School Science

Had we used these vocabulary displays, we might have included "Engineering Education" (related to "Science Education") as a MATHEMATICS AND TEACHERS OR SCIENCE AND TEACHERS term, and thereby retrieved eight additional records, with the following titles:

1. The crisis in engineering education: a dissenting view.

2. Plan may ease faculty shortage in engineering.

3. One tenth of engineering faculty slots vacant.

4. Grim tidings on U.S. engineering education.

5. The faculty shortage: the 1982 survey.

6. Engineering education quality in decline, NASULGC panel says.

7. New faculty survey puts shortage at 9.1 percent.

8. Gathering up the parts.

An advantage of subject term searching, in comparison to title textword searching, is that precision based on subject terms is more predictable. That is, if the concepts in your query can be expressed fairly directly by subject terms, and if your search formulation is rather specific, your retrieval sets can be extremely precise. If your search formulation is more general, your retrieval sets will be less precise (but your recall may improve). However, because of the consistency of meaning of controlled vocabulary terms, it is easier to characterize your search formulation, in advance, in terms of how specific or general your retrieval is likely to be.

In contrast, the meaning of title textwords is dependent on the meaning ascribed to it by any writer that might use it. This uncontrollability, with regard to what a search term might mean in a title, makes it difficult to predict the precision of a retrieval set based on title textwords.

Title textword searching is invaluable for searching concepts that have no directly equivalent subject term in the vocabulary and are not easily represented by the coordination of subject terms. On the other hand, we have seen the necessity for controlled subject terms for retrieving records with titles whose informational content is of limited use in developing a search formulation. The following are examples, displayed previously in this chapter, of this type of title:

1. Association affairs.

2. A national problem.

3. Gathering up the parts.

At the end of Chapter 9, we will resume development of this search formulation by illustrating the use of search statements as search terms; negation of search statements to avoid redisplaying records; use of other search keys for search terms; qualifying search terms according to a specific search key, such as subject term; and omitting search key qualifiers, thereby searching textwords by default.

EXERCISES

1. As stated in this chapter, no two records have the same value in the field that contains the official version of a subject term. If FRIENDSHIP is an official subject term, does that statement mean that the search key value FRIENDSHIP will never locate more than a single record according to the index? If not, then explain what is meant. (Hint: Assume the following portions of two vocabulary records, and think of how they might be indexed.)

SUBJECT TERM [SU]: FRIENDSHIP

SUBJECT TERM [SU]: PEER RELATIONSHIP
RELATED TERM [RT]: FRIENDSHIP

2. Devise a small controlled subject indexing vocabulary (10-15 terms) other than the one described in this chapter. Include at least one of each of the following: three-level hierarchical classification, entry term (with corresponding backward reference), and mutual relatedness. Display the terms in the following formats:

   a. Alphabetic display showing two-level hierarchical classifications, relatedness, and entry terms.

   b. KWIC index.

   c. KWOC index.

   d. Hierarchical tree display.

3. Devise a computer vocabulary file record for one of the terms in the vocabulary you have developed. Include a definition field, with a value. Show all fields even though some may have no value.

4. Assign an address to the record you have devised in 3, and construct an index to the record. Assume that most search key values locate other vocabulary records as well. Identify the entry in the index that will never locate more than a single vocabulary record.

5. Propose (or ask someone else to propose) a search query based on the subject of the controlled subject indexing vocabulary you have created in Exercise 2. Develop a search strategy and formulation, in response to this query, based entirely on subject terms in your vocabulary. Contrast the strategy and formulation with one that would be based entirely on title textwords. Construct your final formulation, and describe how you derived it.

Expansion of Search Keys

9

The computer automatically numbers search statements sequentially (first search statement number = 1, second = 2, and so on). Each search statement number labels a retrieval set, which is actually the union of addresses of a set of records located by a previous search statement. Previous search statement number is a search key, just as subject term and title textword are search keys.

A particular search statement number is a search key value that locates the retrieval set that resulted from that search statement. When used as a search term in a later search statement, it will locate that retrieval set, in the same way that a subject term in a search statement locates records during index searching. For example, in the following series of search statements, the search term "1" is equivalent to the search term GAMES, and the search term "2" is equivalent to the intersection GAMES AND CHILDREN. Can you tell which search statements in this series are equivalent; that is, which search statements will result in identical retrieval sets?

SEARCH STATEMENT 1
    GAMES
SEARCH STATEMENT 2
    1 AND CHILDREN
SEARCH STATEMENT 3
    2 OR HOPSCOTCH
SEARCH STATEMENT 4
    GAMES AND CHILDREN OR HOPSCOTCH
SEARCH STATEMENT 5
    3 OR 4

If you answered that SEARCH STATEMENTS 3, 4, and 5 are equivalent, you are correct. We will show a common use of specifying the complement of a search statement number at the end of this chapter in our continuing development of a search strategy and formulation begun in Chapter 7.

**INDEX
INCLUDING
SUBJECT
TERMS**

To the previous complete index displayed in Chapter 5 we have added subject term values to our bibliographic records, as follows:

37.
AU- Smith, John
TI - Guide to enjoying the teenage years.
PL - Chicago, Illinois
PU- Atlas Publishing Company
PY- 1983
SU - Adolescents
    Family Relationships
    Hygiene
    Peer Relationships
    Recreational Activities
    Student School Relationship

24.
AU- Jones, Mary
TI - Guide to enjoying yourself on a rainy afternoon.
PL - Dallas, Texas
PU- Tops Publishing Company
PY- 1983
SU - Adolescents
    Arts Activities
    Children
    Games
    Hobbies
    Recreational Activities
    Recreational Reading

The following is the new version of the complete index:

SEARCH KEY VALUE	SEARCH KEY	ADDRESS OF RECORD	NUMBER OF RECORDS
ADOLESCENTS	SU	24,37	2
AFTERNOON	TW	24	1
ARTS ACTIVITIES	SU	24	1
ATLAS PUBLISHING COMPANY	PU	37	1
CHICAGO, ILLINOIS	PL	37	1
CHILDREN	SU	24	1

(cont.)

SEARCH KEY VALUE	SEARCH KEY	ADDRESS OF RECORD	NUMBER OF RECORDS
DALLAS, TEXAS	PL	24	1
ENJOYING	TW	24,37	2
FAMILY RELATIONSHIPS	SU	37	1
GAMES	SU	24	1
GUIDE	TW	24,37	2
GUI/T/E/T	TF	37	1
GUI/T/E/Y	TF	24	1
GUIDE TO ENJOYING THE TEENAGE YEARS	TI	37	1
GUIDE TO ENJOYING YOURSELF ON A RAINY AFTERNOON	TI	24	1
HOBBIES	SU	24	1
HYGIENE	SU	37	1
JONES, MARY	AU	24	1
PEER RELATIONSHIP	SU	37	1
RAINY	TW	24	1
RECREATIONAL ACTIVITIES	SU	24,37	2
RECREATIONAL READING	SU	24	1
SMITH, JOHN	AU	37	1
STUDENT SCHOOL RELATIONSHIP	SU	37	1
TEENAGE	TW	37	1
TOPS PUBLISHING COMPANY	PU	24	1
YEARS	TW	37	1
YOURSELF	TW	24	1
1983	PY	24,37	2

In the preceding index, the textword search key consists only of words from titles, but the computer could index as textwords, using the same search key abbreviation [TW], words from multiple fields. The following version includes a textword [TW] search key consisting of words from the author, title, place of publication, publisher, and subject term fields.

INDEX INCLUDING TEXTWORDS FROM MULTIPLE FIELDS

SEARCH KEY VALUE	SEARCH KEY	ADDRESS OF RECORD	NUMBER OF RECORDS
ACTIVITIES	TW	24, 37	2
ADOLESCENTS	SU	24,37	2
ADOLESCENTS	TW	24,37	2
AFTERNOON	TW	24	1
ARTS	TW	24	1
ARTS ACTIVITIES	SU	24	1
ATLAS	TW	37	1
ATLAS PUBLISHING COMPANY	PU	37	1

(cont.)

SEARCH KEY VALUE	SEARCH KEY	ADDRESS OF RECORD	NUMBER OF RECORDS
CHICAGO	TW	37	1
CHICAGO, ILLINOIS	PL	37	1
CHILDREN	SU	24	1
CHILDREN	TW	24	1
COMPANY	TW	24,37	2
DALLAS	TW	24	1
DALLAS, TEXAS	PL	24	1
ENJOYING	TW	24,37	2
FAMILY	TW	37	1
FAMILY RELATIONSHIPS	SU	37	1
GAMES	SU	24	1
GAMES	TW	24	1
GUIDE	TW	24,37	2
GUI/T/E/T	TF	37	1
GUI/T/E/Y	TF	24	1
GUIDE TO ENJOYING THE TEENAGE YEARS	TI	37	1
GUIDE TO ENJOYING YOURSELF ON A RAINY AFTERNOON	TI	24	1
HOBBIES	SU	24	1
HOBBIES	TW	24	1
HYGIENE	SU	37	1
HYGIENE	TW	37	1
ILLINOIS	TW	37	1
JOHN	TW	37	1
JONES	TW	24	1
JONES, MARY	AU	24	1
MARY	TW	24	1
PEER	TW	37	1
PEER RELATIONSHIP	SU	37	1
PUBLISHING	TW	24,37	2
RAINY	TW	24	1
READING	TW	24	1
RECREATIONAL	TW	24,37	2
RECREATIONAL ACTIVITIES	SU	24,37	2
RECREATIONAL READING	SU	24	1
RELATIONSHIP	TW	37	1
RELATIONSHIPS	TW	37	1
SCHOOL	TW	37	1
SMITH	TW	37	1
SMITH, JOHN	AU	37	1
STUDENT	TW	37	1
STUDENT SCHOOL RELATIONSHIP	SU	37	1
TEENAGE	TW	37	1
TEXAS	TW	24	1
TOPS	TW	24	1

(cont.)

SEARCH KEY VALUE	SEARCH KEY	ADDRESS OF RECORD	NUMBER OF RECORDS
TOPS PUBLISHING COMPANY	PU	24	1
YEARS	TW	37	1
YOURSELF	TW	24	1
1983	PY	24,37	2

If the same search key value appears more than once in the index, with different search keys, how might you search them individually? For example, suppose a file consists of two bibliographic records with the following values in the title and subject term fields:

SPECIFYING SEARCH KEYS

45.
TI - Getting the most out of watching football games.
SU- FOOTBALL

52.
TI - Games for two people.
SU- GAMES

The following are entries in the index to these records:

SEARCH KEY VALUE	SEARCH KEY	ADDRESS OF RECORD	NUMBER OF RECORDS
FOOTBALL	SU	45	1
FOOTBALL	TW	45	1
GAMES	SU	52	1
GAMES	TW	45,52	2

You could retrieve only the record with GAMES as the subject term by using the search key abbreviation in your search statement, as follows:

GAMES [SU]

Searching single-term textwords is a form of free text searching. Free text searching is searching text as it occurs naturally in the record rather than units of compound words, such as controlled subject terms. Most of the time, free text searching refers to searching textwords originating from titles, abstracts, and full text of documents stored in the computer. Since the textword search key includes title textwords, the retrieval set resulting from the following search statement would locate any record having "activities" in the title.

FREE TEXT SEARCHING: SINGLE-WORD INDEX SEARCHING

[TW] ACTIVITIES

However, subject terms may also be searched as free text. For example, since individual words in the subject term field are included in the textword search key, the preceding search statement would illustrate free text searching of subject terms, since it would locate any record that has a subject term with the word ACTIVITIES (including ARTS ACTIVITIES and RECREATIONAL ACTIVITIES).

Free text searching of textwords might be enhanced by the use of positional operators, which are special types of logical operators, similar to the intersection operator AND. There is the further restriction, however, that terms connected by a positional operator occupy a specific physical position in the record with respect to one another as defined by the operator. An example of a positional operator is ADJACENT-TO. When combining title textwords using this operator, you are requiring that these words be in the title in direct sequence. Free text searching is a form of index searching that requires the computer to store the relative positions of words within a record.

Another form of free text searching is stringsearching, for matching sequences of characters directly against records, in contrast to index searching. Stringsearching enables you to specify and match character strings that are not indexed, such as stopwords, parts of words, and sequences of words (phrases).

Stringsearching and free text searching of multiple textwords, using positional operators, are discussed in detail in the following chapter.

SEARCHING TEXTWORD FROM ONE OF MULTIPLE FIELDS

If a textword search key indexes words from different fields, how might you search them individually? For example, suppose a file consists of two bibliographic records with the following values in the title and publisher fields:

78.
TI - How to form your own company.
PU - Anderson Publishing Company

60.
TI - How to plan your summer vacation.
PU - Jefferson Publishing Company

The following is an entry in the index to these records:

SEARCH KEY VALUE	SEARCH KEY	ADDRESS OF RECORD	NUMBER OF RECORDS
COMPANY	TW	60,78	2

You may want to search COMPANY only as a title textword, but if your search term were COMPANY [TW], both records would be retrieved. As currently constructed, the index would not enable you to search COMPANY only as a title textword. However, the index could have been designed to enable you to retrieve only the record with COMPANY as a title textword. The computer could have established different textword search keys from different fields, with search key abbreviations that show the field from which the textword originated, as follows:

SEARCH KEY VALUE	SEARCH KEY	ADDRESS OF RECORD	NUMBER OF RECORDS
COMPANY	TWTI	78	1
COMPANY	TWPU	60,78	2

Based on the preceding entries in the index, the search statement for retrieving only the record with COMPANY as a title textword would be:

COMPANY [TWTI]

The same result may be achieved, even with the multiple-field textword search key, by sequentially searching the title field using stringsearching (discussed further in the next chapter).

More than one search key may be specified for a search term, as follows (the comma implies union of search keys):

ADOLESCENTS [SU,TW]

The computer may allow you to apply the complement operator to a search key specification, as follows:

PUBLISHING [NOT SU]

UNION OF SEARCH KEYS AND COMPLEMENT OF SEARCH KEY

This search term would not be matched against subject search key values in the index.

OMITTING SEARCH KEYS

If no search key is specified for a search term, the computer may match the search term against the union of search key values identical to the search term, regardless of search key. For example, if GAMES were in the index both as a subject search key value and as a textword search key value, the search statement GAMES would retrieve records located by either search key value, as if the search statement had been GAMES [SU] OR GAMES [TW]. An alternative would be for the computer to display search key options for your selection. For the same example, the computer would display:

1 - GAMES [SU]
2 - GAMES [TW]
SELECT BY NUMBER, OR SPECIFY ALL OR NONE

DEFAULT SEARCH KEYS

Another possibility is that the computer may establish certain default search keys, that is, search keys assumed by the computer when you don't specify them. For example, if the default search keys are AUTHOR [AU] and SUBJECT TERM [SU], the search statement

ATLAS PUBLISHING COMPANY

would not retrieve the following record:

37.
AU- Smith, John
TI - Guide to enjoying the teenage years.
PL - Chicago, Illinois
PU- Atlas Publishing Company
PY- 1983
SU - Adolescents
       Family Relationships
       Hygiene
       Peer Relationship
       Recreational Activities
       Student School Relationship

However, specifying the search key would cause default search keys to be overridden. Therefore, even given the preceding default search keys, this record would be retrieved by the following search statement:

ATLAS PUBLISHING COMPANY [PU]

If the existing search key default is not convenient, the computer may permit you to cancel it, or establish your own.

A search key may be specified for all terms in a search statement. For example, the search key abbreviation [SU] applies to each term in the following search statement:

SEARCH KEYS APPLIED TO SEARCH STATEMENT

[SU] CHILDREN OR ADOLESCENTS OR ADULTS

The search key could be overridden for an individual search term. For example, in the following search statement, the search key abbreviation [SU] applies to each term except the last, where [TW] applies instead.

[SU] CHILDREN OR ADOLESCENTS OR ADULTS OR ADOLESCENTS [TW]

A search key may qualify a search term that is a previous search statement number. For example, suppose you enter a search statement without specifying a search key, as follows:

SEARCH STATEMENT 1
     INFANTS OR CHILDREN OR ADOLESCENTS OR ADULTS

If the search statement result is too large, you may wish you had specified a search key such as SUBJECT TERM [SU]. Instead of re-entering the complete search statement, this time specifying [SU], you may enter the next search statement as follows, where "1" is used for searching the search key value SEARCH STATEMENT 1:

1 [SU]

Chapter 4 discussed computerized tables for automatically changing alternate forms entered in a record into the official form. In Chapter 8, we discussed entry terms in the controlled indexing vocabulary that were in the form of "see" cross references such as "TEENAGERS see ADOLESCENTS," for helping indexers locate official subject terms. We also noted that indexers and searchers might actually use entry terms in place of the official form. For example, indexers could use the entry term TEENAGERS with full assurance that the computer would convert it to the official term ADOLESCENTS.

ENTRY TERM AS SEARCH TERM

Let's examine how this feature might be used for searching the subject term TRACK AND FIELD. If TRACK AND FIELD is entered as a search term, the computer will not recognize it as a single term since it will consider AND to be the logical operator for intersection. If, however, you enter TRACK (a legitimate entry term), the computer would replace it with the official form TRACK AND FIELD.

The additional search keys described so far do not really stand for information that is unfamiliar to you; that is, title, subject term, publisher, textword, and search statement have been discussed prior to this chapter. We will now define additional search keys that come from new fields that we will add to the record in our bibliographic file, namely, call number, unique identifier, entry date, and update file code. These will be followed by a discussion of the weight category subfield for searching subject terms according to their importance in items being indexed.

BOOK CALL NUMBER

If you were indexing a collection of books in a library, you would want books on the same subject to be shelved together, and books on similar subjects to be shelved near each other. Shelving books on the same subject together would save the library patron time and effort when locating books on the same subject, as well as facilitate browsing.

A record about a book would have a *call number* [CA] field as the source for the call number search key. A call number is a code that gives the location of a book on the shelf. It is placed on the outside of books, and informs shelvers of their proper location. A call number consists of subcodes. For example,

- subject subcode
- author subcode
- publication year subcode

Books would be shelved using the first subcode as the primary sort, the second subcode as the secondary sort, and the third subcode as the tertiary sort. Therefore, all books with the same subject subcode would be shelved together and sorted by the author subcode. Books on the same subject by the same author would be sorted by publication year.

Since a book can have only one location on the shelf, the subject subcode, which is selected from a classification schedule, reflects the topic of the book. In the Library of Congress' *LC Classification Schedules,* the subject subcode for the teenage years book would correspond to "youth and adolescence," and for the rainy afternoon book, "indoor games and amusements." Call numbers for these books might be GV796.S553 1983 ("teenage years" book by John Smith) and GV1229.J63 1983 ("rainy afternoon" book by Mary Jones). (Application of the call number search key to a library inventory problem is presented in the next chapter.)

UNIQUE IDENTIFIER (ACCESSION NUMBER)

The remaining fields to be mentioned as sources for search keys are numeric fields whose values are automatically assigned by the computer after the record is accepted. The first computer-assigned field we'll call the *unique identifier* [UI] field. The first four digits could be the year that the record goes into the computer, and the remainder of the code could be a sequentially assigned accession number. For example, the unique identifier field value for the first record put into the computer in 1983 might be 1983000001, the value for the second record would be 1983000002, and so on.

The important thing about the unique identifier is that its value should be unique for the record; that is, no two records would have the same unique identifier. Another characteristic of the unique identifier is that, after it is assigned to a record, as long as the record is in the computer, it would never be changed or deleted from the record and therefore always point to the same record addresses in the index.

The unique identifier might be a search key for retrieving a record having a known unique identifier. It may be used in a search statement to check if a specific record is in a previous retrieval set. For example, if you locate a set of records with the search statement

FAMILY RELATIONSHIPS

and then you find that the search statement

FAMILY RELATIONSHIPS AND 1983000089

locates only one record, you know that the record with the unique identifier 1983000089 is in the set of records located by the term FAMILY RELATIONSHIPS. If the result of the intersection is zero, then you know that the record with that unique identifier is not in the retrieval set located by that term.

The unique identifier might be used in a search statement for adding a single record to a retrieval set that doesn't already include the record. For example, if no records are located by the search statement

FAMILY RELATIONSHIPS AND 1983000089

you may produce a new retrieval set, which has added that record to the retrieval set located by FAMILY RELATIONSHIPS, by entering the search statement

FAMILY RELATIONSHIPS OR 1983000089

ENTRY DATE AND UPDATE FILE CODE

The remaining numeric computer-assigned fields are related to when a record was accepted by the computer. The first is *entry date* [ED], the actual date (year, month, day) the record was accepted by the computer, for example 19830302 for March 2, 1983. The second is *update file code* [UF], which is a code for the set of records belonging to an update file. If a file is updated monthly, each record in an update file might be coded with the year and month of the update file in the update file code [UF] field, for example 198304 for the April 1984 update file.

Search key values indexed from these date fields may be used as search terms, particularly for intersection with other search terms in order to limit the search statement to searching records in a particular update, or set of updates. Relational operators, such as GREATER THAN (a number), may be used for "ranging" of dates (as discussed and illustrated in the next chapter).

WEIGHT (IMPORTANCE) CATEGORIES

The final new category of information in our bibliographic file is the weight category subfield. A record may have as part of the subject term field a weight category subfield for entering values that indicate the importance of the search term in relation to the topics presented in the item being indexed. For example, "Adolescents" and "Recreational Activities" might be selected as the subject terms for our two bibliographic records that best describe the content of the respective book. In other words, "Adolescents" represents the central concept of the "teenage years" book, and "Recreational Activities" represents the central concept of the "rainy afternoon" book. In general, anywhere from one to three weight categories might be established when the file is designed.

In order to use weighting in a search statement, the importance weights assigned to subject terms in the weight subfield must be copied to the index. In the index, weights may be displayed as symbols directly following the search key value. For example, a central concept indicator, symbolized by the asterisk (*), might be displayed as follows:

SEARCH KEY VALUE	SEARCH KEY	ADDRESS OF RECORD	NUMBER OF RECORDS
ADOLESCENTS*	SU	37	1
RECREATIONAL ACTIVITIES*	SU	24	1

An alternative is for weights to be displayed as symbols directly following the search key abbreviation and thereby defining subject-term-with-specific-weight-category as a separate search key. For example, a central concept indicator, symbolized by the asterisk (*), might be displayed as follows:

SEARCH KEY VALUE	SEARCH KEY	ADDRESS OF RECORD	NUMBER OF RECORDS
ADOLESCENTS	SU*	37	1
RECREATIONAL ACTIVITIES	SU*	24	1

If the weight category is represented by a symbol attached directly to the search key value, the symbol might directly follow a subject search term in a search statement. In the following example, the asterisk (*) is used as a central concept indicator for locating records indexed with the subject term RECREATIONAL ACTIVITIES as representing the main topic of the book:

*RECREATIONAL ACTIVITIES AND CHILDREN [SU]

If the weight category is part of the search key abbreviation, the subject-term-with-specific-weight-category search key is specified in the usual way that search keys are specified in a search statement. The following is a version of the preceding search statement using the abbreviation for the subject-as-central-concept [SU*] search key:

RECREATIONAL ACTIVITIES [SU*] AND CHILDREN [SU]

We have now completed our two-record bibliographic file and index, which include the call number [CA] field and search key, unique identifier [UI] field and search key, entry date [ED] field and search key, update file code [UF] field and search key, and central concept (*) subfield and "search key," as follows:

COMPLETE INDEX

37.
AU- Smith, John
TI - Guide to enjoying the teenage years.

PL - Chicago, Illinois
PU- Atlas Publishing Company
PY - 1983
SU - Adolescents*
    Family Relationships
    Hygiene
    Peer Relationship
    Recreational Activities
    Student School Relationship
CA- HQ796.S553 1983
UI - 1983120488
ED- 19830522
UF- 198306

24.
AU- Jones, Mary
TI - Guide to enjoying yourself on a rainy afternoon.
PL - Dallas, Texas
PU- Tops Publishing Company
PY - 1983
SU - Adolescents
    Arts Activities
    Children
    Games
    Hobbies
    Recreational Activities*
    Recreational Reading
CA- GV1229.J63 1983
UI - 1983060104
ED- 19830302
UF- 198304

The following is the final version of the complete index:

SEARCH KEY VALUE	SEARCH KEY	ADDRESS OF RECORD	NUMBER OF RECORDS
ACTIVITIES	TW	24,37	2
ADOLESCENTS	SU	24,37	2
ADOLESCENTS	TW	24,37	2
ADOLESCENTS*	SU	37	1
AFTERNOON	TW	24	1
ARTS	TW	24	1
ARTS ACTIVITIES	SU	24	1
ATLAS	TW	37	1

(cont.)

SEARCH KEY VALUE	SEARCH KEY	ADDRESS OF RECORD	NUMBER OF RECORDS
ATLAS PUBLISHING COMPANY	PU	37	1
CHICAGO	TW	37	1
CHICAGO, ILLINOIS	PL	37	1
CHILDREN	SU	24	1
CHILDREN	TW	24	1
COMPANY	TW	24,37	2
DALLAS	TW	24	1
DALLAS, TEXAS	PL	24	1
ENJOYING	TW	24,37	2
FAMILY	TW	37	1
FAMILY RELATIONSHIPS	SU	37	1
GAMES	SU	24	1
GAMES	TW	24	1
GUIDE	TW	24,37	2
GUI/T/E/T	TF	37	1
GUI/T/E/Y	TF	24	1
GUIDE TO ENJOYING THE TEENAGE YEARS	TI	37	1
GUIDE TO ENJOYING YOURSELF ON A RAINY AFTERNOON	TI	24	1
GV1229.J63 1983	CA	24	1
HOBBIES	SU	24	1
HOBBIES	TW	24	1
HQ796.S553 1983	CA	37	1
HYGIENE	SU	37	1
HYGIENE	KW	37	1
ILLINOIS	TW	37	1
JOHN	TW	37	1
JONES	TW	24	1
JONES, MARY	AU	24	1
MARY	TW	24	1
PEER	TW	37	1
PEER RELATIONSHIP	SU	37	1
PUBLISHING	TW	24,37	2
RAINY	TW	24	1
READING	TW	24	1
RECREATIONAL	TW	24,37	2
RECREATIONAL ACTIVITIES	SU	24,37	2
RECREATIONAL ACTIVITIES*	SU	24	1
RECREATIONAL READING	SU	24	1
RELATIONSHIP	TW	37	1
RELATIONSHIPS	TW	37	1
SCHOOL	TW	37	1
SMITH	TW	37	1
SMITH, JOHN	AU	37	1
STUDENT	TW	37	1

(cont.)

SEARCH KEY VALUE	SEARCH KEY	ADDRESS OF RECORD	NUMBER OF RECORDS
STUDENT SCHOOL RELATIONSHIP	SU	37	1
TEENAGE	TW	37	1
TEXAS	TW	24	1
TOPS	TW	24	1
TOPS PUBLISHING COMPANY	PU	24	1
YEARS	TW	37	1
YOURSELF	TW	24	1
1983	PY	24,37	2
19830302	ED	24	1
198304	UF	24	1
19830522	ED	37	1
198306	UF	37	1
1983060104	UI	24	1
1983120488	UI	37	1

SUBDIVIDERS

Chapter 8, on controlled indexing vocabulary, discussed special subject terms for subdividing other subject terms. A slash (/) is used for separating a subject term from its subdivider. The following keywords

SU - GAMES/ADOLESCENTS/ADULTS/CHILDREN
HOBBIES/ADOLESCENTS/ADULTS/CHILDREN

where ADOLESCENTS and CHILDREN are subdividers of the subject terms GAMES and HOBBIES, might be copied to the index, using [SU] for the subject term search key, and [SD] for the subdivider search key, as follows:

SEARCH KEY VALUE	SEARCH KEY
ADOLESCENTS	SD
ADULTS	SD
CHILDREN	SD
GAMES [with or without a subdivider]	SU
GAMES/ADOLESCENTS	SU
GAMES/ADULTS	SU
GAMES/CHILDREN	SU
HOBBIES [with or without a subdivider]	SU
HOBBIES/ADOLESCENTS	SU
HOBBIES/ADULTS	SU
HOBBIES/CHILDREN	SU

A subdivider may be searched either as an individual search term, without specifying the term that it subdivides, or as a combination subject term with its subdivider. The following is a search statement specifying union of subdividers:

[SD] CHILDREN OR ADOLESCENTS

Searching attached subdividers may require special positional operators, such as the forward slash (/) in the following search statement:

GAMES/CHILDREN OR GAMES/ADOLESCENTS OR
HOBBIES/CHILDREN OR HOBBIES/ADOLESCENTS

The first of these last two search statements implicitly includes the second, as well as any other combination of the subject term with either of these subdividers attached to them. The following is a version of the latter search statement illustrating the use of logical operators combining subdividers:

(GAMES OR HOBBIES)/(CHILDREN OR ADOLESCENTS)

An alternate way a record might represent subject terms with subdividers would be as "sentences" within a field, such as:

SU - GAMES ADOLESCENTS CHILDREN. HOBBIES
        ADOLESCENTS CHILDREN.

Searching this form of subject term with attached subdivider would entail the use of the positional operator SAME-SENTENCE-AS (discussed in the next chapter), as:

[SU] (GAMES OR HOBBIES) SAME-SENTENCE-AS (CHILDREN OR ADOLESCENTS)

Files are not necessarily limited to search keys defined in this chapter. The search keys for a file would correspond to categories of information the searchers of the file would find useful for retrieval. Search keys are initially established during the design of a file. The producers of a file may modify the original set of search keys, but searchers have no direct control over the establishment or modification of search keys.

**ESTABLISHING
AND
MODIFYING
SEARCH KEYS**

**DEVELOPING
SEARCH
STRATEGY AND
FORMULATION
(III)**

Let's return to the query APPROACHES TO SOLVING THE SHORTAGE OF MATHEMATICS AND SCIENCE TEACHERS IN THE SCHOOLS, and show how information presented in this chapter might be applied to the search formulation for responding to this query.

During interactive formulation development, involving insertion of new search terms in hopes of improving the resulting retrieval set, we showed how the computer might be used to avoid redisplaying records, by negation of search terms in search statements. However, negating search terms for this purpose may become complicated, causing relevant records to be missed. For example, if the search query were, for the sake of simplicity, THE SHORTAGE OF SCIENCE TEACHERS, we might begin with the following search formulation:

SEARCH STATEMENT 1
    science AND teacher AND shortage

Suppose, after displaying resulting titles of records, we thought of inserting two new search terms simultaneously, "teachers" (for the TEACHER concept) and "physics" (for the SCIENCE concept), as follows:

SEARCH STATEMENT 2
    (science OR physics) AND (teacher OR teachers) AND shortage

In displaying titles of records retrieved by SEARCH STATEMENT 2, we would find titles from SEARCH STATEMENT 1 redisplayed. How, in SEARCH STATEMENT 2, might we have negated search terms to avoid redisplaying these titles? After struggling with this problem, we might have devised the following search statement:

SEARCH STATEMENT 2
    science AND teachers AND shortage AND NOT teacher OR physics AND (teacher OR teachers) AND shortage AND NOT science

Fortunately, however, as described in this chapter, we now have an alternative to the tricky practice of negating search terms. We can regard SEARCH STATEMENT 1 as representing a retrieval set whose titles have already been displayed, and therefore simply negate the complete search statement, as follows:

SEARCH STATEMENT 2
>   (science or physics) AND (teacher OR teachers) AND
>   shortage AND NOT 1

Free text searching of single words, as described in this chapter, may be employed in a search formulation. If the default when search keys are omitted is that all search keys will be searched, then a search statement containing single words might be used for searching textwords indexed from titles [TI], subject terms [SU], and, as in the following example, journal titles [JT].

The following search statement would be an alternate way of expressing the MATHEMATICS AND TEACHERS OR SCIENCE AND TEACHERS concept in the search strategy.

(physics OR mathematics OR science OR chemical) AND (teacher OR education OR school)

If words in journal titles are indexed as textwords, and the default includes the textword search key, this search statement would retrieve references to articles published in the following journals:

School Science and Mathematics
Physics Teacher
Physics Education
Connecticut Journal of Science Education
Mathematics Teacher
Science Education
Journal of Chemical Education

The following might be a revised search formulation:

SEARCH STATEMENT 1
>   [SU] Teacher Shortage AND (Mathematics Teachers OR
>   Mathematics Education OR Mathematics Instruction OR
>   Elementary School Mathematics OR
>   Secondary School Mathematics OR
>   College Mathematics OR Science Teachers OR
>   Science Education OR Science Instruction OR
>   Elementary School Science OR
>   Secondary School Science OR College Science OR
>   Engineering Education)

SEARCH STATEMENT 2

> (shortage OR shortages OR scarcity) AND
> (mathematics OR math OR science OR biology OR
> chemistry OR physics OR engineering OR chemical) AND
> (teacher OR teachers OR teaching OR education OR
> classroom OR classrooms OR school OR schools)

SEARCH STATEMENT 3

> 1 OR 2

Note that SEARCH STATEMENT 1 is restricted to the subject term [SU] search key. We will assume that omission of the search key implies "any search key." Therefore, SEARCH STATEMENT 2, which is our "insurance" search statement, in case relevant records are missed by SEARCH STATEMENT 1, would search textwords in article titles, subject terms, and journal titles.

If the file we are searching is updated monthly, we might, as suggested by the discussion of the update file code [UF] field and search key in this chapter, process this formulation each month against the file update. Assuming that the first time the search formulation was processed, we were searching a file that was most recently updated with the November 1984 file update, the next time the formulation is processed we might intersect SEARCH STATEMENT 3 with the search term 198412 [UF] to restrict the retrieval set to records in the December 1984 file update, as follows:

SEARCH STATEMENT 4

> 3 AND 198412 [UF]

Chapter 12 discusses selective dissemination of information (SDI), a feature for automatically searching file updates. Searching weight categories, a topic of this chapter, will be illustrated in the continuation of the search formulation at the end of the next chapter.

EXERCISES

1. If words in subject terms are indexed as textwords [TW], substitute a single-term search statement for the following:

   LAND ACQUISITION [SU] OR LAND SETTLEMENT [SU] OR LAND USE [SU]

   Under what circumstances might the brief version retrieve records unrelated to the topic suggested by these three subject terms? Propose a method of computer indexing that would reduce this possibility.

2. Based on the search keys and search key values in the complete computer index displayed in this chapter, but assuming these index other records in addition to the two records indexed in this chapter, write a single-statement search formulation resulting in a retrieval set representing books either about games for children (using the subject term [SU] search key) or written by Mary Jones. Assume there are no default search keys.

   Revise this search statement based on subject term [SU] and author [AU] as the default search keys.

   Revise this search statement based on subject term [SU] alone as the default search key.

   Write this search formulation as two search statements.

3. Suggest a library function that might make use of the call number search key. (Hint: Consider the library as a warehouse of books.)

4. How might the unique identifier search key be used by producers of a file in order to maintain the file? (Hint: Consider the maintenance action of modifying a single record.)

5. Assume three categories for weighting, designated * + −, in decreasing order of importance. Show entries in an index where a search key value locates three bibliographic records, assigned the subject term HOBBIES, as follows:

   record at address 1: HOBBIES—concept of highest importance
   in the document

   record at address 2: HOBBIES—concept of intermediate
   importance in the document

   record at address 3: HOBBIES—concept of lowest importance
   in the document

   Include an entry for HOBBIES irrespective of importance. Show two versions of the index, illustrating both methods for representing weight category assignments discussed in this chapter. Show the entries for HOBBIES as a search term, corresponding to each version in the index.

Search Capabilities, Limits and Overflows, Displays to Aid Searching

10

In Chapter 9 we presented information about search keys and some basic techniques required for searching them. This chapter will explain more advanced search techniques, including truncation, searching hierarchical classifications, ranging of numeric search terms, string-searching, and nesting search statements.

Suppose that you were in charge of taking inventory in a library for the purpose of identifying misplaced books. A search capability known as *truncation* could assist you in dividing this task among employees according to sections of bookshelves. For example, an employee might receive a list of bibliographic records for books with call numbers beginning with GV, in order to check these records against the books on the shelf.

TRUNCATION AND VARIABLE CHARACTER SYMBOL

The list would be the output of a retrieval set from a search statement that used right-handed truncation, a shorthand way for searching the union of search terms generated by entering a single search term whose ending characters are unspecified and represented by a variable character symbol. To illustrate, the following is a display of a portion of an index:

SEARCH KEY VALUE	SEARCH KEY	ADDRESS OF RECORD	NUMBER OF RECORDS
GT6060.C7 1980	CA	92	1
GV721.5.A7 1980	CA	58	1
GV721.5.K6 1984	CA	14	1
GV1229.J63 1983	CA	24	1
GV1229.W3 1981	CA	73	1
GV1469.3.A5 1983	CA	66	1
H61.9.W3 1980	CA	11	1

If the variable character symbol, representing any number of unspecified characters, is the backward slash (\), the search statement GV\ would retrieve the five records located by call number search key values starting with GV. The truncated search term is equivalent to the following search statement:

GV721.5.A7   1980 OR
GV721.5.K6   1984 OR
GV1229.J63   1983 OR
GV1229.W3   1981 OR
GV1469.3.A5   1983

Left-handed truncation is a shorthand way for searching the union of search terms generated by entering a single search term whose initial characters are unspecified and represented by a variable character symbol. Embedded truncation is a shorthand way for searching the union of search terms generated by entering a single search term that has one or more middle characters that are unspecified and represented by a variable character symbol.

Truncation may include specifying the maximum number of characters represented by the variable character symbol. For example, the search statement ENJOY\.3, specifying a maximum of three unspecified ending characters, would match against the union of search key values including ENJOY, ENJOYS, ENJOYED, and ENJOYING, but not ENJOYMENT.

If you enter a truncated search term that corresponds to more than one search key value, the computer may return a message dis-

playing them and offering you the option of selecting certain ones. You may be able to avoid this display (for example, by preceding the truncated search term with the word ALL) if you know in advance that you want the union to include each search term generated by the truncated term.

Chapter 8 treated hierarchical classifications in a controlled indexing vocabulary. A concept is usually indexed with the most specific subject term in a classification for that concept; hierarchical displays of the vocabulary may be used not only for locating these specific search terms, but also searching an entire classification as a single search term. For example, when the display shows the term SPORTS with FOOTBALL as a more specific term, and if a book is about football, the record will be indexed with FOOTBALL, not SPORTS. Therefore, if a search query includes the concept "sports," you would translate this concept into the union of all "sports" subject terms. The following is a hierarchical display of sports terms:

HIERARCHICAL CLASSIFICA-TION AS SEARCH TERM

SPORTS
       ARCHERY
       BASEBALL
       BASKETBALL
       FIELD HOCKEY
       FOOTBALL
       GOLF
       GYMNASTICS
       ICE SKATING
       LACROSSE
       ROLLER SKATING
       SKIING
       SOCCER
       SOFTBALL
       SQUASH
       SWIMMING
       TENNIS
       TRACK AND FIELD
       VOLLEYBALL
       WATERSKIING
       WEIGHTLIFTING
       WRESTLING

    A search query on sports injuries might include a search statement consisting of the union of terms in the above SPORTS classification (SPORTS OR ARCHERY OR BASEBALL OR BASKET-BALL OR FIELD HOCKEY OR FOOTBALL OR, and so on), and then intersect this search statement with the subject term INJURIES. A less troublesome way of entering the union of these 22 terms would be to employ truncation, described earlier in this chapter. The computer might store a table equivalent to the SPORTS classification with each more specific term tagged as belonging to the SPORTS classification. These terms might be preceded by SPORTS, as follows:

SPORTS
SPORTS.ARCHERY
SPORTS.BASEBALL
SPORTS.BASKETBALL
SPORTS.FIELD HOCKEY
SPORTS.FOOTBALL
SPORTS.GOLF
SPORTS.GYMNASTICS
SPORTS.ICE SKATING
SPORTS.LACROSSE
SPORTS.ROLLER SKATING
SPORTS.SKIING
SPORTS.SOCCER
SPORTS.SOFTBALL
SPORTS.SQUASH
SPORTS.SWIMMING
SPORTS.TENNIS
SPORTS.TRACK AND FIELD
SPORTS.VOLLEYBALL
SPORTS.WATERSKIING
SPORTS.WEIGHTLIFTING
SPORTS.WRESTLING

In response to the search term SPORTS\, which uses right-handed truncation, instead of matching directly against subject terms in the index, the computer would first access the table and then substitute the union of terms in the SPORTS classification.

The index may include codes for search key values, for example, A1.7 (= SPORTS), A1.7.2 (= BASEBALL), and A1.7.5 (= FOOTBALL), and union of terms in the SPORTS classification might be searched by right-handed truncation of the code, that is, A1.7\. Instead of the usual right-handed truncation format, using a variable character symbol (for example, SPORTS\ or A1.7\, where ''\'' is the variable character symbol), there may be a special command for hierarchical searching, such as EXPLODE (for example, EXPLODE SPORTS or EXPLODE A1.7).

Numeric search keys, especially dates, are frequently searchable as a range of numeric values. Ranging uses relational operators, which include EQUAL TO (a number), NOT EQUAL TO (a number), and three ranging operators GREATER THAN (a number), LESS THAN (a number), FROM (a number) TO (a number), and their complements NOT GREATER THAN, NOT LESS THAN, and NOT FROM (a number) TO (a number).

RELATIONAL OPERATORS (RANGING NUMERIC SEARCH TERMS)

For example, to locate records of books published since 1982, and indexed with the subject term READING, you would enter the search statement:

READING [SU] AND GREATER THAN 1981 [PY]

To locate records of books on this subject published from 1978 to 1981, the search statement would be:

READING [SU] AND FROM 1978 TO 1981 [PY]

To locate records of books on this subject published before 1978, the search statement would be:

READING [SU] AND LESS THAN 1978 [PY]

To illustrate ranging the update file code [UF] search key, suppose you had searched the subject term READING against a file extending through June 1983, and six months later you needed to retrieve records on the same subject that had been input to the file from July 1983 through December 1983. You could use ranging to retrieve only the new records indexed with the subject term READING, by intersecting the subject term with a GREATER THAN (update file code value) expression, as follows:

READING (SU) AND GREATER THAN 198306 [UF]

Chapter 3, on noncomputerized files, treated searching a file sequentially (one record at a time), that is, without using an index. In computerized retrieval, searching a file sequentially for a specified sequence of characters in a record is known as stringsearching.

FREE TEXT SEARCHING: STRING-SEARCHING

Stringsearching a small number of records may be more efficient

than searching them using the index. If a retrieval set is small, it may be more efficient to stringsearch them than to intersect the search statement number with an equivalent search term. For example, suppose SEARCH STATEMENT 4 consisted of an author term, as follows:

SEARCH STATEMENT 4
    SMITH, JOHN [AU]

If the search statement result were 10, indicating ten books written by John Smith, and you needed only the record with the word ENJOY-ING in the title, SEARCH STATEMENT 5 could be entered as follows:

SEARCH STATEMENT 5
    4 AND ENJOYING [TW]

However, it may be faster to stringsearch the titles of the ten records in the SEARCH STATEMENT 4 retrieval set using a string-search command, such as SCAN, and specifying the field in the same way search key values are specified in searching against the index, as follows:

SEARCH STATEMENT 5
    SCAN 4 [TI] \ENJOYING\

In this example, both right-handed and left-handed truncation are used for telling the computer it doesn't matter what, if any, characters either precede or follow the string in the title field.

Chapter 9 introduced free text searching (searching text as it occurs naturally in the record rather than units of compound words) and discussed single-word searching of textwords. Stringsearching was mentioned as a type of free text searching that, in contrast to index searching, enables you to specify and match character strings not found in the index, such as stopwords, parts of words, and sequences of words (phrases).

The following is an example of searching a character string that is a portion of a word. Any record retrieved by the previous string-search statement would also be retrieved by the following search statement:

SCAN 4 [TI] \NJOYING\

Since stringsearching is not limited to values in the index, it may also be used for searching multiple words in a specified sequence. For example:

SEARCH STATEMENT 9
    SCAN 8 [TI] \GUIDE\ENJOY\

The preceding search statement, using right- and left-handed and embedded truncation, would retrieve a record from the SEARCH STATEMENT 8 retrieval set, which has the following title:

Guide to enjoying your European tour.

A record in the SEARCH STATEMENT 8 retrieval set, which has the following title, would not be retrieved by SEARCH STATEMENT 9 because the sequence of words does not match the sequence in the search statement.

Enjoying your guided tour of Europe.

A stringsearch statement might include an explicit compound expression, as follows:

SCAN 8 [TI] \GUIDE TO ENJOY\

It doesn't matter if a word in a stringsearch statement, such as "to" in the preceding search statement, is a stopword (a nonindexed word) since the record is being searched directly.

You may use logical operators in a stringsearch statement as in search statements that search the index. For example:

SCAN 4 [TI] \GUIDE\ AND \ENJOY\

Stringsearching may specify the maximum number of characters represented by the variable character symbol in a truncation, or that character strings be in the same sentence. (The same-sentence capability in searching the index is discussed later in this chapter.)

In Chapter 9, we presented an example of textword indexing in which words from more than one field were indexed as values belonging to a single textword [TW] search key. Records in the example were:

78.
TI - How to form your own company.
PU- Anderson Publishing Company

60.
TI - How to plan your summer vacation.
PU- Jefferson Publishing Company

The following is a portion of the index to these records containing the search key value COMPANY:

SEARCH KEY VALUE	SEARCH KEY	ADDRESS OF RECORD	NUMBER OF RECORDS
COMPANY	TW	60,78	2

Since COMPANY is not indexed separately, as title textword and publisher textword, you might use stringsearching to retrieve only the record with COMPANY in the title, as follows:

SEARCH STATEMENT 1
    COMPANY [TW]

SEARCH STATEMENT 2
    SCAN 1 [TI] \COMPANY\

Stringsearching has the following major limitation: If previous retrieval sets against which stringsearch statements are processed are large, stringsearching, which would be slow in comparison to index searching, would take a long time and may not be possible if a certain time limit is exceeded.

Some of the same functions of stringsearching, namely, searching words in a specified sequence or specifying that words be in the same sentence, may be accomplished by searching the index based on positions of words within records. Combining terms according to word position is a special case of logical intersection.

FREE TEXT SEARCHING: MULTIPLE-TERM INDEX SEARCHING

Because they allow more specificity than the intersection operator AND, positional and repeat-word operators (described further on) are particularly useful for searching fields containing much text and indexed as textwords, such as abstracts and the full text of documents. Suppose one of our bibliographic records contained an abstract field, as follows:

37.
AU - Smith, John
TI - Guide to enjoying the teenage years.
PL - Chicago, Illinois
PU - Atlas Publishing Company
PY - 1983
SU - Adolescents*
      Family Relationships
      Hygiene
      Peer Relationship
      Recreational Activities
      Student School Relationship
CA - HQ796.S553   1983
UI - 1983120488
ED - 19830522
UF - 198306
AB - This book contains advice on how to lessen the growing pains
      frequently experienced by adolescents. The authors acknowl-
      edge that growing up can be a painful experience. This book is
      written with sensitivity and understanding.

Word position would be searched using positional operators such as SAME-FIELD-AS, SAME-SENTENCE-AS, and ADJACENT-TO. (The complement operator NOT may be combined with these operators for specifying that two words not have the designated positional relationship.) For example, if words in the abstract field were indexed as textword search key values, the above record would be retrieved by each of the following search statements:

POSITIONAL OPERATORS

ADOLESCENTS [AB] AND UNDERSTANDING [AB]
[AB] ADOLESCENTS AND UNDERSTANDING
ADOLESCENTS SAME-FIELD-AS UNDERSTANDING

The following are equivalent versions that show how the third search statement may be modified, using search key qualifiers, to retrieve only records with both ADOLESCENTS and UNDERSTANDING in the abstract field:

ADOLESCENTS [AB] SAME-FIELD-AS UNDERSTANDING
ADOLESCENTS SAME-FIELD-AS UNDERSTANDING [AB]
ADOLESCENTS [AB] SAME-FIELD-AS UNDERSTANDING [AB]
[AB] ADOLESCENTS SAME-FIELD-AS UNDERSTANDING

Not only may words in records be indexed as textword search key values, but in addition, their word positions in the field may be stored in the computer. For example, the following word positions may be recorded for words in the abstract field.

GROWING is word #10 in sentence #1.
GROWING is word #5 in sentence #2.
PAINS is word #11 in sentence #1.
PAINFUL is word #10 in sentence #2.
UNDERSTANDING is word #8 in sentence #3.
LESSON is word #8 in sentence #1.

The preceding record would be retrieved by the following search statement based on either sentence #1 or sentence #2:

GROWING SAME-SENTENCE-AS PAIN\

But it would not be retrieved by the following search statement:

UNDERSTANDING SAME-SENTENCE-AS PAIN\

However, the record would be retrieved by the following search statement based only on sentence #1:

GROWING ADJACENT-TO PAIN\

In Chapter 9, we noted that subject terms with attached subdividers might be in the record in the form of sentences, as follows:

SU - GAMES ADOLESCENTS CHILDREN. HOBBIES
      ADOLESCENTS CHILDREN.

In this case, a subject term with its subdivider would be searched using the SAME-SENTENCE-AS operator.

Numeric positional operators may be used in a search statement for specifying the maximum number of intervening words between two words in a sentence. For example, the following search statement would retrieve the preceding record based on intervening word specifications applied to textword search key values from the abstract:

NUMERIC POSITIONAL OPERATORS

LESSON 2-WORDS PAINS

In our examples the ADJACENT-TO operator and operators for specifying the maximum number of intervening words assume that the computer stores and utilizes positions of all words, including stopwords, words not indexed as search key values that should therefore not be used as search terms in search statements connected by positional operators.

In searching the index, the computer may provide a repeat-word operator, a logical operator for specifying intersection of the same word, counting each word separately. Suppose you need to retrieve records having a repetition of the word PERSON in the same sentence, as, for example:

REPEAT-WORD OPERATOR

PERSON-PERSON
PERSON TO PERSON
PERSON TO ANOTHER PERSON
PERSON COMMUNICATING WITH ANOTHER PERSON
PERSON TRIES TO COMMUNICATE WITH ANOTHER
   PERSON

Records having these phrases in the title field may be retrieved by the following search statement:

[TW] PERSON REPEAT-WORD PERSON

Positional operators may have a repeat-word capability. Based on the above phrases, adjacency of the same word PERSON would retrieve only PERSON-PERSON, and specifying that the same word PERSON have no more than two intervening words would retrieve only PERSON-PERSON, PERSON TO PERSON, and PERSON TO ANOTHER PERSON.

Since indexing the abstract field, which may have a relatively large amount of text, would greatly increase the size of the index by increasing the number of records retrieved, this field could be made searchable only by stringsearching. There is another mechanism for retrieval from a previous retrieval set that entails neither stringsearch-

SEARCHING TEMPORARY INDEX TO RETRIEVAL SET

ing nor searching the complete index to the file. It would require a special searching command causing the computer to instantaneously generate a temporary index to the previous retrieval set. A search statement using this special command would then search the index to this retrieval set, which would be considerably smaller than the complete index.

NESTING

In the discussion of logical operators in Chapter 6, we used parentheses for clarifying the order of operations or for specifying the order when the order without parentheses is intentionally against the computer rule for the order of logical operations. Computers may allow nesting, which uses parentheses for embedding search statements containing logical operators within other search statements. In the following example, the first three search statements are equivalent to SEARCH STATEMENT 4, which illustrates nesting; that is, either SEARCH STATEMENT 3 or SEARCH STATEMENT 4 would result in the same retrieval set.

SEARCH STATEMENT 1
    CHILDREN OR ADOLESCENTS
SEARCH STATEMENT 2
    1 AND READING OR RECREATIONAL READING
SEARCH STATEMENT 3
    2 AND GRADES
SEARCH STATEMENT 4
    ((CHILD OR ADOLESCENTS) AND READING OR
    RECREATIONAL READING) AND GRADES

SELECTING SEARCH TERMS FROM NUMBERED DISPLAY

Later in this chapter displays of search key values in the index as search aids will be discussed. If search key values in this display are numbered, it may be possible to select values by number, causing the computer to process the selections as search terms. If more than one number is selected, the computer might assume that you intend to search the corresponding values as search terms in a union relationship. For example, suppose you could request a numbered display of only the subject term portion of an index, as follows:

SEARCH KEY VALUE	SEARCH KEY	NUMBER OF RECORDS
1 - ADOLESCENTS	SU	2
2 - ARTS ACTIVITIES	SU	1
3 - CHILDREN	SU	1
4 - FAMILY RELATIONSHIPS	SU	1
5 - GAMES	SU	1

(cont.)

SEARCH KEY VALUE	SEARCH KEY	NUMBER OF RECORDS
6 - HOBBIES	SU	1
7 - HYGIENE	SU	1
8 - PEER RELATIONSHIP	SU	1
9 - RECREATIONAL ACTIVITIES	SU	2
10 - RECREATIONAL READING	SU	1
11 - STUDENT SCHOOL RELATIONSHIP	SU	1

ENTER ALL, NONE, OR NUMBERS SEPARATED BY A SPACE

In response to the computer instruction at the end, you might enter the following:

2   5   6   9   10

Instead of having to enter the following search statement:

ARTS ACTIVITIES OR GAMES OR HOBBIES OR
RECREATIONAL ACTIVITIES OR RECREATIONAL READING

This type of search term entry is part of the trend toward user-friendliness (discussed in Chapter 14).

In our discussion of stringsearching earlier in this chapter, we mentioned the possibility of a time limit on the processing of search statements. Computerized retrieval operates under the time sharing principle, that is, the continous allocation of successive slices of time to multiple simultaneous users. Switching from one user to another occurs at such high speeds that usually users cannot detect any reduction of response time, which is the time needed by the computer to respond to messages from users.

TIME SHARING

TIME LIMIT AND TIME OVERFLOW MESSAGE

There are some time-consuming operations, such as stringsearching a large retrieval set, that may not be completed in the time slice allotted. When a slice of time is exceeded, the computer may respond with a time overflow message, offering you the option to cancel the operation or to use another time slice to continue the operation. Normally you would continue receiving as many additional slices of time as you need, although you may reach an absolute limit if there are many simultaneous users making the same request for additional time.

It may be possible for the computer to provide an intermediate search statement result at the end of each time slice. For example, in stringsearching 300 records from a previous retrieval set, if only about 100 records could be searched in the first time slice, the computer would display the number of records searched and the search statement result. This retrieval set would be your final retrieval set for that search statement should you choose not to request additional time. If you cancel a stringsearch after some processing has occurred but before completion, the computer may allow you to re-enter the stringsearch statement later, specifying that processing begin where it left off in the previous stringsearch statement.

If time overflow/continuation cue messages are not provided, the computer may require you to wait until processing is complete. On the other hand, the computer may allow you to preselect from a set of time overflow options, as follows: completion of the operation without interruption by time overflow messages; notification of a time overflow only once, and then offering the option of either cancelling or continuing without interruption; notification of the first time overflow and then offering the option of continuing without interruption, receiving time overflows as needed; or cancelling. The computer may provide a continuous signal on your terminal screen indicating that the search statement is still being processed.

WORKSPACE LIMIT

Another computer limitation is the physical workspace limit. Each user is reserved a certain amount of space in the computer for storing information during the search session. Information stored in your workspace may be limited by the number of search statements, the number of search terms or number of characters entered at the terminal, or the number of records in all the retrieval sets combined. There may also be a workspace limit for each search statement, such as the number of search terms or the number of records in the retrieval set. Limits for the number of records the computer will list at the terminal or in an offline printout (a listing produced by a high-speed printer attached to the computer you are accessing for retrieval) resulting from an output instruction are discussed in the next chapter.

When a workspace limit is exceeded, processing of the current search statement will be aborted (terminated), and the computer will send you an explanatory message. If processing is aborted, there may be some other options available to you, such as subdividing the search statement into two or more search statements, or re-entering the search statement after removing from your workspace previous search statements, with their retrieval sets, that are no longer needed.

The computer may prevent you from potentially exceeding a limit by forbidding certain operations at the outset. For example, you may not be allowed to use the complement operator (NOT) unless the complement of the search term is intersected with another search term. According to this restriction, NOT GUIDE as a complete search statement would be forbidden, as would the complete search statement TEENAGER OR NOT ADULT. The computer might permit these types of search statements but prevent you from using them as search terms in subsequent search statements or as the basis for stringsearching.

COMPUTER RESTRICTIONS ON OPERATIONS

We've already mentioned several forms of controlled subject indexing vocabulary, specifically, an alphabetic display, a hierarchical display, and keyword in context (KWIC) and keyword out of context (KWOC) displays. These displays are usually available in published form. Sections of vocabulary may be requested as computer displays, followed by options for continuing the display in either direction, whether alphabetically or among levels of hierarchical displays. Similar displays may be available for other types of authority files, such as name authority files containing official names of individuals or organizations, or serial authority files containing titles, title abbreviations, or codes for journals or other serial publications.

COMPUTER DISPLAY OF VOCABULARY

Computer displays of the index to the retrieval file are helpful for searching. Since the complete index to the file would be too large to display all at once, a small section of the index would be available for display, and, as for displays of authority files discussed previously, options would be offered for continuing the display in either direction.

How can a display of the index help in searching? The display will show you if a search term under consideration is a search key value. If the term is absent from the display, there would be no point in using it as a search term to be matched against the index. The display of search term results (counts of records) associated with each

COMPUTER DISPLAY OF INDEX

search key value may be used in developing search strategies and formulations.

The display will help you locate search key values related to a search term, such as different forms of the term, different spellings, and misspellings. For example, the following display illustrates variations of search key values in an index:

SEARCH KEY VALUE	SEARCH KEY	NUMBER OF RECORDS
ADVERTISING	SU	16
ADVERTISING	TW	10
ADVERTIZING	TW	2
.		
.		
.		
HGIH	TW	1
HIGH	TW	22
HIGH SCHOOLS	SU	28
.		
.		
WRITE	TW	9
WRITING	TW	40
WRITING SKILLS	SU	32
WRITINGS	TW	2
WRITTEN	TW	9

You may restrict the display to specific search keys. For example, to locate an author's name, you may restrict the index display to the author search key. On the other hand, to locate subject terms in the index, you might restrict the display to the subject term search key. Using displays of numbered search key values for selecting search terms from the index was illustrated earlier in this chapter.

SEARCH HISTORY DISPLAY

Another kind of display at a terminal is the search history display, which consists of a set of previously processed search statements, with their search statement results. In developing a search formulation, you may need to be reminded of previous search statements. A second use of search history displays would be for interactively displaying search formulations as hard copy (in printed form).

HARD COPY OF SEARCH FORMULATION

Hard copy of the search formulation may be for your personal use or for distribution. When obtaining hard copy output of retrieval sets, whether a list of records printed at your terminal or an offline printout, it may be convenient to have the accompanying search formulation in hard copy as well. Keeping a hard copy of your search formulation is particularly important once you have requested, but not yet received, an offline printout; if for some reason you never receive the printout, you will have an exact copy of the search formulation as a source for re-entering it. The printed search formulation could be used for evaluating the retrieval set for determining why the retrieval set contains an unexpected record, or why it does not contain a record that you expected. Obtaining hard copy of search formulations generated during batch processing is discussed in Chapter 11.

We will now show how three search capabilities discussed in this chapter—truncation, searching hierarchical classifications, and string searching—might be applied to our ongoing search formulation in response to the query APPROACHES TO SOLVING THE SHORTAGE OF MATHEMATICS AND SCIENCE TEACHERS IN THE SCHOOLS. We will also discuss use of computerized displays of the controlled indexing vocabulary, the index, and the search history.

DEVELOPING SEARCH STRATEGY AND FORMULATION (IV)

The following is the final version, from the previous chapter, of SEARCH STATEMENT 1 of the formulation:

SEARCH STATEMENT 1

> [SU] Teacher Shortage AND (Mathematics Teachers OR
> Mathematics Education OR Mathematics Instruction OR
> Elementary School Mathematics OR
> Secondary School Mathematics OR
> College Mathematics OR Science Teachers OR
> Science Education OR Science Instruction OR
> Elementary School Science OR
> Secondary School Science OR College Science OR
> Engineering Education)

This search statement contains a number of subject terms from the controlled indexing vocabulary. Suppose a computerized or published display of the indexing vocabulary listed hierarchical classifications, where each subject term was coded, as follows. (The ERIC® thesaurus does not contain hierarchical classification codes, which were devised here for illustrative purposes.)

Mathematics Curriculum		MathCurric
Narrower Term:	College Mathematics	MathCurric.1
	Elementary School Mathematics	MathCurric.2
	Modern Mathematics	MathCurric.3
	Secondary School Mathematics	MathCurric.4

Science Curriculum		SciCurric
Narrower Term:	College Science	SciCurric.1
	Elementary School Science	SciCurric.2
	General Science	SciCurric.3
	Secondary School Science	SciCurric.4

These classifications include six of the search terms in SEARCH STATEMENT 1 that had been assigned to the MATHEMATICS AND TEACHERS OR SCIENCE AND TEACHERS concept in the search strategy. While the four remaining subject terms in the classifications—Mathematics Curriculum, Modern Mathematics, Science Curriculum, and General Science—are not in the search statement, it might be reasonable to include them as terms for the concept MATHEMATICS AND TEACHERS OR SCIENCE AND TEACHERS as well.

We might, therefore, in SEARCH STATEMENT 1, use these codes and the truncation capability in order to save the time and effort of entering the search terms individually. The following are the truncated codes and their equivalencies in a search statement:

MathCurric\ = Mathematics Curriculum OR College Mathematics OR Elementary School Mathematics OR Modern Mathematics OR Secondary School Mathematics

SciCurric\ = Science Curriculum OR College Science OR Elementary School Science OR General Science OR Secondary School Science

The following is the revised search statement, with truncated subject term codes in place of their preceding equivalencies:

SEARCH STATEMENT 1

[SU] Teacher Shortage AND (Mathematics Teachers OR Mathematics Education OR Mathematics Instruction OR MathCurric\ OR Science Teachers OR Science Education OR Science Instruction OR SciCurric\ OR Engineering Education)

The following is the final version, from the previous chapter, of SEARCH STATEMENT 2 of the formulation, which was oriented toward textword searching:

SEARCH STATEMENT 2

(shortage OR shortages OR scarcity) AND (mathematics OR math OR science OR biology OR chemistry OR physics OR

engineering OR chemical) AND (teacher OR teachers OR teaching OR education OR classroom OR classrooms OR school OR schools)

Truncation might be used for saving time and effort in entering words in this search statement, by truncating words beginning with the same sequence of characters. The following are the truncated words and their equivalencies in this search statement:

```
    shortage\ = shortage OR shortages
        math\ = mathematics OR math
       chemi\ = chemistry OR chemical
     teacher\ = teacher OR teachers
   classroom\ = classroom OR classrooms
      school\ = school OR schools
```

We might consider truncating "teacher" earlier in the word as "teach\" thereby implicitly incorporating "teaching" as well. Similarly, we might truncate "education as "educat\". The following is the revised search statement, with truncated words in place of their preceding equivalencies:

SEARCH STATEMENT 2

(shortage\ OR scarcity) AND (math\ OR science OR biology OR chemi\ OR physics OR engineering) AND (teach\ OR educat\ OR classroom\ OR school\)

In Chapter 8 the strategy was suggested of intersecting the concept of SOLVING with the final strategy up to that point in order to first display a retrieval set that appeared to be more relevant to the query, which had specified SOLVING. The formulation might accomplish this strategy in the series of search statements following, which are a continuation of SEARCH STATEMENT 1 and SEARCH STATEMENT 2, and which include search terms based on words in titles and subject terms identified from displays of records during development of the formulation.

SEARCH STATEMENT 4 uses stringsearching to efficiently retrieve records with SOLVING terms in the title. Note the form for "\ cope\" with a space between the first variable character symbol and the first character in the string. This format would ensure consideration of "cope" as the initial characters in a word or a sentence and thereby avoid stringsearching for words such as "scope."

Since SEARCH STATEMENT 4 stringsearches titles of records, it seemed to be in parallel to specify that the subject terms for

SOLVING be searched as central concepts. (Searching weight categories is described in Chapter 9.) Assuming a separate "subject-term-as-central-concept" field, we have specified the corresponding search key abbreviation [SU*] for search terms in SEARCH STATEMENT 5.

SEARCH STATEMENT 3

    1 OR 2

SEARCH STATEMENT 4

    SCAN 3 [TI] \bonus\ OR \ cope\ OR \coping\ OR \solv\ OR \correct\ OR \policy\ OR \policies\ OR \plan\ OR \plans\ OR \planning\ OR \solution\ OR \strengthen\ OR \incentive\

SEARCH STATEMENT 5

    3 AND (Teacher Recruitment OR Retraining OR Inservice Teacher Education OR Merit Pay OR Premium Pay OR Master Teachers OR Cooperative Programs OR School-Business Relationship OR Financial Support OR Government Role OR Federal Aid OR Federal Programs OR Research Needs OR Policy Formation) [SU*]

SEARCH STATEMENT 6

    4 OR 5

SEARCH STATEMENT 7

    3 AND NOT 6

The retrieval set for SEARCH STATEMENT 6 will be the list of records of primary relevance to the search query. This retrieval set constitutes a more precise response to the query than the more comprehensive retrieval set produced by SEARCH STATEMENT 3. A retrieval set of the remaining records is produced by SEARCH STATEMENT 7, which intersects SEARCH STATEMENT 3 (the comprehensive search statement) with the complement of SEARCH STATEMENT 6 (the precise search statement).

During the development of this search formulation, we have shown displays from the controlled indexing vocabulary, for displaying hierarchical classifications and related-term cross references. These might also be viewed as computer displays of the vocabulary file. However, if consulting vocabulary displays by computer requires

changing to a different file, causing us not to be able to return to the search formulation in progress, then published forms of the vocabulary would be preferred.

The following is a display of a search term as a search key value in the index that we might have requested when we began to develop the formulation:

SEARCH KEY VALUE	SEARCH KEY	NUMBER OF RECORDS
TEACHER SHORTAGE	SU*	86

Based on this display, our complete search formulation might simply have consisted of the following single-term search statement:

Teacher Shortage [SU*]

The search statement result, as indicated in the index display, would have been 86 records. Each record in the retrieval set would be indexed with "Teacher Shortage" as a central concept of the journal article, as indicated by the asterisked search key [SU*]. This retrieval set would include many of the relevant records returned by the detailed formulation, but a large proportion would consist of records of little or no relevance to the query. Moreover, although weight indicators were not included in displays in Chapter 8, in actuality, seemingly relevant titles did not always guarantee the indexing to "Teacher Shortage" as a central concept. Therefore, this single-term search formulation would miss retrieving a number of relevant records.

This simple formulation exemplifies an approach designed to produce easily and quickly a retrieval set that contains highly relevant records. In this type of searching, characterized as quick-and-dirty, recall is knowingly sacrificed for precision, although even the degree of precision may not be great.

We might request a search history display of the detailed formulation as follows:

1   [SU] Teacher Shortage AND (Mathematics Teachers OR
     Mathematics Education OR Mathematics Instruction OR
     MathCurric\ OR Science Teachers OR Science Education OR
     Science Instruction OR SciCurric\ OR Engineering
     Education)
RESULT   36

2   (shortage\ OR scarcity) AND (math\ OR science OR
     biology OR chemi\ OR physics OR engineering) AND
     (teach\ OR educat\ OR classroom\ OR school\)

RESULT   10

3   1 OR 2
RESULT   35

4   SCAN 3 [TI] \bonus\ OR \ cope\ OR \coping\ OR \solv\
       OR \correct\ OR \policy\ OR \policies\ OR \plan\ OR
       \plans\ OR \planning\ OR \solution\ OR \strengthen\ OR
       \incentive\
RESULT   6

5   3 AND (Teacher Recruitment OR Retraining OR
       Inservice Teacher Education OR Merit Pay OR
       Premium Pay OR Master Teachers OR Cooperative
       Programs OR School-Business Relationship OR Financial
       Support OR Government Role OR Federal Aid OR
       Federal Programs OR Research Needs OR
       Policy Formation) [SU*]
RESULT   13

6   4 OR 5
RESULT   17

7   3 AND NOT 6
RESULT   18

EXERCISES

1. Using truncation, substitute a single-term search statement for the
   following:

   (LAND ACQUISITION [SU] OR LAND SETTLEMENT [SU] OR
   LAND USE [SU]) AND NOT LANDFILLS

2. Write an actual search statement for the sports injuries query described in this chapter.

   Note the format of the computerized SPORTS table, equivalent to
   the hierarchical classification. Write a search statement for the
   union of specific sports search terms (not including the term
   SPORTS).

3. Answer the following, based on the passage in the Exercises for
   Chapter 6. Use parentheses to clarify the order of operations in
   search statements.

   a. Using the search terms IMMUNE and SYSTEM, write a search
      statement that would retrieve the set of sentences {1 3 4}, but
      not also sentence 8.

b. Using the search term MILLIONS, write a search statement that would retrieve sentence 7, but not also sentence 4.

4. Assume that words in the title [TI] field are indexed as textwords [TW], and that the computer does not permit left-handed truncation for index searching. Write search statements that would retrieve the set of all records with "million" or "billion" or "trillion" in the title field.

5. Stopwords may be counted for determining word position, but cannot be used as search terms for index searching. Assuming that words in the title [TI] field are indexed as textwords [TW], devise a search formulation to retrieve all records with "vitamin C" in the title field.

   Would your formulation retrieve records with "vitamin A and C" in the title field? If not, how could you revise the formulation to retrieve these records as well?

6. What is time sharing? How might the computer respond to time overflows?

7. What does it mean to exceed a workspace limit? How might you respond to exceeding a workspace limit during processing of a search statement? How might the computer prevent this eventuality?

8. Examine the index display at the end of this chapter. How could each of the three segments of the display assist you in devising a specific search statement? Write the resulting search statements.

9. Revise the search formulation you constructed in Exercise 5 at the end of Chapter 8 by using specific search keys presented in Chapter 9 (such as search statement number, weight category, textword from multiple fields) and applying new search capabilities presented in this chapter (such as truncation, hierarchical searching, string-searching, multiple-term index searching using positional operators, and ranging using relational operators).

Displaying Output, Offline Printout, Searching in Batch Mode

11

When the computer responds with a positive search statement result, you may then elect to display the records at your terminal. Displays of retrieval sets at the terminal are a form of output. The message you send the computer for producing this output is in the form of an *output instruction*. Output instructions begin with a command, followed by specifications. Assuming the command is PRINT, let's begin divising an instruction.

OUTPUT INSTRUCTION

Your first specification would be the search statement number of the retrieval set containing the records to be displayed. If five search statements have been processed during the session so far, you may display output from any of their retrieval sets. To display output from the retrieval set of SEARCH STATEMENT NUMBER 4, your output instruction would begin as follows:

SEARCH STATEMENT NUMBER SPECIFICATION

PRINT SEARCH STATEMENT 4

Suppose the retrieval set consists of bibliographic records, as follows:

FIELD AND FIELD ORDER SPECIFICATION

37.
AU- Smith, John
TI - Guide to enjoying the teenage years.
PL - Chicago, Illinois
PU- Atlas Publishing Company
PY - 1983
SU - Adolescents*
    Family Relationships
    Hygiene

      Peer Relationship
      Recreational Activities
      Student School Relationship
CA- HQ796.S553   1983
UI - 1983120488
ED- 19830522
UF- 198306

24.
AU- Jones, Mary
TI - Guide to enjoying yourself on a rainy afternoon.
PL - Dallas, Texas
PU- Tops Publishing Company
PY - 1983
SU - Adolescents
      Arts Activities
      Children
      Games
      Hobbies
      Recreational Activities*
      Recreational Reading
CA- GV1229.J63   1983
UI - 1983060104
ED- 19830302
UF- 198304

To display portions of records, you would select and specify certain fields in the output instruction. For locating books, you usually need to display only author, title, and call number fields. Using field abbreviations, your output instruction would now appear as follows:

PRINT SEARCH STATEMENT 4 FIELD AU TI CA

The order of these fields within an individual record may follow the order of the field abbreviations in the output instruction. This instruction would produce the following output based on the preceding retrieval set:

AU - Smith, John
TI - Guide to enjoying the teenage years.
CA - HQ796.S553   1983

AU - Jones, Mary
TI - Guide to enjoying yourself on a rainy afternoon.
CA - GV1229.J63   1983

For the call number to appear first, you would enter one of the following output instructions:

PRINT SEARCH STATEMENT 4 FIELD CA AU TI
PRINT SEARCH STATEMENT 4 FIELD CA TI AU

The first instruction would produce the following output:

CA - HQ796.S553   1983
AU - Smith, John
TI - Guide to enjoying the teenage years.

CA - GV1229.J63   1983
AU - Jones, Mary
TI - Guide to enjoying yourself on a rainy afternoon.

The second instruction would produce output as follows:

CA - HQ796.S553   1983
TI - Guide to enjoying the teenage years.
AU - Smith, John

CA - GV1229.J63   1983
TI - Guide to enjoying yourself on a rainy afternoon.
AU - Jones, Mary

Besides specifying that call numbers be displayed as the first field in a record, locating books would be facilitated by specifying that records in the output be sorted by call number, so that you could proceed along the shelves without backtracking. For example, suppose the retrieval set consists of the following five records, displayed as two versions each sorted differently. Output #2 is sorted by call number, whereas Output #1 is sorted by some other field. Output #2 would be more useful for locating books.

**SORT
SPECIFICATION**

OUTPUT #1	OUTPUT #2
CA - HQ796.S553 1983	CA - BF719.R2 1984
AU - (author)	AU - (author)
TI - (title)	TI - (title)
CA - BF719.R2 1984	CA - GV1229.J63 1983
AU - (author)	AU - (author)
TI - (title)	TI - (title)
CA - P90.N4 1982	CA - HQ796.S553 1983
AU - (author)	AU - (author)
TI - (title)	TI - (title)

(cont.)

OUTPUT #1   OUTPUT #2

CA - GV1229.J63   1983   CA - ML67.B3   1982
AU - (author)   AU - (author)
TI - (title)   TI - (title)

CA - ML67.B3   1982   CA - P90.N4   1982
AU - (author)   AU - (author)
TI - (title)   TI - (title)

For output to be sorted by call number, as in Output #2, you would specify the sort in your output instruction, as follows:

PRINT SEARCH STATEMENT 4 FIELD CA AU TI SORT-BY CA

NUMBER OF RECORDS SPECIFICATION

Suppose the retrieval set consists of many records, and you're not sure if these records are relevant to the search query. You could specify in your output instruction to display a sample consisting of the first five records in the retrieval set, as follows:

PRINT SEARCH STATEMENT 4 FIELD CA AU TI SORT-BY CA RECORD 1–5

You could then display the next five records using the following instruction:

PRINT SEARCH STATEMENT 4 FIELD CA AU TI SORT-BY CA RECORD 6–10

RECORD NUMBERING SPECIFICATION

Normally the records in a retrieval set, when displayed as output, would be numbered in sequence starting with the number 1. If the retrieval set consists of 50 records, and the output instruction specifies RECORD 1–5, records in the resulting display will be numbered 1 to 5, as follows:

1
CA- HQ796.S553   1983
TI - Guide to enjoying the teenage years.

2
CA- GV1229.J63   1983
TI - Guide to enjoying yourself on a rainy afternoon.

3
CA- GV1201.4.H8   1984
TI - Games for two people.

4
CA- GV950.6.E6   1984
TI - Getting the most out of watching football games.

5
CA- GV1469.3.L7   1984
TI - Video games.

Specifying RECORD 6–10 results in records numbered 6 to 10, and so on. However, you may display records 26–30, numbering them 1 to 5, using an output instruction that specifies the number of records and record numbering, as follows:

PRINT SEARCH STATEMENT 4 FIELD CA AU TI SORT-BY CA
RECORD 26–30 STARTING NUMBER 1

To display records 1–5, numbering them 26 to 30, the output instruction would specify the number of records and record numbering, as follows:

PRINT SEARCH STATEMENT 4 FIELD CA AU TI SORT-BY CA
RECORD 1–5 STARTING NUMBER 26

Suppose that the retrieval set consists of 50 records, and rather than display them at your terminal, you prefer them to be listed on a printer connected to the computer being accessed for retrieval. Since the output would not be displayed through the connection ("line") between the computer and your terminal, this type of output is called an *offline printout*.

**OFFLINE
PRINTOUT
SPECIFICATION**

To obtain an offline printout, you would specify this request in your output instruction as follows:

PRINT SEARCH STATEMENT 4 FIELD CA AU TI SORT-BY CA RECORD 1–50 OFFLINE

When you specify OFFLINE, the computer will proceed to solicit additional information, such as mailing address and search title. Immediately before accepting output instructions requesting offline printouts, the computer will offer you the option of cancelling the instruction. The computer may limit the number of records it will display in an offline printout. Offline printouts resulting from batch processing are discussed later in this chapter.

SPECIFICATION DEFAULTS AND STANDARD SPECIFICATIONS

In order to save time, instructions for displaying output may have specification defaults, that is, specification values assumed by the computer unless otherwise specified. You already know of two specification defaults. If you don't specify OFFLINE, the computer assumes that you want records displayed "online" at your terminal; thereby ONLINE is the default. The other default is that the number for the STARTING NUMBER specification is always the same as the first number for the RECORD specification. For example, in an output instruction with the specification RECORD 26–50, the first record in the output will be numbered 26 if the instruction does not include a different STARTING NUMBER specification.

What would be a useful SEARCH STATEMENT default? The SEARCH STATEMENT default could be the search statement number of the last search statement that resulted in a positive search statement result. If the last positive search statement result is for SEARCH STATEMENT 4, and you need to display records from that set, this default would enable you to omit the SEARCH STATEMENT specification from your output instruction.

The FIELD dafault may be AU TI PL PU PY CA, so you could omit this specification as well. The SORT-BY default may be the order in which the record was added to the file, with the most recently input record sorted at the beginning.

The RECORD default could be ALL, standing for all the records in the retrieval set, but the display would probably be interrupted at certain intervals when you would be offered the option to discontinue; or you may be able to discontinue by striking a special key, such as the BREAK or ESCAPE key, on your terminal. Even though ALL may be the default, or ALL or a large number may be specified, for example RECORD 1000, the computer may impose a limit to the number of records it will display.

If each specification default described above applies, the output instruction PRINT would be sufficient for the online display of the AU, TI, PL, PU, PY, and CA fields of all records in the most recent retrieval set, numbered starting with 1, and in the order they were accepted by the computer starting with the most recently accepted record.

The computer may provide standard specifications; for example, RECORD ALL defined above, or FIELD ALL for displaying all fields of a record, to save you the trouble of entering the following FIELD specification:

FIELD AU TI PL PU PY SU CA UI ED UF

Another standard specification might be FIELD BR (where BR = BRief) to display only CA, AU, TI. Standard specifications might be used as defaults. For example, if FIELD BR were the default, the computer could store different definitions of "brief," which would be applied according to the file being searched.

If the specification defaults or standard specifications offered do not suit you, it may be possible to establish your own defaults, or define and name standard specifications according to your individual need.

If you are using a terminal that includes a printer, you may want to display search formulations with their search statement results in hard copy. Hard copy display of a search formulation could be produced by requesting a search history display of specified search statements with their search statement results, as discussed toward the end of Chapter 10.

BATCH PROCESSING OF SEARCH FORMULATIONS

Chapter 4 covered real time and batch processing for creating and maintaining records. Real time processing and batch processing may also apply to searching. So far we have assumed that search formulations are processed in real time, where search statements are processed and result in retrieval sets as soon as they are entered into the computer. It may also be possible to enter a search formulation into the computer as a batch process, where the computer processes it later and returns the retrieval set as output in the form of an offline printout.

Why would you instruct the computer to process a search formulation in batch? When searching interactively, you are connected to the specific file you wish to search, but batch processing would enable you to enter a search formulation when the file to be searched is not "up," that is, when the file is not available for real time proc-

essing. Although not connected to the file to be searched, you may nevertheless enter a search formulation that will be processed against that file later.

Another reason for batch processing is that it may be at a time of day when search processing on the computer is scheduled to be "down," that is, inoperative, and when there is not enough time for the computer to process and respond to every search statement. Even if both the file and search processing will be up long enough for processing a search formulation in real time, you may not have the time to wait for it. Batch processing is particularly useful for processing the same search formulation against more than one file. After entering it only once, you may then specify that it be processed against several files.

As a search formulation is being entered for batch processing, the computer may or may not require that it be processed interactively at the same time. If processed interactively, it would be processed only against the file to which you are currently connected, and as such may provide complete search statement results, partial results such as indicating only the absence of search terms from the index, or no search statement results.

OUTPUT INSTRUCTION IN BATCH PROCESSING

Earlier in this chapter we mentioned the possibility of receiving offline printouts resulting from search statements processed in real time. This was done by specifying OFFLINE in the output instruction, along with other output specifications, for selecting retrieval sets, or selecting, sorting, formatting, and numbering records. Processing search formulations in batch mode also requires output instructions with similar specifications. Furthermore, these output instructions may offer an option for offline display of search formulations with their search statement results, using an output specification equivalent to DISPLAY SEARCH STATEMENT RESULTS. This display would be part of the offline printout. (Uses of hard copy displays of search formulations appear in the discussion of interactive search history displays toward the end of Chapter 10.)

The output instruction could specify that the offline printout consist only of the search statement results display, that is, without any output of records. This type of offline printout might be requested if the counts associated with search statements would be sufficient to answer the search query; or, if the computer could display search statement results in an offline printout, yet save the retrieval set, then after reviewing the counts you could request an offline printout of the retrieval set, and the computer would have only to print it according to an output instruction. Saving retrieval sets is discussed in the next chapter.

HARD COPY OF SEARCH FORMULATION IN BATCH PROCESSING

A limit of the number of records in an offline printout would have different implications for batch processed search formulations in contrast to search formulations processed in real time. In a real time search formulation, you know the search statement result at the time you enter an output instruction, and you therefore also know whether the number of records you intend to specify exceeds the limit. In a batch search formulation, you don't yet know the final search statement result when you enter the output instruction, so that the computer will send you an incomplete listing unless you can tell it to ignore the output instruction if the limit is exceeded. If you expect a search statement result that might exceed the limit, you could select the option for displaying search statement results only, save the retrieval set in the computer, and then request it as output in an offline printout if the limit was not exceeded.

NUMBER OF RECORDS LIMIT IN OFFLINE PRINTOUT

Cancelling offline printouts would also differ for search formulations processed in batch in contrast to search formulations processed in real time. For search formulations processed in real time, you could cancel an offline printout, but you could not cancel processing of the search formulation, which has already occurred by the time you enter the output instruction with the OFFLINE specification. For batch processed search formulations, cancellation of processing would be possible. After the batch search formulation is processed at the computer site, you could not cancel the offline printout.

CANCELLING OFFLINE PRINTOUT

1. What is the purpose of output specification defaults?
2. Of the following output specifications, select the ones that would employ defaults that are easily defined without regard to knowl-

EXERCISES

edge about the particular file. Define specification defaults for these.

SEARCH STATEMENT
FIELD
SORTED-BY
RECORD
ONLINE/OFFLINE
STARTING NUMBER

3. The specifications not selected in Exercise 2 might employ defaults that are standard specifications defined according to the file being searched. Using records from a bibliographic file and a controlled indexing vocabulary file, define a "brief" record for each file, and show a sample record that would be displayed from each file in response to an output instruction containing FIELD BRIEF. If FIELD BRIEF were the default, you could omit the FIELD specification from the output instruction. How would the output appear if you did this, compared to the previous sample output?

4. RECORD ALL might be a standard specification. Name legitimate mechanisms that would decrease the danger of including RECORD ALL in an output instruction.

5. List the conditions that would favor entering a search formulation for batch processing.

6. Name two retrieval methods that would result in offline printouts.

7. In batch processing, when might you specify an offline printout consisting only of the search formulation with search statement results? Why is this capability especially useful if there is a limit on the number of records that can be displayed in an offline printout?

8. Compare real time with batch processing in terms of the possibilities for cancelling search formulation processing and for cancelling offline printouts. Include explanations.

Saving Searches, Saving Output

12

A search formulation can be saved in the computer by entering it at the terminal without requiring that it be processed immediately. It is thereby stored in the computer so that you can execute it in the future, i.e., have the computer locate and automatically process the saved search. For example, a saved search may be executed against update files (new records that have been added to the file).

When a search formulation is saved, the computer stores a record you have created. Each saved search would therefore constitute a record in your personal file of saved searches. To be most effective, a saved search should be maintainable on the computer; that is, you should be able to use the computer to add, delete, and modify the search statements in a saved search record. A newly created saved search will be assigned a name so the computer can locate it. You would use this name, from then on, to call up (tell the computer to locate) a saved search in order to execute, maintain, display, or delete it.

SDI

The computer may process a saved search automatically in batch mode against new update files as soon as they become available, which is usually prior to the time when they become available for interactive retrieval. This automatic procedure is known as *selective dissemination of information* (SDI). The purpose of an SDI search is to assist you in maintaining current awareness about the topic of a search query. An SDI search would require storing in the computer not only a search formulation but also an output instruction.

SAVING IN BATCH MODE

Saving a search formulation may be accomplished in batch mode. You would first enter a command instructing the computer to call a special program to assist you in creating saved searches. The program would cause the computer to prompt you for each statement, and after you indicate that you are finished, the search would be saved by the next workday.

A disadvantage of saving a search formulation in batch mode is that it requires you to decide to save it in advance of entering it. After entering a search formulation processed interactively, you may then decide to save it, but in order to save it in batch, you would need to request the saved search program and, interacting with that program, re-enter the complete search formulation.

SAVING AFTER INTERACTIVE PROCESSING

You could avoid re-entering the search formulation if the computer permits saving immediately after interactive processing of the last search statement. However, the problem with this method is that your workspace may also contain search statements that you would not want included in the saved search. For example, the following search statements may have been processed interactively:

SEARCH STATEMENT 1
        CHILDREN OR ADOLESCENTS

SEARCH STATEMENT 2
        READING AND 1

SEARCH STATEMENT 3
        RECREATIONAL READING AND 1

To save the search formulation resulting in the retrieval set of SEARCH STATEMENT 3, you don't need to save SEARCH STATEMENT 2 since processing it is not necessary in order for SEARCH STATEMENT 3 to be processed. Before saving a search formulation, you could instruct the computer to delete from your workspace the search statements that would not be needed for processing the saved search.

You should be careful, however, not to delete needed search statements. For example, if you delete SEARCH STATEMENT 1 from your workspace, the saved search could not be processed because SEARCH STATEMENT 3 uses SEARCH STATEMENT 1 as a temporary search key value, and the deletion would remove that search key value from the index. Furthermore, you should retain a needed search statement even if the search statement result was zero when it was processed interactively, since it may have positive results when the search is executed later against a file update or an otherwise different file.

**KEEPING
NEEDED
SEARCH
STATEMENTS**

Suppose you execute the following saved search, named S39, interactively:

**EXECUTION OF
SAVED SEARCH**

SAVED SEARCH STATEMENT 1
     CHILDREN OR ADOLESCENTS

SAVED SEARCH STATEMENT 3
     RECREATIONAL READING AND 1

You would execute the search by entering its name, which would instruct the computer to locate and begin processing it. If you execute it at the beginning of a search session (at SEARCH STATEMENT 1), there are two processes for execution of a saved search, as follows:

1. The computer executes SAVED SEARCH STATEMENT 1 and SAVED SEARCH STATEMENT 3 as if they were search statements in the current workspace, and displays the results for each as SEARCH STATEMENT 1 and SEARCH STATEMENT 3 in the current workspace. At the end of the execution, the next available search statement number would be SEARCH STATEMENT 4.

2. The computer executes SAVED SEARCH STATEMENT 1 and SAVED SEARCH STATEMENT 3, but displays only the result of SAVED SEARCH STATEMENT 3, which then becomes the search statement result for the current search statement.

    The following is an example of execution and processing of the saved search, at SEARCH STATEMENT 1, according to the first method. SAVED SEARCH STATEMENT 1 and SAVED SEARCH STATEMENT 2 are automatically displayed and processed. SEARCH STATEMENT 4 was entered after execution of the saved search, and uses SAVED SEARCH STATEMENT 1 as a search term.

SEARCH STATEMENT 1
     S39 (SAVED SEARCH NAME)

SAVED SEARCH STATEMENT 1
        CHILDREN OR ADOLESCENTS
    RESULT = 500 RECORDS

SAVED SEARCH STATEMENT 3
        RECREATIONAL READING AND 1
    RESULT = 25 RECORDS

SEARCH STATEMENT 4
        3 OR HOBBIES AND 1
    RESULT = 75 RECORDS

The following is an example of execution and processing of the saved search, at SEARCH STATEMENT 1, according to the second method. SAVED SEARCH STATEMENT 3 is indexed as the current SEARCH STATEMENT 1. SEARCH STATEMENT 2 was added after execution of the saved search. It is equivalent to SEARCH STATEMENT 4 in the previous version, except that it cannot use the saved search statement numbers since these have not been indexed. Therefore, it uses SEARCH STATEMENT 1 as a search term (which is equivalent to SAVED SEARCH STATEMENT 3), and since it cannot use SAVED SEARCH STATEMENT 1, the equivalent union (CHILDREN OR ADOLESCENTS) is entered instead.

SEARCH STATEMENT 1
        S39 (SAVED SEARCH NAME)
    RESULT = 25 RECORDS

SEARCH STATEMENT 2
        1 OR HOBBIES AND (CHILDREN OR ADOLESCENTS)
    RESULT = 75 RECORDS

An advantage of the first method is that you are shown the results of each search statement of the saved search. Moreover, since each search statement was entered into your workspace, its search statement number is a temporary search key value that can be used as a search term in later search statements. In this case, after executing the saved search at the beginning of the search session, SAVED SEARCH STATEMENT 1 was used as a search term in SEARCH STATEMENT 4.

In contrast, if the saved search were executed according to the second method, you would be shown the search statement result of only the final search statement of the saved search, and only that search statement would be indexed to a current search statement number and therefore usable as a search term in a later search statement.

The first method has a limitation that results in the second method's having an advantage. To illustrate, using the previous example, if you are at SEARCH STATEMENT 2 in the current search session, and SEARCH STATEMENT 1 is already occupied, then the saved search cannot be executed by the first method. The second method therefore has the advantage that it can be executed at any point in the session, since the final retrieval set of the saved search is, in effect, transferred to the search statement number used for executing the saved search.

In contrast to saved searches, let us now consider saved output. After you log onto the computer and begin searching, your outputs are being saved temporarily during that session, that is, until you are no longer logged onto the computer. This temporarily saved output permits the use of a previous search statement number as a search term (described at the beginning of Chapter 9). For example:

SAVING ADDRESSES OF RECORDS

SEARCH STATEMENT 4
    GAMES

SEARCH STATEMENT 5
    4 AND CHILDREN

In discussing this type of automatic saving of output during a session, we really mean saving the addresses of records, not the records themselves. If the computer did save output in the form of records, it would need to save every record of every retrieval set since it would not know in advance which records you might ultimately display. Moreover, it would need to save the complete record since it would not know in advance which fields you might want to display, or which fields you would require for sorting the output.

It would be a waste of computer space to save records in a retrieval set instead of their addresses, especially since many search statements are intended to furnish intermediate results or to be combined with search terms in a future search statement. These intermediate results may involve huge numbers of records.

Automatic saving of output as addresses to records therefore allows the computer to locate and display records according to specific information in an output instruction, for example:

PRINT SEARCH STATEMENT 4 FIELD CA AU TI SORT-BY CA
RECORD 1-5

SAVING OUTPUT AS RECORDS

There are situations, however, in which saving output as records rather than as addresses might be preferred. You may want to postpone displaying the output of a processed search formulation by entering an output instruction specifying that the output be saved, and then display it later. Saving output would also enable you to again display an output quickly and easily, that is, without reprocessing of the search formulation. As in saving searches, saving output includes assigning a name to the saved output so that the computer can locate it for future display.

TRANSFERRING AND TRANSMITTING SAVED OUTPUT

The computer may locate saved output in order to transfer it to another computer electronically. For example, if output were retrieved on a microcomputer used as a terminal, the output may be stored by the microcomputer on a transportable disk and the disk then used for displaying or permanently storing the output on another microcomputer. Saved output stored on a microcomputer may be transmitted to other computers by electronic mail.

APPLICATIONS OF SAVED OUTPUT

There are many possible applications of saved output. Saving output would assist you in cumulating outputs by computer, that is, merging outputs, based on searching update files, with previous outputs. Saved output may be used for electronically reserving a book from the library by transmitting a bibliographic reference to a library that has a computer. Saved output would enable you to share the output with others; it may be distributed to other computers, or published by computer (described later on).

EDITING AND REPROCESSING OF SAVED OUTPUT

The computer may locate saved output in order to maintain it, not only to add, delete, or change information in the output, but also to reformat or re-sort it, or merge it with other saved output. These procedures are discussed in the example of saving output for publication treated further in this chapter.

COMPUTER INDEXING OF SAVED OUTPUT

So far we have been regarding saved output only as a retrieval set resulting from a search formulation. It might also be considered a file, not unlike the retrieval file from which it originated. If saved output is to function as a file that someone may want to search, it might be indexed by the computer for retrieval as was the original file.

PUBLISHING A COMPUTER INDEX

Saving output, and computer indexing of saved output, constitute a method for producing published indexes by computer. As an example, we will consider computerized publication of a bibliographic subject index on sports from an indexed file. Each record in the output would be a reference to a book, and the subject headings in the published index would be subject terms assigned to the record from a controlled indexing vocabulary.

The first step in producing this publication would be to enter a search formulation for processing against a retrieval file that contains records to be included in the saved output. The search terms in the formulation would be subject terms for sports from the controlled indexing vocabulary.

You would then save the output, and a publication program would produce the index for publication. This program would require the following information: the search key for sorting the records in the publication (sort key), fields to be selected for a published record, the format of the record, and the format of a published page.

Since the bibliographic index is to be a subject index, the sort key would be subject term. We could instruct the computer to use all the subject search key values in the index, or we could furnish the program with a more restricted list of subject terms. For example, we may elect to use only the terms for sports (ARCHERY, BASEBALL, BASKETBALL, and so on), and thereby not include other subject headings in the publication (such as CHILDREN, INJURIES, COMPETITION), even if these are search key values in the index.

In proofreading the published form, you may notice an error in a reference. This would indicate an error in a record in the saved output that produced the publication. This, in turn, would indicate an

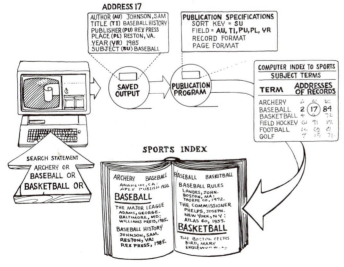

PRODUCING A SUBJECT INDEX BY COMPUTER

error in that record in the original retrieval file. To correct the error in the publication, you would need to notify the producer of the retrieval file, wait until the error is corrected in that file, reprocess the search formulation against the corrected retrieval file, save the new output, and then use the new saved output in reprocessing the publication.

Correcting errors by computer directly in the saved output would be preferable. (You would still notify the producers about errors in the retrieval file.) Modifying saved output entails an editing capability, and might also include adding information to records or adding new records from other sources.

Modifications to saved output involving search key values used for sorting the index (published subject headings) would require the edited version to be re-indexed by the publication program. Furthermore, if new fields have been added to the record through editing, you may need to supply the publication program with new specifications for fields selected for publication, or new formatting specifications, and then reprocess the publication according to the revised specifications.

PUBLISHING CUMULATED COMPUTER INDEXES

If the bibliography is published four times per year, you may want to merge each saved output with the previous one during the year; each issue will then be a cumulation of all the records for the year up to that point. The final output would be an annual cumulation. On the other hand, you may not want to merge the four outputs as they are produced but instead produce a fifth publication at the end of the year, as the annual cumulation, by merging the noncumulated quarterly outputs. Publishing cumulations, regardless of the schedule, would always require computerized indexing of merged output.

Saving output for retrieval is related to the notion of distributed database subsets discussed at the end of Chapter 15.

EXERCISES

1. What is SDI? Why would an SDI search require an output instruction?

2. What are the advantages and disadvantages of saving search formulations in batch, and saving search formulations directly after they have been processed interactively?

3. What are the advantages of saved searches that can be executed visibly statement by statement? Devise an example of a saved search that illustrates these advantages.

4. What is the advantage of saved searches that, when executed, dis-

play only the result of the final search statement? Devise an example of a saved search that illustrates this advantage.

5. What information does the computer save automatically that enables you to use a search statement as a search term later in the session? Contrast this with the topic of this chapter, saving output.

6. What are the benefits of saving output? Name some applications of saving output.

7. What process should be applied to saved output in order for it to function as a retrieval file?

8. What is the role of computer indexing in producing a published index from saved output? What information does a publication program need in order to produce an index?

Database Retrieval

13

Information storage and retrieval, more commonly known as *information retrieval,* refers to the techniques for managing (storing, maintaining, and updating) and retrieving records. If the retrieval file is large, it is known as a *database.* The retrieval function is also known as *database retrieval,* and the management function as *database management,* although sets of computer programs known as database management systems (DBMSs) generally incorporate both functions. The interactive mode is inherent in the retrieval function.

In previous chapters, we have used as examples records that comprise a bibliographic file, without emphasizing the organization that administers the retrieval function. One such organization might be the library. Libraries create, maintain, and update bibliographic files that form catalogs of the libraries' collection. The goal of retrieval from the catalog may be to locate a particular book in the library or to compile a bibliography on a topic that is represented in the collection. In this and the remaining chapters, however, we will focus on retrieval from databases offered by retrieval services.

A *retrieval service* is an organization that manages a number of databases and provides customers with the facility for database retrieval. Files offered by retrieval services are usually known as databases regardless of their size. A retrieval service provides remote access to databases by telephone via a *telecommunications network.*

A database may cover a particular discipline, such as education, business, or medicine, or constitute a general reference work, such as an encyclopedia. Customers of retrieval services expect a broad range of information, even within a particular discipline, that is not limited to a physical collection of documents, such as a library. Although libraries everywhere are computerizing their catalogs into databases

**INFORMATION
RETRIEVAL**

**RETRIEVAL
SERVICES**

known as online public access catalogs (OPACs), libraries will not be considered retrieval services in the sense discussed in this chapter.

DATABASE SUPPLIERS AND DATABASE MANAGEMENT

A *database supplier* is an organization that manages (creates, updates, and maintains) databases, and then turns them over to a retrieval service that administers the database retrieval function. The database management function performed by suppliers includes retrieval to some degree since maintaining records necessitates retrieval for isolating a record from other records prior to modifying or deleting it. However, this type of retrieval is internal to the organization and therefore different in many respects from retrieval performed by outsiders.

Conversely, database management is a behind-the-scenes function of retrieval services, but as discussed later in this chapter, retrieval services generally do not perform file maintenance that would substantially change the content of a database. The primary database management function of a retrieval service is aimed toward ensuring that a database exists in the computer in a form that is accessible for retrieval.

UNIT OF SERVICE: THE SESSION

The function of retrieval services that directly affects you, as a customer, is database retrieval. The basic unit of service is a user-initiated *session,* a session that begins when your terminal, a device for entering and displaying messages transmitted between you and a computer, is connected to the retrieval service computer after you have entered a valid *password,* and it ends when the computer subsequently breaks the connection.

HOST COMPUTER AND TELECOMMUNICATIONS NETWORK

You begin a session by "calling up" a computer on the telephone. The retrieval service computer, also known as the *host computer,* may be called directly. If, however, the host computer is not in your local calling area, you may call up a small computer belonging to a telecommunications network, which, using special telephone lines and a battery of small computers, then connects your terminal to the host computer. The effective use of telephone lines by these networks

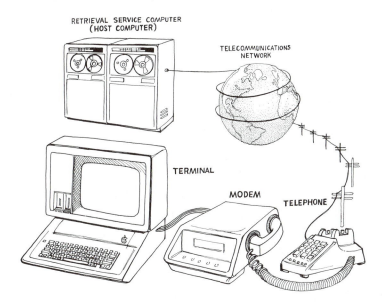

greatly reduces your cost for telephone communications. The direct customer of a telecommunications network is the retrieval service, but the retrieval service will forward you the telecommunications network charges, and these will be paid to the retrieval service along with your direct charges.

When the call is completed to the initial computer, you will then attach the telephone receiver to the terminal by means of a *modem,* a device within the terminal, or wired to it, for interconverting digital signals, transmitted and received by computers and terminals, and audible signals (tones), transmitted over communications lines. To summarize, assuming that you are not in the same building as the retrieval service computer (if you were, your terminal may be *hardwired,* that is, connected to the computer directly without requiring a telephone), your immediate equipment needs would include a telephone line, terminal, modem, and cable to connect the terminal to the modem.

If your terminal is a microcomputer, you may also need a communications interface card that plugs into the microcomputer, and a communications software package for communicating with other computers. Software packages are available for *downloading,* that is, copying information received from the host computer to a disk for storage, or to a capture buffer. The buffer enables you to save the information in your microcomputer's memory and later copy it to a disk or display it. If your microcomputer modem is internal (not a

MICRO-COMPUTERS AS TERMINALS

free-standing unit separate from the microcomputer), you would not need the communications interface card and cable.

LOGGING ON, PASSWORD, AND USER PROFILE

If you are calling through a network, you will be asked by the network computer to enter the name of the host computer. When the connection between the two computers has been completed, the host computer will ask you for a password, a unique identification code authorizing you to use the retrieval service. This procedure for initiating a session for interacting with the host computer is known as *logging on*. If everything has gone well up to this point, you will be greeted with a message indicating that your session has begun.

You will receive passwords, probably at least two (one for connecting to the telecommunications network and one for the host computer), and information about logging on once you have signed a contract with the retrieval service, thereby becoming an authorized subscriber. The password for logging on the host computer may be stored in your user profile, a confidential file established for each retrieval service account. You may access this private file to change your password as well as display or change other information (described under "user profile" in the glossary).

LOGGING OFF

A session includes all interactions between you and the host computer and terminates after you instruct the computer to disconnect in a brief procedure known as *logging off*. Logging off disconnects your telephone from the retrieval service computer. If you are using a telecommunications network, you will probably continue to be connected to the network computer for a short time in order to reconnect to the host computer, or connect to another host computer, without redialing. The retrieval service may offer a restart capability. Restarting is a procedure that simulates logging off and immediately logging back on to begin a new session, but without requiring a password.

If you are improperly disconnected from the host computer, you may need to call the retrieval service (usually a toll-free number) to cancel the session. You may then receive the option of restarting (a different use of the word from that above) the session with your workspace saved, and therefore resuming. After an improper disconnect, the computer may automatically offer this option when you log back on later during the day. Retrieval services may, however, automatically cancel your session after the computer has been inactive for a specified time. When you log off normally or are disconnected due to inactivity, there may be a grace period for retaining your workspace. Your workspace might not be saved if the computer goes down during a session.

IMPROPER DIS-CONNECTION

Once the host computer sends you the standard greeting acknowledging that the connection has been completed, you may automatically receive, or be given the option to receive, a brief broadcast message, which is of immediate relevance to all users as they log on.

BROADCAST MESSAGE AND NEWS FILE

The broadcast message may refer you to a more comprehensive news file. When you select the news file, the result may be a table of contents consisting of numbered topics, which you may select for display, or a continuous display of dated news items beginning with the most recent, and interrupted at intervals with an option to continue. News items typically provide information about specific databases, price changes, lists of available databases, computer schedules, training schedules, retrieval capabilities, and accessing the computer.

A retrieval service usually offers a number of databases. (Selected major retrieval services in the United States with the databases they offer are listed in Appendix A. Appendix B cites a number of database directories as well as periodicals featuring database updates.) Databases are generally classified as to whether another source is required for complete information (retrieval databases) or whether they contain complete information (source databases). Referral databases include bibliographic databases, catalogs of nonprint media such as audiovisuals, microcomputer software packages, and databases, and locational directories. Source databases include handbooks, encyclopedias, and full text documents such as books, journal articles, and newspaper items.

DATABASE CLASSIFICA-TION

Databases may be classified according to data type: numeric, graphic, or textual. Numeric databases include survey or statistical information or reference values. Patent drawings and chemical structures of compounds are examples of graphic information. Handbooks may combine all data types. Databases may also be classified by subject or by the purpose of the information.

DATABASE DESCRIPTIONS

Retrieval services provide database catalogs and manuals offering detailed descriptions of their databases. These materials may classify databases as described above. Descriptions that specify features of databases that affect retrieval, such as searchable categories (search keys), may be displayed by computer. Database descriptions may require frequent updating primarily to provide information about new databases and databases that have been expanded or reorganized and to announce databases that have been discontinued.

DATABASE SELECTION AND CROSS-DATABASE SEARCHING

After you have logged on and viewed the broadcast message, you may begin retrieval. The computer may automatically connect you to a database, or you may be asked to select a database. Assistance in deciding on the most appropriate database may be provided by selecting a special database that serves as a master index to the record counts for search key values across all the databases. When you enter a search term in this database, the computer matches it against the master index and displays the search statement result for each database, or each database in a predefined subset of subject-related databases, or each database in a personally defined subset. You might then elect to search the database that posted the greatest number of records. This type of cross-database searching may allow search statements containing logical operators.

After being connected to a database, you may switch to a different one. The search statements and retrieval sets for the first database will be lost once you switch to another database, unless the computer was told to save them.

RETRIEVAL SERVICES AND DATABASE MANAGEMENT

Databases consist of files and indexes, similar to those described throughout the book up to now. However, as produced by suppliers, databases are usually not in a form immediately acceptable by the host computer. Therefore, a major database management function of retrieval services is to convert databases into a form that can be read and indexed by the host computer and processed by its retrieval programs.

Database management functions such as reorganization of fields, records, or files, or changes in computer indexing (automatic generation of search key values) are performed by retrieval services. These include transferring records from one file to another. For example, when a file gets too large, older records may be relegated to a separate backfile, with the more recent records remaining in the current file. A new backfile may be created when the most recent backfile is filled.

A retrieval service may combine one or more fields, making each a subfield, or convert a subfield into a field, or strip the file of certain fields or subfields. The eligibility of a field for computer indexing may be changed. For example, words in a field previously only string-searchable may subsequently begin to be indexed by the computer as textword search keys.

Even when databases are in an acceptable form for retrieval, they may contain significant differences. For example, the search key for controlled indexing terms may be IT (Indexing Term) for one database and DE (Descriptor) for another; similarly, the unique record identifier search key may be UI (Unique Identifier) for one database and AN (Accession Number) for another. Furthermore, two databases may both have an Accession Number (AN) field displayed in the record, but its value may be a search key value in one database, but only stringsearchable in the other.

DIFFERENCES AMONG DATABASES OF A RETRIEVAL SERVICE

Database updates consist of new records periodically added to a database. The database is updated when the database supplier sends the retrieval service a computer tape containing the new records. Another function of the database supplier is modifying or deleting records. Database suppliers perform individual record maintenance, usually interactively, to correct sporadic errors in the database; for example, the misspelling of a person's name or the incorrect assignment of a subject term from a controlled indexing vocabulary. Database suppliers also perform systematic maintenance of sets of records (class maintenance), usually in batch mode, as described further on.

UPDATING AND MAINTAINING DATABASES

In most cases, retrieval services offering databases supplied by others do not apply these types of changes, which are essentially content changes (changes in field values). The results of file maintenance of this kind become evident when the database supplier furnishes the retrieval service with a new tape, consisting of the file-maintained version. If the retrieval service and the supplier of a database are the same, the database available on that retrieval service is more likely to be more current and better maintained than the version of the same database available on another retrieval service.

A type of file maintenance performed on databases indexed with controlled subject terms is *class maintenance* of subject terms in records to ensure that they match official subject terms in the current version of the controlled indexing vocabulary. For example, COMPUTER may be a subject term in a number of records. If that term is changed to COMPUTERS in the controlled indexing vocabulary, the database supplier may also change COMPUTER to COMPUTERS in each record of the database containing the subject term COMPUTER.

CLASS MAINTENANCE OF CONTROLLED SUBJECT TERMS

Class maintenance of subject terms in retrieval files is a service to you as a searcher since, unless this change is made, you would need to use COMPUTER as a search term for retrieving the older records, and COMPUTERS as a search term for retrieving new records. Why are changes made to subject terms in controlled indexing vocabularies?

CHANGES IN CONTROLLED SUBJECT INDEXING VOCABULARY

Changes in terminology may be precipitated by low usage in indexing. For example, if the term LEMON was hardly ever used for indexing, it could be deleted from the controlled indexing vocabulary, and the subject term LEMON could be replaced in the database with the broader term CITRUS FRUIT. The same procedures may be followed if the usage for LEMON is adequate, but the usage for CITRUS FRUIT is too low.

If usage is not a factor, it may be that the subject term is not the best form. For example, it may be preferable for RETRIEVAL, COMPUTERIZED to be in the direct form as COMPUTERIZED RETRIEVAL so that it lines up alphabetically in the neighborhood of the term COMPUTERS.

If low usage or preferred form is not a factor, the change could be attributed to a discrepancy between the subject term and its meaning. For example, if a vocabulary contains the terms SEARCH KEY VALUE and INDEX POINT, both having the same meaning, then one of these should be deleted from the vocabulary and replaced by the other term in the database.

Conversely, a term could be ambiguous for purposes of retrieval. For example, the search term PAINTING could refer to either artistic painting or industrial painting. In this case, PAINTING might be deleted from the vocabulary and two new terms, ARTISTIC PAINTING and INDUSTRIAL PAINTING, added. The appropriate new term would replace PAINTING in records in the database.

CLASS MAINTENANCE OF CONTROLLED NONSUBJECT TERMS

Class maintenance of controlled indexing terms is not restricted to subject terms but may be performed on other authority-based fields. For example, if the official abbreviation for AMERICAN is changed from AMER to AM, then all journal title abbreviation field values in a bibliographic database, as well as the search key values derived from this field, should be changed accordingly. This change would cause the abbreviation of the journal title AMERICAN HOBBYIST to be changed from AMER HOBBYIST to AM HOBBYIST.

This chapter has presented an introduction to basic functions and configurations that affect users of retrieval services. The next two chapters will focus on more advanced topics of information retrieval in areas undergoing rapid change due to the increasing use of micro-computers for database retrieval.

1. What are the functions of retrieval services and database suppliers?

2. Diagram the components needed for accessing a retrieval service.

3. How are databases classified?

4. What is "cross-database" searching?

5. What types of database management are performed by retrieval services?

6. How might databases offered by a single retrieval service differ significantly for searching (other than differences in subject content)?

7. What is the practical reason for performing file maintenance of a retrieval file to reflect changes in the controlled indexing vocabulary? Who usually performs this type of maintenance?

Friendly Computers, Intelligent Computers

14

With rapidly increasing numbers of microcomputer users, retrieval services are attempting to attract this new segment of the market by making their computers user-friendly. A computer is user-friendly to the extent that you can "converse" with it with little physical or mental effort. The friendly computer is patient and forgiving and sometimes knows what you intend to convey even if you didn't express it properly, and it offers you any assistance you might need for locating the information you want. User-friendly features for novices differ from those intended for experienced users.

USER-FRIENDLY COMPUTER

Regardless of the user's familiarity, user-friendly commands are mnemonic (easy to remember), brief, and unambiguous, entered without physical awkwardness (such as use of the shift key), avoid the need for remembering syntax (for example, the sequence of specifications in output instructions), employ defaults, and automatically accept reasonable alternatives. A command that would result in the deletion of stored information may have a complementary command that reverses the action; if deletion is irreversible, the computer might give the user the opportunity to reconsider.

USER-FRIENDLY COMMANDS

USER-FRIENDLY COMPUTER MESSAGES

In general, messages from the computer should be clear, simple, and concise. The most user-friendly computer message is the briefest message the user can properly interpret. (Error messages are discussed in this context further on.) If messages from the computer are directive, the requested responses should exhibit the characteristics of commands previously specified. For novice users, messages from the computer may branch optionally to text that provides additional guidance; or user-requested assistance may be provided on an as-needed basis (help messages are discussed later).

PROMPTING AND ERROR MESSAGES

Retrieval programs need not be particularly sophisticated to offer user-friendly features. Two of the most common are prompting messages and error messages. A prompting message invites a response from the user. An error message is displayed when the user has entered a command that is misspelled, improperly formatted, or inappropriate to the situation, and therefore unable to be processed.

Prompting messages may range from general user cues to menus that define the options for selection (discussed later). General user cues may be single words (such as USER) or symbols (such as ? or :). Examples of prompting messages of intermediate specificity and complexity are:

ENTER AUTHOR'S LAST NAME
CONTINUE DISPLAY? (YES/NO)

The latter message might permit Y (for Yes) or N (for No), or employ a YES default, thereby permitting users to simply strike the ENTER key to continue the display.

The degree of user-friendliness of error messages frequently is measured by the extent to which the computer provides instructions for revising the erroneous command. For example, if you mistype the PRINT command as PRITN, the error message CANNOT PROCESS THAT would be less friendly than THAT IS NOT A VALID COMMAND. As another example, if you enter an output instruction PRINT RECORD 1–20, based on the preceding search statement number as the default, but the retrieval set consisted of 10 records, the error message RECORD NUMBER SPECIFIED EXCEEDS THE NUMBER OF RECORDS IN THE RETRIEVAL SET would again be preferable to a nonspecific error message.

A greater degree of friendliness would be exhibited if the computer could recognize but nevertheless process misspelled commands, for example, accept PRITN and PRINT as equivalent inputs. In the other example, a more specific error message than that shown above would be RETRIEVAL SET CONTAINS 10 RECORDS. YOU MAY ENTER A REVISED RECORD SPECIFICATION ONLY. Experienced users might know how to correct the output instruction and not require the second sentence of the error message.

User-friendliness for novices may be achieved by a scaled-down version of a more comprehensive retrieval program, the friendly version offering a few easily understood commands. Another user-friendly mechanism is the menu, whereby the computer prompts users to select from a list of options. (An example of a menu for retrieving information from a computerized library catalog was presented in Chapter 1.) Menus intended for novices usually include explanations of the options. For example, instead of a general user cue, a novice may require the following menu:

SIMPLIFIED COMMAND LANGUAGE AND MENUS FOR NOVICES

ENTER THE LETTER S OR C, FOR THE FOLLOWING, AND STRIKE THE "ENTER" KEY
S - TO BEGIN A SEARCH STATEMENT
C - TO ENTER A COMMAND

If C is selected, the computer might display a menu of the possible commands with their functions. If S is selected, the computer might display a sequence of menus to guide users in devising search statements. Mnemonic selections, as in this example, are preferred over numbered selections.

Messages from the computer in response to a user's request for help are a user-friendly feature. Help messages fall into two categories: contextual (providing information specific to the immediate situation), and addressable (providing information on a requested topic at any point during the session). The format and context of help messages may be assessed in terms of user-friendliness. Help messages

HELP MESSAGES

may prompt users to receive additional help or to perform certain functions.

ERASING AND INTERRUPTING WITHOUT DIS-CONNECTION

A common user-friendly feature is the provision for erasing. This includes immediately deleting individual characters or immediately deleting the entire line of input provided it has not been sent to the computer. Another feature is deliberate interruption of computer messages or displays, without disconnecting, by striking a BREAK or INTERRUPT key.

MULTIPLE VERSIONS

A retrieval service may offer more than one version of retrieval: a comprehensive version for experienced users, and a version for novices based on menus or fewer and simplified commands. Versions for novices simplify retrieval at the expense of offering a variety of search capabilities and commands and flexibility in applying them. The slowness and rigidity of menus, in particular, would soon become intolerable for experienced users. In the comprehensive version, messages from the computer may provide less (unnecessary) information. However, help messages on request would be available in any version, should users become uncertain about how to proceed. Multiple levels of familiarity may be accommodated within a retrieval program that has multiple versions and permits users to explicitly change versions at any point during the session.

USER-FRIENDLY SEARCHING

Up to now, the discussion has focussed on the command language. Another application of user-friendliness involves entering and formulating search statements. Requesting displays from the index or from the controlled indexing vocabulary, followed by selecting search key values as terms from these displays by number, would constitute user-friendly searching. Truncation, searching subject hierarchies without entering subordinate terms individually, automatic application of a spelling error correction program to search terms, and automatic search term completion are user-friendly features.

AUTOMATIC TERM COMPLETION

Automatic search term completion, the opposite of truncation, is a feature whereby the computer automatically completes a search term as soon as it recognizes that the portion of the term entered is unique in the index. For example, the search key value INTERPERSONAL RELATIONSHIP may be unique at the second E, enabling you to enter INTERPE as a search term, resulting in its being completed automatically.

The computer may employ user-friendly techniques for processing search statements in the form of naturally written search queries; that is, without requiring users to know the usual conventions and rules for term matching and logical operations. When the computer processes input in this way, it does not process it as natural language; it does not use semantics (meanings of words in the query), but processes the words in the query as search terms to which it automatically applies rules for matching and logically combining terms. (Knowledge-based natural language processing for intelligent computer retrieval is discussed later in this chapter.)

NONSEMANTIC NATURAL LANGUAGE QUERY PROCESSING

A common feature of nonsemantic computer processing of natural language queries is *word stemming*. This uses a set of rules for reducing words to their root forms by stripping them of their suffixes and then automatically searching a root form as the union of all forms of the word in the index. The program may contain rules for exceptions due to the language of a particular discipline (sublanguage). For example, in the sublanguage for medicine, removal of the suffix -ATORY from RESPIRATORY correctly leaves RESPIR- as the root form. However, its removal from LABORATORY to produce the root LABOR- (as in childbirth) would be erroneous.

WORD STEMMING

Along with word stemming, the computer may automatically intersect the root forms from the natural language search statement. The computer may permit users to rank search terms in this type of search statement according to importance and consider these rankings in a formula for automatically ranking records in a retrieval set according to their relevance (discussed later in the chapter).

INTERSECTION OF ROOT FORMS

Related to word stemming is the application of rules for automatic inclusion of spelling variants (COLOR and the British variant COLOUR), acronyms and their equivalents (NIOSH and National Institute for Occupational Safety and Health), and variations in romanization of Chinese (Peking and Beijing). The computer may automatically include the inverted form, resulting, for example, in the conversion of the incorrect controlled subject term NEWBORN INFANT to the correct form INFANT, NEWBORN. Punctuation may be removed from search terms automatically for matching against search key values in the index, which has also been stripped of punctuation by the computer; for example, the search terms FULL TEXT and FULL-TEXT would be equivalent as input for matching against the search key value FULL TEXT.

SPELLING AND OTHER VARIANTS

SEARCH FORMULATION LOGIC

The computer may provide user-friendly assistance in developing the logic of a search formulation by prompting users for sets consisting of unions of search terms, and then intersecting the sets. If the resulting formulation consists of several sets of intersections, the computer might complete the search statement as the union of these sets. Another feature would invoke computer prompting for individual search terms that are labeled alphabetically (A=TERM-1, B=TERM-2, C=TERM-3), and allow users to form intersections by combining two alphabetic characters (D=AB would be equivalent to TERM-1 AND TERM-2; E=CD would be equivalent to TERM-3 AND TERM-1 AND TERM-2).

ASSESSING AND REVISING SEARCH FORMULATIONS

User-friendliness also plays a role in using search statement results of retrieval sets for assessing and revising search formulations. The computer may ask you in advance how many records you expect. If the search statement result for the retrieval set varies considerably from this number, the computer may make general suggestions for reducing the discrepancy. For example, if the search statement result for an intersection is lower than expected, which would indicate poor recall, the computer might suggest expanding one of the concepts of the intersection, although it could not tell you specifically if you should broaden the concept or merely add synonyms. This type of computer assistance may be offered prior to viewing the records in a retrieval set.

COMPUTERIZED RANKING OF RETRIEVED RECORDS

The computer may employ a formula for ranking the records in a retrieval set according to their relevance to the search formulation. It may list the record with the greatest number of matches between search terms and search key values derived from the record, based on the notion that the greater the number of matches, the more relevant the record. Computerized ranking of retrieved records might apply user rankings of search terms that may have been assigned earlier.

SEARCH TERMS SELECTED FROM KEYWORDS BY NUMBER

Records in retrieval sets often provide additional search terms. The manual process would be for users to examine the keywords in records judged relevant and select from these additional search terms for incorporation into a revised or supplementary formulation. These keywords may be selected in a user-friendly procedure whereby the computer would number keywords in the display of a record and permit their selection as search terms by number.

In another approach to search term selection, the computer might remove the keywords from the retrieved records, rank them by frequency within the retrieval set (by applying a special formula that reduces the rank of keywords appearing frequently in the database) and present the ranked keywords in a separate numbered display for selection.

COMPUTERIZED RANKING OF RETRIEVED KEYWORDS

User-friendliness may include editing the search formulation interactively, including the addition of search terms suggested by the computer, as well as any other type of modification. A friendly computer might avoid unnecessary processing by automatically saving segments of the search formulation, with their results, so that as you edit the formulation and try new versions, segments of the new formulation that remain unchanged would not be reprocessed. Finally, the computer may remember the records it has already shown you, and in response to your output instruction, offer you the option of whether or not they should be redisplayed.

EDITING FORMULATIONS AND AVOIDING REPEAT PROCESSING

To summarize, user-friendly retrieval for entering search statements, assessing retrieval sets, revising search formulations, and suggesting additional search terms are forms of computer-assisted search formulation based on similarities among word forms in the index, retrieval set counts, the number of matches against the index, and conventional logical operations. These techniques may be augmented by the application of word processing capabilities, avoidance of reprocessing of unchanged segments of revised search formulations, or elimination of redundancy in displaying records. User-friendly features are also elaborated in the next chapter in the discussion of marketing retrieval services for microcomputer users.

SUMMARY OF USER-FRIENDLY RETRIEVAL

Intelligent computer retrieval and indexing are areas of research in the field of *artificial intelligence,* which is the study and implementation of techniques for programming computers to perform activities that are considered to require intelligence when performed by people. Artificial intelligence applications frequently entail computerized natural language processing of queries and text based on semantics. To be an ''expert searcher'' and ''expert indexer,'' the computer should be able to explain its reasoning, acquire new knowledge, and modify existing knowledge.

ARTIFICIAL INTELLIGENCE

INTELLIGENT COMPUTER RETRIEVAL

User-friendly retrieval employs knowledge about searching based on word matching and logical operations. In contrast, intelligent computer retrieval depends on domain knowledge, that is, knowledge about the subject matter covered by the database and about the subject matter that would be expected in search queries of the database.

KNOWLEDGE BASE

Domain knowledge, with rules for applying the knowledge, is known as a *knowledge base*. The knowledge base is represented in the computer using data structures that are more complicated than the records, fields, and indexes of conventional retrieval files. The data structures in a knowledge base permit the representation of semantic relationships among concepts (relationships based on meaning). In intelligent computer (i.e., knowledge-based) retrieval, queries are matched against semantic relationships stored in these data structures. For example, let's assume that the following record is in a bibliographic database:

AU- Jones, Mary
TI - Guide to enjoying yourself on a rainy afternoon.
PL - Dallas, Texas
PU- Tops Publishing Company
PY - 1983
SU - Adolescents
      Arts Activities
      Children
      Games
      Hobbies
      Recreational Activities*
      Recreational Reading
CA- GV1229.J63 1983
UI - 1983060104
ED- 19830302
UF- 198304

The subject of a query of this database might be "indoor activities for summer camp." Intelligent computer retrieval would automatically process this query and retrieve the preceding record; that is, the computer would employ artificial intelligence techniques for natural language understanding by indirectly matching a natural language query against search key values that index the record, using the knowledge base to interpret the meaning of the query.

Intelligent computer retrieval would require the computer to "read" the query statement and categorize it. A representation of the query would be devised by the computer, which records the concepts in the query and their interrelationships in terms of the knowledge base, that is, as instances of the knowledge represented in the knowledge base. Correlating concepts in the query and representing them, as relationships, in the computer would require the computer to perform inferencing based on certain premises, as defined by knowledge and rules stored in the knowledge base. The conclusions drawn might not be guaranteed, but highly probable; these types of rule are known as *heuristics*.

The knowledge base would need classification hierarchies for generalization–specialization relationships similar to those in a controlled indexing vocabulary, but more extensive. It would contain autonym–synonym relationships, as do controlled vocabularies. Furthermore, using linking terms, it would store many other types of relationships. Using linking terms for where activities are performed, it might store a relationship that specifies that reading is usually thought of as an indoor activity, for example:

(Reading WherePerformed (Indoors Usually))

In processing our sample query, the knowledge base would be used for recognizing the relationship between "indoor activities" and "summer camp" (indicated by "for" in the query statement), and causing records to be retrieved that are indexed under terms for recreational activities normally taking place indoors, such as "Arts Activities" or "Recreational Reading." The knowledge base would infer that "summer camp" implies children, and thereby require that retrieved records be indexed also under "Children."

Intelligent computer retrieval is still ultimately a matching process, but the computer first recognizes the meaning of the query using the knowledge base. As exemplified above, once the concepts and relations in the query have been represented in terms of the knowledge base, the computer will, still according to directions in the knowledge base, match this representation against search key values that index the title and subject terms in the record.

Intelligent computer indexing would entail using artificial intelligence techniques to automatically index records based on text from documents, such as the title, abstract, or the body of the document. As in retrieval, a knowledge base would be used for categorizing and inter-

CLASSIFICATION, INFERENCING, AND HEURISTICS

INTELLIGENT COMPUTER INDEXING

preting the meaning of text and systematically storing the outcome of these processes as an organized version of the text, which would then be available for retrieval.

In the preceding record, the subject terms have been assigned by a human indexer, but they are listed as keywords that do not show relationships. The goal of intelligent computer indexing might be to automatically derive from concepts and relations in a document, not a set of keywords as in conventional indexing but a representation of the relationships that have been identified during the indexing process.

These computerized representations would come closer to representing the richness of the original text than would keywords, primarily because they would store relationships. As an organized form of natural language text, the stored representations might then become the basis for extremely precise and comprehensive retrieval of information from large bodies of text.

EXERCISES

1. Define user-friendly. Does this definition apply to both novices and experienced users?

2. Can all features of computerized retrieval be defined in terms of user-friendliness independently of user experience? Name some features of command languages for retrieval that seem to be user-friendly regardless of user familiarity. In general, how may user-friendly messages from the computer be characterized?

3. Define prompting message. Describe three categories of prompting message discussed in this chapter.

4. Define error message. How may user-friendliness of error messages be assessed? How would error messages for novices and for experienced users differ?

5. Name two general approaches to achieving user-friendly messages for novice users.

6. Design a menu that would guide a novice user in devising a search formulation. Demonstrate your menu by illustrating how it would assist a novice user in devising a two-statement search formulation where SEARCH STATEMENT 1 consists of the union of three search terms, and SEARCH STATEMENT 2 consists of the intersection of SEARCH STATEMENT 1 with another search term, as follows:

SEARCH STATEMENT 1
        TERM-1 OR TERM-2 OR TERM-3
SEARCH STATEMENT 2
        1 AND TERM-4

7. Design a menu that would guide a novice user in devising an output instruction. Demonstrate your menu by illustrating how it might assist a novice user in devising the following output instruction:

PRINT SEARCH STATEMENT 2 FIELD BRIEF SORTED-BY CA RECORD ALL STARTING NUMBER 1

8. Differentiate between contextual and addressable help messages.

9. Describe the trade-off between versions of retrieval for novices and comprehensive versions of retrieval designed for experienced users. How might a retrieval program effect a compromise?

10. Describe user-friendly features for entering search terms.

11. Describe user-friendly features for developing the logic of search formulations.

12. Describe user-friendly features for assessing and revising search formulations. An example was given of user-friendly assistance to improving recall. Give an example of user-friendly assistance to improve precision.

13. Differentiate between nonsemantic processing of natural language queries and natural language query processing.

14. Differentiate between user-friendly retrieval and intelligent computer retrieval. What is contained in a knowledge base?

The Microcomputer Influence: Developments in Database Retrieval

15

The single most important influence on computerized database retrieval is the microcomputer—in the home, in the schools, and in the workplace. While microcomputers have various uses in these environments, they also function as terminals that may be connected by telephone to the host computers of retrieval services.

Retrieval services have identified specific professions as potential markets for their services. The predominating professional target areas are business and finance; science, technology, and medicine; education; law; and news. In order to satisfy the needs of professional users, retrieval services are employing the following general strategies (discussed in this chapter in detail):

- Packaging databases appropriate to the target group
- Facilitating retrieval of source, as opposed to reference, information
- Providing automatic current awareness services
- Building electronic mail networks for delivering retrieval sets and promoting interprofessional communication
- Offering private database services
- Offering special software for entering and displaying graphics, retrieving from high-density storage media (optical disks), and repackaging and re-using retrieved information
- Improving electronic accessibility of their services
- Providing retrieval systems that are easy to learn and use

- Ensuring the quality, coverage, and timeliness of information in databases

- Offering these services at an affordable cost

In addition to the retrieval services, other organizations are aware of the potential market for database retrieval by microcomputer, namely, the traditional database suppliers (indexing and abstracting services), microcomputer software companies, electronic publishers, and telecommunications networks.

MICRO-COMPUTER REVOLUTION AND INFORMATION FLOW

The microcomputer revolution has disrupted the usual organizational flow whereby end-users (individuals who ultimately apply the retrieved information) access databases by first going through intermediary users. The traditional model—forwarding end-users' requests for documents through intermediary users, telecommunications networks, and retrieval services to document delivery services—is depicted in Figure 15.1. In this model, each organization is an independent entity.

With the advent of microcomputers, organizations involved in computerized retrieval, especially retrieval services and database suppliers, are now identifying direct users of retrieval services as end-users employing microcomputers for retrieval. They recognize that direct relationships with multiple end-users are more profitable than indirect relationships through fewer intermediaries. Furthermore, organizations having direct relationships with end-users as well as direct responsibility for databases would be better able to control development of the products and services these clients require.

Configurations of information flow are currently in a state of transition. Retrieval services are supplying their own databases. Database suppliers are providing retrieval services. Both are produc-

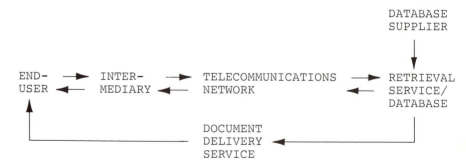

FIGURE 15.1. Traditional model of database retrieval.

ing retrieval software for microcomputers, or forming relationships with software producers for that purpose. Retrieval services are establishing their own dedicated telecommunications networks, or forming new relationships with existing telecommunications networks for providing mail services such as electronic document delivery and messaging. International retrieval networks are being formed by retrieval services whose respective databases are complementary.

At this time, retrieval services maintaining a host computer for interactive database retrieval, regardless of their organizational past, have the most direct relationship with users and the most control over products and services they need. We will assume this situation to be the case, although later on we will mention what appears to be the beginning of a trend toward distributed databases, whereby microcomputer users receive database subsets directly from database suppliers.

ELECTRONIC PUBLISHERS

Electronic publishers are a new type of database supplier, mainly for supplying full text databases. They are forming relationships with retrieval services or with traditional database suppliers. Electronic publishers may exhibit an interest in information retrieval, but will certainly become directly involved in electronic document delivery.

GROUPING DATABASES FOR PROFESSIONALS

Retrieval services are approaching target professions by grouping the databases of interest to a profession. In most cases, the databases in a group cannot be merged physically, but access to them may be offered as a package, including special access or retrieval capabilities, or special prices. Users may simultaneously search the indexes to all databases in a group, using cross-database searching (as discussed in Chapter 13), and make a selection based on displays of retrieved record counts from each database.

SOURCE DATABASES FOR PROFESSIONALS

Each profession has a need for particular types of information, in addition to that provided traditionally (indexes and abstracts). Full text databases are being offered to meet the needs of business and financial analysts, legal researchers, newspeople, patent and trademark searchers, medical personnel, and chemists. A database of full text newsletters provides professionals in all areas with advance information. In the display of full text output, the screen may highlight search terms wherever they appear in the text.

Handbook databases are an important source of information in science and technology. A unique type of database consists of back-of-the-book indexes to hundreds of reference works, including handbooks, in science, engineering, and medicine, published by over 20 major publishers. A number of full text chemical journals are available in a single database. A database package for medicine includes a combination of bibliographic information, full text information from selected medical specialty texts, and selected medical journals in full text. Directory databases apply to all fields. They include directories for locating individuals, organizations, services, projects, programs, databases, software packages, and educational tests. Comprehensive (encyclopedic) directories may function as source databases.

STATISTICS AND GRAPHICS

Business and financial analysts need statistical databases of economic indicators. Retrieval services provide databases in the form of graphics for displaying these statistics, as well as for displaying graphics for other disciplines, such as patent diagrams and chemical structures. They may accept as search terms diagrams of chemical structures drawn on the screen, using the keyboard or a pointing device such as a lightpen. Technology is being developed for high-density storage of text and graphics on optical disks, and direct interactive retrieval of this information is envisioned.

Databases may include analyses and evaluations; for example, economic forecasts, evaluated software packages, or evaluated educational programs and products. Special programs are provided that display and analyze financial and investment information, and produce customized reports.

CURRENT AWARENESS SERVICES

Retrieval services provide customized current awareness services. Chapter 12 discussed SDI (selective dissemination of information) searches, which retrieval services process against updates of databases. Full text newsletter databases are subject to an electronic clipping service based on user-selected search terms. Later in this chapter we will mention the new role of database suppliers as direct providers of current awareness services through distribution of databases directly to users.

ELECTRONIC MAIL, DOCUMENT ORDERING AND DELIVERY

Current awareness retrieval sets are usually mailed to users as are other retrieval sets produced offline. Retrieval services will soon have the capability to deliver retrieval sets electronically, and users will be able to exchange retrieval sets by electronic mail. Electronic mail facilitates messaging among users, database suppliers, and the retrieval services, as well as furnishing electronic newsletters and bulletin boards.

Retrieval services may feature computerized ordering of full text documents. If the database is a directory of microcomputer software packages, the retrieval service may also accept orders. After receiving orders, retrieval services may soon be relaying them to electronic mail services, which will then be responsible for printing the request at a center closest to the recipient and delivering it by paper delivery.

Orders for documents may be received by publishers or document delivery services, which then mail documents to users by manual delivery, and bill them directly. Electronic document delivery to end-users is not being provided at this time, although one database supplier will soon be delivering documents electronically from certain full text databases to an interlibrary loan service, which will receive requests for documents from libraries and will then transmit documents electronically to requesting libraries via its own telecommunications network. Royalty payments will be made to publishers for electronically delivered documents. In the ordering of software packages, directory publishers act as brokers for the software producers by receiving these orders, mailing the packages directly to users by manual delivery, and billing them.

PRIVATE DATABASES

Some retrieval services are offering a private database service, which is the use of the host computer and its software for individuals and groups who wish to create and update private, guaranteed secure databases and control who can access them. Retrieval would be performed using the usual programs that operate on the host computer. Private databases would be updated by providing retrieval services with updates on a computer tape. Retrieval services may allow interactive updating of private databases from the user's local facility. They may assist users in establishing databases on their own computers by selling them the database management and retrieval software that is used on the host computer.

MICROCOMPU-TER SOFTWARE FOR RETRIEVAL

Retrieval services are creating or participating in the development of software packages for accessing their databases by microcomputer. The following software features may be included:

- Automatic dialup and logon.

- Substitution of the software's user-friendly command language for command language of the retrieval service.

- Storage of search formulations on microcomputer disks.

UPLOADING

- Uploading information from microcomputer to host computer; for example, copying locally prepared search formulations from microcomputer storage into the host computer for subsequent execution, perhaps allowing interruptions for interactive processing, such as discontinuing, inserting search statements or commands, or displaying retrieval.

DOWNLOADING

- Downloading information from host computer to microcomputer; that is, copying retrieved information from the host computer into microcomputer storage for further computer-based manipulation or re-use, such as analysis, editing, reformatting, or redisplaying using microcomputer software. Information may be uploaded again to take advantage of processes available on the host computer not available locally, followed by redownloading.

- Searching using graphics input, and displaying graphics in retrievals.

- Retrieval of information stored on optical disks.

IMPROVING ELECTRONIC ACCESSIBILITY

Three major developments in electronic accessibility of retrieval services entail the opening of gateways between interactive systems, improvements in telecommunications networks, and international cooperation.

Gateways (paths for electronic access) are being established to profession-oriented retrieval services from interactive videotex systems, which emphasize home computer services such as shopping, banking, mail, entertainment, games, classified ads, and frequently updated directories. Gateways are also being formed from one retrieval service to another, especially if their respective databases are complementary. Gateways may also be in the form of microcomputer software packages that connect to several retrieval services, providing many of the features just described (automatic dialup and logon, a substitute command language, uploading locally prepared or stored search formulations, and text editing and reformatting of downloaded information).

Retrieval services are forming private telecommunications networks for improved response time, increased reliability, higher speeds, special services such as electronic mail for delivering retrieval sets or documents, and connecting with internal corporate networks.

Retrieval services in the United States and Europe with complementary databases are combining their services using international networks, including establishing dedicated telecommunications facilities. Access to databases produced in Europe but not available on a United States host will be provided by intermediaries, who will search these databases on European hosts for United States clients.

Retrieval services recognize the need for a system that is easy to learn and use. Some services offer simple systems that enable users to rely on information provided by the program as the system is being used, especially in the form of menus and explanatory messages. Others offer advanced systems that rely more on manuals, newsletters, and other tools, and toll-free telephone numbers for assistance during business hours. These provide formal training programs for various levels of expertise and may offer computer-assisted instruction programs or training and practice files for certain databases.

Recognizing that menus may be time-consuming and tedious as constant users become more proficient, retrieval services that offer simple systems may permit direct commands as alternatives to menu options. The trade-off in simplified systems results in less sophisticated retrieval capabilities than in advanced systems.

Retrieval services that initially offered only advanced systems have developed simplified versions in addition, aimed at microcomputer users in the professional markets, for use during off-peak hours. These services may initiate efforts to incorporate the simplified versions as daytime options as well. It is expected that retrieval services will continue to produce, or cooperate with producers of, microcomputer software with features described earlier in this chapter. Database suppliers are developing microcomputer software for retrieval from their databases that is compatible with certain retrieval services.

Retrieval services and database suppliers as sources of documentation and training are discussed in the introduction to Appendix B. Other sources of training include local online user groups, which sponsor seminars, workshops, tutorials, lectures, and featured topics at meetings; regional (state or multistate) library networks authorized by major retrieval services to conduct seminars and workshops and provide consultation throughout their regions; and university graduate schools of information/library science, which offer short courses and training sessions. (Chapter 16 contains additional information about training.)

There is a clear trend toward full text databases. The result will be an increase in searchable information, but in many cases this information will not be indexed for retrieval. It would be desirable for electronic texts to be indexed with back-of-the-book type indexes, as their published counterparts. These indexes would function as controlled indexing vocabularies. Retrieval based on huge textword indexes should also be available. With these types of subject access in mind, retrieval programs will need to retain the advanced features developed over the past decade.

MAKING RETRIEVAL EASIER TO LEARN AND USE

We anticipate a concomitant trend toward user-friendliness in the best sense, not by imposing simple but rigid conventions that thwart the opportunity to retrieve information creatively, but instead offering the following types of features:

- Command language characterized by brief, unambiguous, and easy-to-enter-commands, computer acceptance of errors and variations, computer-defined and user-defined defaults, and user-defined commands.

- Easy entry of search terms, including automatic word completion, truncation, and word stemming, and computer acceptance of spelling errors and variations.

- Messages from the computer offering explicit assistance and explanations.

- Ready transfer of information between computers, or from computers to other media.

- Convenient and easy-to-read standard formats for screen displays and hard-copy output from the computer, computer-designed and user-defined format defaults, and user-defined formats.

- Automatic saving of workspace when processing is interrupted, either deliberately or inadvertently, and automatic saving of workspaces from previous sessions.

- Sophisticated editing and formatting for preparing search formulations and for processing resulting retrieval sets.

- Special devices and software that reduce extensive typing or file switching, such as pointing devices (mouse, lightpen, cursor disk, joydisk, joystick, trackball, touch screen, digitizing or graphics tablet, etc.) and windowing, which is a division of a screen into segments, called windows, each of which may be used for examining and interacting with a different file as displayed in the window.

DATABASE QUALITY, COVERAGE, AND TIMELINESS

As the number of databases and public access to them grow, some imperfections, specifically in the information they contain, will probably become more obvious. These imperfections are in the areas of quality, coverage, and timeliness. Quality may be classified in terms of the causes of problems in the quality of database information: errors in form (dirty data), intellectual errors, and poor quality of source material.

DIRTY DATA

Dirty data usually refers to errors committed as errors in the form of information, rather than errors of interpretation. These may be one-time careless errors or systematic errors. In Chapter 4 we mentioned that errors in the index, when the records are correct, are usually due to an error in that part of the system that performs the computerized indexing (that is, the automatic generation of the index), and would affect the indexing of many records. A source of systematic error, then, is faulty computer indexing, resulting, for example, in absent search key values or search key values that fail to point to the appropriate records. Another source of systematic error is absent, inadequate, or inoperative computerized validation of information entered into the database (discussed in Chapter 4).

A database contains dirty data if indexing using unauthorized forms is permitted, for example COMPUTER instead of the current authorized form COMPUTERS. Suppose, however, the policy is not to file-maintain databases in order to change indexing terms of previously indexed records to current versions of these terms (as described in Chapter 13). These databases, which are not file-maintained to reflect current versions of indexing terms, would contain subject terms not currently authorized for indexing. These should not be considered to contain dirty data, provided that users are informed of the history of these terms and are instructed in their use. For example, if the former authorized indexing term COMPUTER had been changed to COMPUTERS starting with 1984, there should be a note under the COMPUTERS entry of the controlled vocabulary display that gives the year when COMPUTERS became the authorized version, gives the range of years when COMPUTER was the authorized version, and informs users that they should use both versions when searching the portion of the database that includes records entered before 1984.

What appears to be a one-time careless error may, in fact, be caused by a systematic error because validation did not take place. For example, misspellings in ordinary (nonspecialized) text that originated from the source document may undergo validation using spelling error correction programs. Failure to validate for reasonableness of information, such as ranges for dates, would allow 9184 as a year instead of 1984. Failure to validate for reasonable length for a field could allow misplaced information. For example, the text of an abstract could appear in a field meant for titles instead of the abstract field, and thereby be indexed incorrectly by the computer, causing retrieval problems.

Subject indexing errors, in contrast to dirty data, are errors that involve misapplication of subject terms to concepts in documents. Subject indexing errors may be classified as follows:

**QUALITY OF
SUBJECT
INDEXING**

- Assignment of wrong term. The assigned term is either too general or not related to the concept it stands for.

- Indexing too exhaustive; that is, concepts are indexed that are not substantively discussed.

- Substantively discussed concept not indexed.

Subject indexing requires indexers to maintain sufficient knowledge about the domain and familiarity with the controlled indexing vocabulary and indexing rules. Other requirements are in the areas of establishing and maintaining indexing policy and the controlled indexing vocabulary. The overriding criterion in assessing these factors (indexers' skills, indexing policy, and the indexing vocabulary) is the degree to which they ensure satisfactory retrieval.

Subject indexing involves the application of an official set of rules that form indexing policy. These include rules for coordinate indexing (assigning multiple subject terms for indexing a single concept); rules about weighting subject terms; guidelines for identifying indexable concepts (what topics in a document might be emphasized or ignored, what constitutes substantive discussion of a topic); and even common-sense rules. Indexing policy should strive for completeness, accuracy, currency, and consistency and be readily conveyed to indexers.

The indexer's personal "knowledge base" and indexing policy are established prior to the assignment of subject terms to a document. The quality of the controlled indexing vocabulary is another pre-existing factor. Ideally, the vocabulary should exhibit an optimum degree of specificity for retrieval. It should contain definitions of terms and their hierarchical classification, and relationships between terms (for example, cross references from entry terms to their official form, and related-term cross references). Subject terms should be unambiguous and unique. A controlled indexing vocabulary should reflect real-world use of terminology according to the domain and should strive for consistency.

QUALITY OF DATABASE SOURCE MATERIAL

The quality of information in databases is also determined by the quality of information in source materials prior to input to the database. Source material may be dirty, and resulting dirty data that could not be detected by validation would be transferred into the database. Furthermore, source material may be intellectually suspect. Control for dirty data and intellectual quality usually takes place during preparation of the source material. For example, the quality of author abstracts in a bibliographic database to journal articles is determined during the publication of the article. Electronic publishers prepare full text source materials (registries, handbooks, encyclopedias, textbooks, journals, newsletters, newspapers) in order to make them available to outsiders as databases for computerized retrieval, and they are responsible for quality assurance of these electronic texts.

Databases receiving particular attention to quality of source materials include directories to software packages for business applications where the database supplier uses stringent editor criteria (support, operation, and actual installation of the software package) in deciding whether to allow the product to be cited in the database.

Database coverage refers to the information a database is expected to contain. Problems in coverage are usually due to exclusion of specific source material resulting from a formal selection process. If selection decisions are made on a case-by-case basis using general guidelines, source materials may be omitted due to variations in individual judgment. Omissions may result from ineffective mechanisms alerting to new sources. Inadequate technical procedures for acquiring, checking in, and internally forwarding source materials may result in gaps in coverage.

DATABASE COVERAGE

Most databases are updated monthly or more frequently, in some cases daily. If there is a published counterpart, the computerized version of referral databases may be available well in advance of the published form. Except for certain newsletter databases, full text databases usually follow their published counterparts; this situation may be reversed as problems involving proper compensation to publishers are resolved. The same problems in technical procedures that result in gaps may also cause inordinate delays in updating. Furthermore, delays may be caused by malfunctioning computer software or hardware.

DATABASE TIMELINESS

The problems of quality, coverage, and timeliness of databases are sometimes the subject of articles in journals that cover the computerized retrieval literature. There may be editorials, or specific criticisms may be voiced by individuals in letters or short essays. Articles may compare databases for retrieving information on specific topics. New databases may be the subject of critical reviews. There is no one source that systematically keeps track of these database problems. However, the competitive market is a strong inducement for responsibility and responsiveness in these hidden aspects of computerized database retrieval.

RESPONSIBILITY FOR QUALITY, COVERAGE, AND TIMELINESS

The pricing methods of computerized retrieval services are in a state of transition. Their objective is to make retrieval both attractive and affordable to microcomputer owners, and at the same time meet the demand of database suppliers for a share in the anticipated profits.

PRICING OF RETRIEVAL SERVICES

The pricing method should also be based on a measure that is understandable and that can be controlled by the customer. If the cost is a flat fee, customers should understand the allowable usage corresponding to this expense. If the fee is not predetermined and based on usage, customers should understand how their use affects the fee, so that they can exert some control, such as use the computer less or use it more efficiently in order to minimize their expense. There may, however, be a periodic subscription fee in addition to charges for usage.

Retrieval services may charge for storage of saved searches, including SDI searches, in the computer. There would also be a charge each time the SDI search is processed automatically against a database update.

CONNECT-TIME RATES

The traditional basis for assessing charges has been by *connect time,* that is, the amount of time you are connected to the computer. The connect-time rate is usually expressed in terms of dollars per hour. Users with slower speed terminals are thereby charged higher fees for the same amount of retrieval as users with faster terminals. Some retrieval services charge a higher connect-time rate during prime time, that is, peak hours of usage. If the number of users during prime time is great, the computer may be slower and thereby cause an even greater increase in cost at those times. Furthermore, when charge by connect time was originated in the mid-seventies, terminals, printers, and computers were considerably slower; current rapid processing is resulting in reduced revenues for retrieval services.

DATABASE ROYALTIES

Connect-time rates may include royalties when certain databases are being searched, or royalties may be charged separately. Royalties are paid to a database supplier as publishing royalties are paid to a publisher when a book is sold to a customer. If assessed separately, the royalty is usually a charge per print hit; for bibliographic databases, a print hit is the display of a bibliographic record. If offline printouts are produced, there may be an additional charge per print hit for each record in the printout, as well as a per page charge for each page of the printout.

PRICING BY AMOUNT OF COMPUTER WORK

Retrieval services are experimenting with new bases for pricing. One of these is the amount of work performed by the computer. The disadvantage of this type of charge is that it requires users to be computer processing experts to ascertain whether a retrieval function will result in harder work for the computer.

A basis for pricing that is gaining popularity is the number of characters prepared for transmission to the terminal. Output instructions (PRINT commands) would be expected to have the greatest effect on the amount of this type of charge. In a bibliographic database, for example, if you display a large number of bibliographic records, you could pay more than someone who displays fewer. The per character rate would, however, take into account the fullness of the record being displayed; if you routinely display abstracts, you would pay more than someone who displays the same number of records but without displaying abstracts. In per character pricing, it may be possible for the retrieval service to ensure that per character costs not be assessed for display of messages in response to requests by users for assistance, explanations, or news.

PRICING BY NUMBER OF CHARACTERS FOR TRANSMISSION

Because of the possibility of downloading information from the database on the host computer to a microcomputer for storage and later re-use of the information in the microcomputer's local environment (or some other environment that is not under the control of the retrieval service), pricing based on the amount of information transmitted from databases is expected to increase in prevalence.

Since unauthorized downloading may be in violation of their copyright, the downloading capability has caused some database suppliers to offer licensing agreements, through the retrieval service, with users of their databases to permit limited downloading, that is, storage and subsequent re-use of information only at a specified site. The downloading cost for a bibliographic database, for example, would be an annual prepaid fee based on the number of bibliographic records to be downloaded per year. There may be different charges for records with fuller information, such as records with abstracts versus those without abstracts.

PRICING AND DOWNLOADING

Whether the basis for pricing is connect time, computer work, amount of information transmitted, or some combination, retrieval services may offer discounts for high-volume use subject to terms in special agreements.

Pricing for computerized retrieval may be based on a flat fee without limitation as to the amount of either time or information transmitted. This type of pricing may apply to a specific subset of databases intended for a particular professional market, for example, a set of business-oriented databases. Flat fee pricing may be offered to specific institutions, for example, academic rates for colleges and universities. Flat fee agreements may, however, include restricted ca-

DISCOUNTS AND FLAT FEE AGREEMENTS

pabilities, such as no offline printouts or document ordering requests, or restriction to usage only during nonprime time.

TELE-COMMUNICA-TIONS PRICING

As mentioned in Chapter 13, charges by telecommunications networks are paid by retrieval service customers through the retrieval service. These are usually connect time charges, but may be based on per character transmission in the future.

DISTRIBUTED DATABASE SUBSETS

The distribution of databases by database suppliers directly to microcomputer users is one of the new configurations in computerized database retrieval mentioned earlier in this chapter. Database suppliers in the areas of biology, medicine, and education are offering subsets of their databases on floppy disks, sometimes along with microcomputer software specifically for retrieving information from these subsets. (These suppliers may also offer distributed subsets on tape for minicomputer and mainframes.) The database supplier may impose certain restrictions on the re-use of distributed databases, such as prohibitions against publishing or duplicating them or offering them for resale to others.

The contents of a distributed subset may be predetermined by the database supplier if it is expected to be of use to a sizeable number of people, or the contents may be selected by the individual user. In the latter case, the database supplier assists in defining a search formulation that would result in a subset appropriate to the user's need. Distributed subsets may be offered on a one-time basis or on a continuing basis entailing periodic updates as new records are added to the database from which the subset is derived.

The development of optical disk technologies for high-density storage, including storage and retrieval of graphics, may lead to the distribution of large database subsets, complete databases, and sets of complete databases, many of them full text, which would then be available for retrieval via mini- and microcomputers at local installations.

COMPUTERIZED LIBRARIES

Although the emphasis of this book has been retrieval from databases supplied by retrieval services, the same types of computer programs used for accessing these databases are beginning to be utilized via microcomputers in university and public libraries. The efficiency of the computerized library will greatly enhance library use. Patrons will retrieve references by subject to a greater extent than before. Location and loan of library items will be streamlined. The university library will provide current awareness services to faculty, students, and administrators by maintaining personalized interest profiles. The development of computerized libraries is occurring in parallel to the functioning of retrieval services, but their immediate objective is improvement of access to and distribution of information from local collections.

1. Identify general approaches being used in the marketing of retrieval services.

2. Diagram the traditional user–organizational model for the provision of retrieval services. Identify the trends that are altering this model.

3. Name reasons why retrieval services and database suppliers might favor direct relationships with end-users.

4. Identify methods of document delivery. Include methods of ordering and methods of delivering.

5. Name the software features of packages for microcomputers being developed for using retrieval services.

6. Name features that might characterize "user-friendliness in the best sense."

7. Differentiate between dirty data and "intellectual" subject indexing errors. Identify the causes of dirty data. How might subject indexing errors be categorized? Give specific examples, using actual subject terms, of each. Name and describe three factors preliminary to the immediate process of assigning subject terms that might affect the quality of subject indexing. What is the overriding criterion in assessing these factors?

8. Identify the causes of problems in database coverage and timeliness.

9. Identify pricing methods used in charging for retrieval services.

10. What is a distributed database? Relate distributed databases to saved output (as discussed in Chapter 12).

11. The following are thought questions relating to issues in 4, 7, 9, and 10 above:

    a. What factors do you think account for the delay in implementing electronic document delivery?

    b. How would you compare the role of indexing policy and controlled indexing vocabulary in intellectual indexing by humans to the function of a knowledge base in intelligent computer indexing described in Chapter 14?

c. Which pricing method would you prefer? Why? What is the dilemma of retrieval services in establishing the basis for pricing?

d. What do you think would be the potential advantages and disadvantages of retrieval services based on distributing optical disks containing large databases to users for local retrieval, compared with centrally located databases accessed through telecommunications networks?

Selecting a Retrieval Service

16

If you think that retrieving information by computer is for you, there are two approaches you might consider for accessing computerized databases:

ACCESSING DATABASES

1. Using a retrieval service to which an institution in your area such as an office, laboratory, school, or library, already subscribes.

2. Subscribing to a retrieval service either personally or as a representative of an organization.

In either case, your objective is to find the service that best suits your needs. How you proceed may differ depending on whether you have already identified an institution that subscribes to a specific service. If you have, you may begin by investigating that service according to the criteria discussed later in this chapter.

If the service is suitable, you may wish to stay with it; that is, you may use it as a client or member of the institution that subscribes to the service, or you may subscribe to it yourself. If the service is not suitable, or if you want a basis for comparison, you may then investigate other services either available to you at another local institution or available to you as a subscriber. The subscribers of the service you start with may be a source of additional information about other services.

If you do not know an institution that subscribes to a specific retrieval service, you might want to request help from the following sources:

ORGANIZA-TIONAL SOURCES OF ASSISTANCE

- Local libraries. These include public libraries, academic (college or university) libraries, school library departments of city or county public school systems, or special libraries such as government libraries or libraries of professional societies.

225

- University graduate schools listed in the "Graduate Schools of Information/Library Science" section in Appendix B.

- Professional societies, regional library networks, and local online user groups listed in the "Organizations" section in Appendix B. In addition to national headquarters, most societies have regional chapters in cities throughout the United States.

- The editorial staff of publications listed in the "Periodicals" section in Appendix B.

- Database hotline administered by the service listed in the "Comprehensive Database User Service" section in Appendix B.

DIRECTORIES AND DOCUMENTATION

You might want to begin your investigation more directly by contacting the retrieval services listed in Appendix A. They will provide information about the availability of their service in your area, as well as material addressed to the needs of potential subscribers. While these retrieval services are among the most well known and widely available, the list is not complete. Comprehensive listings of retrieval services are provided in directories listed in "Directories" and "Comprehensive Database User Service" sections in Appendix B. You may purchase these directories and subscribe to their updates, but generally they are available in the reference sections of most public or university libraries.

Directories are oriented primarily toward databases and their suppliers and secondarily toward the services that are available. They usually do not contain detailed information about retrieval services but rather enable you to identify retrieval services that offer the databases you need, so that you may contact those services for further information.

Directories contain information about databases, such as their classification, content, language, geographic coverage, time coverage, size, and update schedule, but you should also write to database suppliers for more detailed descriptions of databases you are interested in, as well as user training information, references to tools (database guides, vocabulary lists for searching the database, lists of periodicals covered by the database) and other documentation, and a sample newsletter.

The main criterion for selecting a retrieval service is whether it offers the databases you need. While information about databases is available from database directories and database suppliers, you should not rely solely on these sources since the same database may be processed differently by various retrieval services. There may be differences in coverage, in how the database is indexed in the computer, in how the database is searched, and in how much of the database is displayable.

The initial documentation requested from retrieval services may not contain sufficiently detailed information about its databases. The information you need is probably available in database guides that are prepared by, and may be purchased from, the retrieval service. Subscribers should have these types of documentation on hand for inspection and may also have other search aids available for review such as guides, manuals, workbooks, and training materials.

The best way to gain familiarity with a retrieval system is to be involved in an encounter with the system, either by observing someone else interacting with the system or preferably by using it yourself. The mechanism for this is locating a subscriber to the service as mentioned above or obtaining formal training that includes hands-on practice.

ASSESSMENT BY DIRECT ENCOUNTER

Sources for formal training include retrieval services, database suppliers, graduate schools of information/library science, regional library networks, and local online user groups. Refresher, advanced, and subject- or database-specific training sessions and workshops are available from the same sources that provide introductory and beginner's training. Other methods of keeping up include documentation updates and newsletters provided by retrieval services and database suppliers, database directory updates (see the "Directories" and "Comprehensive Database User Service" sections in Appendix B), and scanning periodicals (see the "Periodicals" section in Appendix B).

AVAILABLE TRAINING

Methods of self-training include workbooks, practice files, computer-assisted instruction, or other training materials and programs provided by retrieval services. Most retrieval services and some database suppliers have toll-free telephone numbers for providing assistance, answering questions, and solving problems.

The remainder of this chapter will present criteria for selecting a retrieval service; it is in the form of an extensive checklist. The items in this list refer to records as the units of information in databases. The criteria take the form of questions that need to be considered, at times supplemented by descriptive or explanatory information.

CRITERIA FOR SELECTING A RETRIEVAL SERVICE

Does the retrieval service offer databases that cover the subject matter you want? Some retrieval services are specialized, whereas some offer a wide range of databases. Coverage is determined largely by the selection of source material by the database supplier, for example, the choice of periodicals to be indexed in bibliographic databases.

Database Subject Coverage

Database Type

Is the database a source or a referral database? If it is a bibliographic referral database, does it offer, for display, the abstracts of documents indexed? Abstracts are helpful in determining the content of the document. Are the abstracts searchable? Words in abstracts may provide useful access points for searching. (See also "Search Key Availability" and "Sequential Searching.")

Database Time Coverage

Does the database go back far enough in time? Some databases are segmented by time, with the most recent years constituting the current database and with older records relegated to a separate backfile database.

Database Timeliness

How frequently is the database updated? Monthly? Bi-monthly? Quarterly? However, a database may still not be current despite frequent updating.

Most databases have a publication year search key, so that a quick way to assess timeliness is to use as a search statement the current publication year or, if it is still early in the year, the previous year. The search statement result and actual publication dates (month and year) in a display of the resulting retrieval set will reveal the timeliness of the database.

For example, if in July there are few records in the database to documents published during the current year, you can conclude that there is at least a six-month time lag between when a document is published and when a record of it is added to the database. Furthermore, a display showing a large number of documents published in October of the previous year as compared to November or December indicates that the latest update did not include many documents published since October, which would mean a nine-month lag.

Database Indexed Using Controlled Vocabulary

See also "Controlled Vocabulary Search Terms." Is the database indexed using a controlled indexing vocabulary? This type of indexing provides access by pointing to all records on a subject regardless of the actual words and phrases of the document.

Is the indexing vocabulary adequate? Are the terms too general, too specific, or ambiguous? Do their meanings overlap? Are the terms classified hierarchically and cross referenced to each other? Are these classifications and cross references correct?

Is a document indexed to the most specific controlled indexing term available? Does the controlled indexing vocabulary include required tags that are always applied for frequently occurring concepts, such as age group terms: INFANTS, CHILDREN, ADULTS, and so on? Does it include subdividers, that is, a relatively small set of subject terms that qualify other subject terms according to recurring aspects of a subject?

Is validated authority-based information used for names, such as journal titles, language names, geographic names, names of organizations, or abbreviations in these names? (See also "Database Quality.")

Database Contains Validated Authority-Based Information

Is the database well maintained? Does it contain errors and inconsistencies due to absent, inadequate, or inoperative computerized validation of authorized information entered into the database?

Database Quality

Does the database contain errors that originate from the source material, such as misspellings and typographic errors in titles or abstracts?

If the database is indexed using a controlled vocabulary, are the controlled indexing terms maintained to reflect the current vocabulary, or do records contain outdated controlled indexing terms? If there are outdated controlled indexing terms (terms no longer used for indexing, but still available for searching) on older records, does the thesaurus assist you in selecting current search terms for corresponding concepts in newer records? When searching current search terms, does the thesaurus alert you to outdated controlled indexing terms you need for searching corresponding concepts in older records?

If the retrieval service contains a number of databases, is a combined index to all the databases available for searching so that the results of a search statement are displayed separately for each database? Are there options for searching combined indexes for preselected or user-defined groups of databases? Search statement results from searching combined indexes alert you to databases containing the most number of records in response to your search statement. What are the limitations of search statements used for searching combined indexes?

Database Selection Assistance

Is the database guide, containing descriptions for each database, available as a database for retrieval?

Is most of the information in records available as search keys? Are individual words in most fields, such as titles and abstracts in bibliographic databases, indexed as search key values? Are these fields indexed as separate search keys (title textwords separate from abstract textwords)? Are portions of certain fields, such as journal titles in a field that includes the entire bibliographic source, available as search keys? In multiword search keys such as controlled vocabulary indexing terms, are the individual words also indexed as search key values?

Search Key Availability

Is the unique identifier (a number that uniquely identifies a record, usually an accession number) a search key? Are diagrams of chemical structures available as search keys?

Availability of search keys within a specific database may differ from one retrieval service to another offering that database. Availability of search keys within a retrieval service may differ from one database to another. For example, the unique identifier may be a search key in one database offered by a retrieval service but not be a search key in another database offered by the same service.

Entering Search Terms

See also "Controlled Vocabulary Search Terms." Do certain search keys have special formats for entry as search terms, such as hyphenated forms for compound terms, for example, SMITH-A-B as an author's name? Is a special mechanism needed for entering search terms that contain a logical operator (AND, OR, NOT) or other system keyword?

Can search key values be selected by number from displays? These include displays of terms from the index to the database, displays of individual search terms from a previous search statement, displays of terms used for indexing a set of retrieved records, or displays of terms from a list of index terms that you have built in a special workspace.

Can you use abbreviations, synonyms, or other authorized alternate forms of authority-based search terms as surrogates for those terms? Can you search a reserved word as a literal? For example, can you search AND literally, instead of as the AND logical operator, in entering the magazine title BETTER HOMES AND GARDENS as a search term?

Limiting Search Terms and Search Statements by Search Key

Can you limit a search term to a specific search key or set of search keys? Can you limit an entire search statement in the same way? In limiting a search statement, can you override the limitation with a different one for any search term in the statement? Can you limit a previous search statement by applying the limitation to a search statement number? Can you apply the limitation negatively, for example, specifying that a search term not be indexed as a particular search key?

What is the result when you enter a search term without limiting by search key when the term is indexed as more than one search key value? Does the computer default to searching the union of these values, or does it notify you of these values? Can you initially instruct the computer to ignore the search key and default to the union of search key values?

Can you request a display at the terminal of the index to a particular database that includes the number of records indexed to each search key value? Are the search key values in the display labeled according to the search key value, for example GAMES [SU] and GAMES [TW]? Can you specify that the display be limited to a particular search key or set of search keys? Can the display be used for selecting search terms? (See also "Entering Search Terms.")

Display of Index to a Database

Is there a variable character symbol for replacing single characters or multiple characters? Are there limitations as to their location in a search term; that is, can they be used for right-handed, left-handed, or internal truncation? Can you specify in a truncated search term the maximum number of characters you want represented by the variable character symbol?

Variable Character Symbol, Truncation

What is the result when you enter a truncated search term that corresponds to more than one search key value? Does the computer default to searching the union of these values? Can you initially instruct the computer to default to searching the union?

Are the three basic logical operators (AND, OR, NOT) available? Are combinations (AND NOT, OR NOT) available? Are other logical operators (XOR, NOR, NAND) available? Are positional operators, such as SAME-FIELD-AS, SAME-SENTENCE-AS, and ADJACENT-TO, available for free text index searching? Is there a positional operator for specifying the maximum number of intervening words between two words? If the database is indexed with a controlled indexing vocabulary containing subdividers, is there a special positional operator for specifying a controlled indexing term/subdivider combination as a search term? Is there a REPEAT-WORD operator for intersecting the same word repeated, counting each word separately? Is there a repeat-word feature associated with the positional operators?

Logical and Positional Operators

What is the normal order of precedence of logical and positional operators within a search statement? Can parentheses be used for clarifying or overriding the normal order? Is nesting of search statements permitted? If so, to how many levels?

Are certain logical operators forbidden, such as the complement operator NOT unless it is combined with the intersection operator AND? Can you at least enter the search statement TERM OR NOT TERM in order to get a count for the number of records in the database?

**Controlled
Vocabulary
Search Terms**

Are individual words in controlled vocabulary search terms available as search key values? For example, would a record indexed with the controlled vocabulary search term STUDENT SCHOOL RELA-TIONSHIP also be indexed with the three search key values STU-DENT, SCHOOL, and RELATIONSHIP?

Does the controlled indexing vocabulary search key entail special formats for entering search terms, such as hyphenated forms for com-pound terms, for example ADOLESCENT-DEVELOPMENT as the form required for entering the term ADOLESCENT DEVELOP-MENT? Is a special mechanism needed for entering controlled vo-cabulary search terms that contain a logical operator (AND, OR, NOT) or other system word? Are controlled indexing terms in the form of numeric codes, for example 13203 as the code for MAL-NUTRITION?

Can you use abbreviations, synonyms, or other authorized alter-nate forms as surrogates for controlled vocabulary search terms? For example, is entering TEENAGERS limited by the controlled indexing vocabulary search key equivalent to entering the controlled vocabu-lary search key value ADOLESCENTS, if TEENAGERS is an au-thorized synonym for ADOLESCENTS in the controlled vocabulary?

Can controlled vocabulary search terms be weighted to corre-spond to weight designations assigned to a term during indexing that reflect the importance of the concept in the item being indexed?

If the controlled indexing vocabulary includes subdividers, what is the mechanism for specifying a controlled vocabulary indexing term/subdivider as a search term? Can a union of subdividers be at-tached to an indexing term? Can subdividers be searched alone as any other controlled vocabulary indexing term? Can subdividers be weighted when used as search terms, either in combinations or alone?

Can the union of controlled indexing terms in a specified hier-archical classification be searched as a single search term, for exam-ple, a search term representing a SPORTS classification equivalent to SPORTS OR ARCHERY OR BASEBALL OR . . . and so on? Searching hierarchical classifications in this way may be considered a special form of truncation.

Are displays of hierarchical classifications and cross references available as search aids, without disrupting retrieval from databases indexed using the controlled indexing vocabulary? Is the vocabulary itself available as a database for retrieval? Does the vocabulary database provide scope notes?

Are subject terms that are replaced or deleted from the vocab-ulary maintained in databases to current subject terms? If not, does the vocabulary provide instructions for searching records containing obsolete indexing terms that remain in the database despite having been changed or deleted from the vocabulary? When a new heading is added to the vocabulary, does the vocabulary suggest subject terms for searching the concept before the new term was added?

Is limiting by numeric ranging available? What relational operators are available for comparing numeric values?

    Is limiting by high-volume values for specified fields available, such as ENGLISH (possibly abbreviated ENG) for specifying English-language documents? These fields would not necessarily be search keys in the index to the database.

    Is limiting by stringsearching (sequential searching) of previous retrieval sets available? Stringsearching, a form of free text searching, allows searching of character strings, including phrases or portions of words, in specified fields. Limiting by field in stringsearching is similar to limiting by search key in a search statement processed against the index.

    Stringsearching is used for searching character strings that are not indexed as search key values, such as phrases embedded in text, parts of words, and words in a field that are not search key values specific to that field. For example, if words in titles and abstracts are indexed together as textword search key values, stringsearching could be used for searching a word only if it is in the title field.

    Stringsearching may be used for searching high-volume search key values that are indexed as search keys in the index, but where it would be more efficient to search them sequentially instead; for example, if the retrieval set being limited is a small one.

    You should note the use of variable character symbols in stringsearch terms, and the use of logical operators in stringsearch statements.

Limiting Retrieval Sets by Ranging, High-Volume Field Values, Stringsearching

Normally a total result (a count of the number of records that qualify for retrieval according to the search statement) is displayed for each search statement. Does the computer also provide the option of displaying intermediate results, that is, results for each individual search term within a statement? If the total result is zero, does the search statement number remain the same for the next statement, or is it advanced by one? The answer has implications for saved searches when you want to save a search statement for future processing even though the total result is zero when processed interactively at the time of saving.

Display of Search Statement Results

Are there time limits for processing search statements, whereby statements require more than one slice of time? Are overflow/continuation

System Limits on Searching

cue messages available for notifying you of time overflows? What options do they offer for continuing? For continuing without further interruption? For continuing with interruptions by additional overflow/continuation cue messages as needed? For cancelling? Are you provided with intermediate search statement results at the end of each time slice? Is there ever a final time limit? If processing of a time-consuming stringsearch statement is canceled before completion, can you subsequently re-enter the search statement so that it resumes stringsearching at the record where it left off?

Are there workspace limitations for processing search statements? Examples of limitations include number of search statements per terminal session, number of terms or characters in all search statements, number of records processed per search statement, number of records retrieved per search statement, number of search terms generated per truncated search term, number of characters per search term, number of records retrieved per terminal session, number of records retrieved per search statement that can be sorted, number of records retrieved and saved for online ordering of corresponding documents, and number of terms in a list of numbered search terms you have built that you can display and select search terms from, by number, for entering into a search statement.

In order to prevent you from exceeding limits, are certain logical operators forbidden at the outset, such as the complement operator NOT unless it is combined with the intersection operator AND? In that case, NOT TERM Y could not be a search statement, nor could TERM X OR NOT TERM Y for displaying a record count for the entire database.

Search History Displays

Can you request a display at the terminal of previous search statements? Can all search statements be displayed as well as certain ones, specified by one or more individual search statement numbers or ranges of search statement numbers? Are search statement results (counts) included in search history displays? Can the order of search statements in the display be specified as either ascending or descending?

Output for Search Statements Processed Interactively

What is the degree of flexibility in specifying output? Can the specifications in output instructions be specified individually, or are you restricted to prespecified formats for interactive display and offline output?

For individualized output instructions, are the following possible specifications: search statement number for identifying the retrieval set; field names of fields to be included; field names of fields to be excluded; field by which output is to be sorted; range of records to be displayed; specifications for offline output; specifications for space-saving formats. For full text databases, can you specify that only paragraphs containing search terms be displayed?

Are there defaults for these specifications; for example, a default to the previous search statement number for identifying the retrieval set? Can you define your own defaults; for example, specify a set of field names for fields to be included in displaying from certain databases? Are there preformatted output instructions, such as PRINT without further explicit specifications, that automatically apply certain defaults for each specification? Are there standard specifications, such as ALL, for specifying that all records be displayed?

If offline output is specified, can you request a listing of the search formulation with search statement results as part of the output? If offline output is specified in an output instruction, can you later cancel the output? is there a maximum limit on the number of records displayed in offline output?

Batch Processing of Search Formulations

See also "Output from Batch Processed Search Formulations." Can you enter a search formulation for batch processing? If the retrieval service segments a database into a current database and one or more backfile databases, batch processing would allow you to enter a search formulation only once and process it against some or all segments as a batch process.

As a search formulation is being entered for batch processing, does the computer require that it be processed interactively at the same time against the database to which you are connected? If simultaneous interactive processing occurs, are you given the options of either complete search statement results, or partial results indicating only the absence of search terms from the index? Although partial results may not apply to the databases to be searched against during batch processing, they may alert you to spelling or typographic errors in search statements. Batch processing saves you time if it allows you to avoid total or partial interactive processing as the search statements are entered.

Are there time or space limits in batch processing of search formulations? If a search formulation to be run as a batch process has been entered, can you later cancel the processing of that search formulation?

Output from Batch Processed Search Formulations

Are the output instruction capabilities available as those available for output from search statements processed interactively? (See also "Output for Search Statements Processed Interactively.")

Can you request a display of search statements with corresponding search statement results as part of the output? Can you request that search statement results be displayed independently of requesting output of retrieved records? Is there a maximum limit on the number of records displayed in offline output from batch processed search formulations?

Can you request that a batch processed search formulation and its output instruction be stored in a holding file so that you can access them later for processing interactively or as a batch process? In accessing from this holding file, can you request a display of search statement results independently of requesting output of retrieved records, or can you override any of the specifications in the output instructions, such as the range of records to be displayed? How long do batch processed search formulations and their output instructions remain in the holding file? Can you ask the computer to identify what you currently have in the holding file?

Merging Offline Output

Can records resulting from more than one offline output request (either from search statements processed interactively or search formulations processed in batch) be merged prior to being output? Can records from different databases be merged?

Sorting Output

Is sorting of interactively produced output available? Is sorting of offline output available (either from search statements processed interactively or search formulations processed in batch)? Can you specify ascending or descending order? Is either ascending or descending order a default? How many sorts (primary, secondary, and so on) are permitted for sorting an output? Are preset sorts available for commonly used multiple sorts? Must the field on which a sort is performed be one of the included fields in the output instruction; that is, can you sort on a particular field even if that field name is not listed in the output instruction as a field to be included in the display?

Delivery of Output Produced Offline, Ordering Source Documents

Output of retrieved records produced offline as a result of an output instruction is usually mailed the following day by first class mail.

Does the retrieval service offer ordering of source documents electronically by transmitting your order over the computer? Documents ordered in this way are usually then mailed to you. How much information about the document (accession number, author, title, and so on) must you enter in a document order? Can you order directly from a retrieval set by transferring records by number to a special database used for ordering?

If the database consists of full text documents that may be viewed interactively, is there an option to request that these documents be produced offline and mailed to you?

Can you save a search formulation? A saved search is a set of search statements assigned a name so that it can be called at a later time.

Saving Search Formulations

Can you enter saved searches in batch mode, that is, without interactive processing as you enter the search statements? This requires you to know ahead of time your intention of saving the search formulation, which is probably not really saved until the following working day.

Can you specify that a search formulation be saved after it has already been input and processed interactively? If so, you will probably want to delete any search statements in the session that you don't want as part of the saved search formulation, being careful not to delete search statements that are necessary, such as search statements whose numbers are later used as search terms in the saved search. Does a saved search that has been processed interactively save search statements even when the search statement result was zero?

Can you delete saved searches? If you delete a saved search, is it deleted immediately or not until the next working day? Can you display or modify a saved search?

For how long is a search formulation saved? Some retrieval services offer two types of saved searches: permanent ones and temporary ones that are deleted by the next day. Can you elect to share saved searches, that is, make them available to other users, or arrange to have access to those saved by others?

Are there certain conventions for naming saved searches that you need to be aware of, or does the computer assign a name, for example a serial number, automatically?

Are there time or workspace limitations in saving searches? Are certain types of searching, for example, stringsearching, or certain commands not allowed in saving searches? Can saved searches be nested; that is, can a saved search contain another saved search in one of its search statements?

Can a saved search be executed either interactively or as part of a batch processed formulation? Does execution of a saved search display search statement results for each search statement? When executed, must a saved search be executed at the point of the first search statement in the session, or can it be executed at any point in the session?

When the latest update file is merged into a database, is it also retained as a separate database? Are update files coded so that the code can be used as a search term? Is the code a permanent search key value for that update file?

Update Files, SDI (Selective Dissemination of Information)

Can you save a search formulation for automatic processing by the computer against updates to the database? This is a special type of saved search known as an SDI search, also known as a current awareness search.

An SDI search requires an output instruction. Are the output instruction capabilities available as those for output from search statements processed interactively? (See also "Output for Search Statements Processed Interactively.") Is there an expiration date specification stipulating when the SDI search is to be deleted automatically? Can the output instructions be displayed or modified?

The same considerations for saving non-SDI search formulations apply to SDI searches: interactive vs. batch entry, deletion and when deletion is effective, displayability, modifiability, time and workspace limitations, restrictions on types of searching, and nesting of saved searches.

Do merging and sorting capabilities apply to SDI searches? Can a single SDI search be established to run against more than one database? If so, is there a limit to the number?

Command Language

Are the commands easy to use? Are they brief, easy to remember, unambiguous, and easy to enter? Does the computer accept abbreviations and other variations for commands? How tolerant is the computer when you make a mistake in entering a command? How tolerant is it when you're uncertain on how to enter it? (See also "Getting Information about the System Interactively.") Can you stack commands, that is, enter several commands in sequence on a line of input using a delimiter, such as ";" or "/", to separate them?

Getting Information about the System Interactively

Does the computer offer interactive assistance when you ask for help or make a mistake? Does the computer seem to know where you are in a procedure so it can prompt you? Are the computer prompts appropriate to your specific situation, or are they general, such as USER or ENTER COMMAND? If they are general, can you then request a display of options of what can be done next?

Keep in mind that user help can be excessive as you become more experienced, that is, tedious, time-consuming, and perhaps costly as well. Can you circumvent unneeded help? Is there more than one version of the retrieval program according to your level of experience?

Can you request time and cost information? Are time and cost displays generated automatically at certain points, such as when changing databases, logging off, or saving searches? After display, are these reset to zero, or are they cumulative? Does the computer store and display statistics pertaining to your usage? Can you check the current level of the system's usage?

Can you display a list of databases that are authorized for access by you? If so, are there options for sorting the databases in this display? Is a news file available? Is the retrieval service newsletter available as a database?

Message System

Is there a message for communicating with the user services desk at the retrieval service? Can you use it to communicate with database suppliers and fellow users as well? Is there a limit to message length? Does the computer automatically notify you if you have received a new message even if you're not currently logged on to message system?

User Profile

Does the computer offer you your own user profile in which you can store, display, and modify the following: security password; mailing address; screen or page parameters such as line width, page length or the number of lines you want displayed at a time on the screen; database-specific output instruction defaults for displaying records; versions for system messages (terse vs. explanatory); names you may have assigned for system words such as command names; and the option for displaying time and cost information?

Access to the Retrieval Service Computer

Are the hours for accessing the host computer convenient? How frequently does the computer go down when it is scheduled to be operational?

Is there telecommunications as well as direct dial access? How good is the performance of the telecommunications network? This can be measured by frequency of line noise (garbage output), disconnects, or inability to connect. A retrieval service may offer a choice of telecommunications networks, so you may compare performance.

Disconnects, Interruption of Processing, File Transfer

If you are inadvertently disconnected, are search formulations entered so far during the session saved so that you can resume at the point of the disconnect? If so, for how long? Will you be charged for the time when you were disconnected? Is there a signal that tells you that the host computer is still active?

Can you intentionally interrupt computer processing? Can the interrupt apply to either a computer display or computer processing of a search statement? Can you temporarily change databases without losing the search statements and search statement results from the original database?

Line Deletion, Purging Search Statements, Restarting

Is there a special character for deleting a line of input any time before you finish entering the line?

Can you purge search statements selectively? If so, are search statements then renumbered? Can you purge all previous search statements at once? Purging search statements is used for making more room if there is a limit to the number of search statements in a session, deleting unnecessary search statements in saved searches, or eliminating unwanted search statements in displaying search formulations.

Can you restart a terminal session from the current session without logging off (that is, actually disconnecting) and then logging back on? Restarting may have an accounting advantage when multiple users are sharing an account with a retrieval service.

Private Database Service

Does the retrieval service offer you the use of its computer and database management programs for creating, updating, and maintaining your private database for interactive retrieval? The security of your private database would be guaranteed, and you would determine who could access it for retrieval. The usual retrieval programs that operate on the host computer would be used for retrieval from your private database as well. Your database would be updated when you send the retrieval service an update on a magnetic tape. Does the retrieval service allow you to update and maintain your private database interactively from your local facility?

Documentation, Training, User Services

Does the retrieval service provide full documentation in the way of manuals, database guides, and updates to these? Does it publish a regular newsletter that offers you practical information for retrieval and alerts you to forthcoming changes in retrieval capabilities and availability of databases?

Does the retrieval service offer regularly scheduled workshops in your area, or onsite custom training programs at your own facility? Does it provide courses designed for various levels of expertise? Does it provide self-training, including workbooks, computer-assisted instruction, or special databases designed for training and practice?

User Services Desk

Does the retrieval service maintain a user services desk for answering questions and helping you with retrieval problems? Can it be called using a toll-free telephone number? What are its hours of operation? Does the staff readily accept responsibility for system problems that result in loss of service? Do they frequently pass responsibility for problems to the database supplier or telecommunications network when they could investigate these problems for you? Do they compensate for inadvertent loss of service by reducing your charges?

Cost

Does the retrieval service offer a variety of contracts, including discount plans for training, pilot programs, or special groups such as academic groups? Does it have contracts with group subscribers that are regional networks you can join so you may qualify for lower rates? Does it offer automatic discounts for high usage?

What is the basis for charging for interactive retrieval? Is it connect time, amount of work the computer performs, or number of characters prepared for transmission by the computer? Do these rates include royalties when certain databases are used? Is there a periodic subscription fee in addition to charges for usage? Instead of usage, is the basis for charging a flat fee?

Are royalties assessed separately as a charge per print hit? Is there a charge per print hit in output produced offline? Is there a per page charge for each page of an offline printout? Is there a charge for storing a saved search, or storing and processing an SDI search? There is usually a charge for ordering source documents if that service is offered.

If the basic cost is determined by usage, is the pricing method based on a measurement that is understandable and therefore can be controlled by you in order to minimize your expense? If connect time is a factor, you might obtain a faster-speed terminal, or use the computer when there are less users on the system, or use abbreviated or less detailed formats for displaying records. Certain types of search statements may result in more efficient internal processing. For example, index searching or stringsearching may be more efficient, depending on previous search statement results, or it might be more efficient to enter as the first search term in an intersection a term that would retrieve fewer records than the other term. On the other hand, the retrieval service may have a way of not charging you for computer displays in response to requests for help, explanations, or news. If the basic cost is determined by a flat fee regardless of usage, do you understand any accompanying restrictions in capabilities or usage?

Does the retrieval service offer licensing agreements, originating from database suppliers, for legally downloading retrieval sets from the host computer into your microcomputer or a computer at your facility?

Are telecommunications costs included in your retrieval services charges? Do you understand the basis for these charges? Are you aware that telecommunications networks may charge different rates, and that you may have a choice of network within a retrieval service? If more than one network is accessible in your area, you may call your local telephone operator to determine if calls to them are "free" (as opposed to toll calls). Avoiding additional telephone charges due to toll calls to a "local" network facility would reduce your telecommunications costs.

Are the bills you receive itemized and easy to understand? You should monitor your use to check the accuracy of the charges in your bill. (For information about time and cost displays see "Getting Information about the System Interactively.") Is the retrieval service staff willing and able to explain your bill to you and arrange compensation for inadvertent loss of service? (See also "User Service Desk.")

There are usually additional costs associated with training and ordering publications such as manuals and database guides.

New Features

The preceding items pertain to criteria for selecting retrieval services based on features that are generally available at the present time. The following categories identify areas under development that will result in new features:

- Telecommunications for messaging capabilities that include sophisticated electronic mail systems, conferencing, and bulletin boards, and for electronic transmission of retrieved output and full text documents.

- Optical disk technologies for high-density information storage, and storage and retrieval of both text and graphics.

- Software packages for microcomputers that enable certain information retrieval processes to be performed locally, that is, on the microcomputer without being connected to the host computer. They include creating and storing search formulations that can subsequently be uploaded to the host computer for execution against databases, downloading retrieval sets from the host computer into microcomputer storage, and word processing designed especially for editing and formatting these types of stored information.

- Internal improvements in retrieval software that make computerized retrieval easier to learn and use without sacrificing advanced retrieval capabilities.

EXERCISES

1. A database supplier might name various retrieval services offering a database. Is there any reason for differentiating between these services for purposes of accessing this database? Explain your answer.

2. Imagine you are an employee who has been assigned the task of selecting a retrieval service. Identify the type of work performed by your company or agency. (You may elect to be self-employed.) Begin a real investigation of retrieval services that would be avail-

able to you. Prepare a report of the procedure you followed, and the outcome.

3. Select a retrieval service that appeared promising based on your investigation in Exercise 2. Find out as much as you can about it. Document your findings and identify the source of information for each finding.

Selected Major Computerized Retrieval Services, with Databases

A

This appendix features eight major computerized retrieval services in the United States. The emphasis is on services that currently offer information for academic, professional, and research use, primarily, although not necessarily exclusively, in the form of textual (as opposed to numeric or graphic) information. The lists of databases under these services illustrate the range of this type of information available for computerized retrieval. They were compiled from documentation published by the services during 1983, supplemented by personal communications from the services. Current comprehensive lists of retrieval services and databases are available elsewhere (see Appendix B, "Directories" section, "Comprehensive Database User Service" section, and content details in "Periodicals" section).

Services, followed by system names and aliases in brackets:

- BRS Information Technologies [BRS; BRS/SEARCH®]
- Chemical Abstracts Service®[CAS ONLINE®; Chemical Abstracts® Chem Abstracts]
- DIALOG® Information Services [DIALOG®; DIALOG® Information Retrieval Service; Lockheed]
- Mead Data Central [LEXIS®; NEXIS®]
- National Library of Medicine [NLM; MEDLINE; MEDLARS®; ELHILL]
- NewsNet®
- SDC® Information Services [SDC®; ORBIT® (Online Retrieval of Bibliographic Information and Text); ORBIT® Search Service]
- WILSONLINE℠

**BRS
INFORMATION
TECHNOLOGIES**

BRS Information Technologies
1200 Route 7
Latham, NY 12110
phone:
800-833-4707 (toll-free in continential U.S. outside NY state)
800-533-5566 (toll-free in NY state)
518-783-7251 (collect calls accepted from Canada)

Information services are available through a wide range of terminals and microcomputers. Telecommunications services are available through TELENET, TYMNET, and UNINET.

BRS offers a private database service. BRS databases with their suppliers (in brackets) followed by topical categories*:

ABI/INFORM [Data Courier, Inc., Louisville, KY]
Business/Financial

ABLEDATA [National Rehabilitation Information Center (NARIC), Catholic University of America, Washington, DC]
Social Sciences/Humanities

ABSTRACTS OF WORKING PAPERS IN ECONOMICS [Department of Economics, University of California San Diego, San Diego, CA]
Business/Financial

ABSTRAX 400 [Information Sources, Ltd., Galway, Ireland; Distribution/Marketing: J. A. Micropublishing, Inc., Eastchester, NY]
Reference

ACADEMIC AMERICAN ENCYCLOPEDIA DATABASE [Grolier Electronic Publishing, Inc., New York, NY]
Reference

ACS JOURNALS ONLINE [American Chemical Society, Washington, DC]
Sciences/Medicine

AGRICOLA [National Agriculture Library, Beltsville, MD]
Sciences/Medicine

ALCOHOL USE AND ABUSE [Drug Information Services (DIS), Minneapolis, MN]
Social Sciences/Humanities

AMERICAN MEN AND WOMEN OF SCIENCE [Jacques Cattell Press, a Division of R. R. Bowker Company, New York, NY]
Reference

ASSOCIATIONS' PUBLICATIONS IN PRINT [R. R. Bowker Company, New York, NY]
Reference

*Courtesy of BRS Information Technologies, Latham, N.Y.

BILINGUAL EDUCATION BIBLIOGRAPHIC ABSTRACTS [National Clearinghouse for Bilingual Education, InterAmerican Research Associates, Arlington, VA]
Education

BIOSIS PREVIEWS and backfile [BioSciences Information Services, Philadelphia, PA]
Sciences/Medicine

BOOKS INFORMATION [Brodart, Inc., Williamsport, PA]
Reference

BOOKS IN PRINT [R. R. Bowker Company, New York, NY]
Reference

BRS BULLETIN ONLINE [BRS, Latham, NY]
BRS Special Files

CA SEARCH and backfile [Chemical Abstracts Service, Columbus, OH]
Sciences/Medicine

CA SEARCH TRAINING [Chemical Abstracts Service, Columbus, OH]
Sciences/Medicine

CALIFORNIA UNION LIST OF PERIODICALS [Cooperative Library Agency for System & Services (CLASS), San Jose, CA]
Reference

CATALYST RESOURCES FOR WOMEN [Catalyst Library, New York, NY]
Social Sciences/Humanities

COMPENDEX [Engineering Information, New York, NY]
Sciences/Medicine

COMPREHENSIVE CORE MEDICAL LIBRARY [BRS/Saunders, New York, NY]
Sciences/Medicine

CROSS (cross-file searching) [BRS, Latham, NY]
BRS Special Files

DATA PROCESSING AND INFO SCIENCE CONTENTS [BRS, Latham, NY]
Sciences/Medicine

DIRECTORY OF GRADUATE RESEARCH [American Chemical Society, Washington, DC]
Sciences/Medicine

DISSERTATION ABSTRACTS ONLINE [University Microfilms International, Ann Arbor, MI]
Reference

DRUG INFORMATION [Drug Information Services, Minneapolis, MN]
Social Sciences/Humanities

DRUG INFORMATION AND ALCOHOL USE AND ABUSE [Drug Information Services, Minneapolis, MN]
Social Sciences/Humanities

DRUG INFORMATION FULLTEXT [American Society of Hospital Pharmacists, Bethesda, MD]
Sciences/Medicine

EDUCATIONAL RESOURCES INFORMATION CENTER [ERIC Processing and Reference Facility, Bethesda, MD]
Education

EDUCATIONAL TESTING SERVICE TEST COLLECTION [Educational Testing Service, Princeton, NJ]
Education

EXCEPTIONAL CHILD EDUCATION RESOURCES [The Council for Exceptional Children, Reston, VA]
Education

EXCERPTA MEDICA [Excerpta Medica, Amsterdam, The Netherlands]
Sciences/Medicine

FAMILY RESOURCES DATABASE [National Council on Family Relations, Minneapolis, MN]
Social Sciences/Humanities

FILE (BRS database directory) [BRS, Latham, NY]
BRS Special Files

FROST & SULLIVAN MARKET RESEARCH REPORTS [Frost & Sullivan, Inc., New York, NY]
Business/Financial

GPO MONTHLY CATALOG [Superintendent of Documents, U.S. Government Printing Office, Washington, DC]
Reference

HARVARD BUSINESS REVIEW ONLINE [John Wiley & Sons, Inc., New York, NY]
Business/Financial

HAZARDLINE [Occupational Health Services, Inc., Secaucus, NJ]
Sciences/Medicine

HEALTH AUDIO-VISUAL ONLINE CATALOG [Northeastern Ohio Universities College of Medicine, Rootstown, OH]
Sciences/Medicine

HEALTH PLANNING & ADMINISTRATION [National Library of Medicine, Bethesda, MD]
Sciences/Medicine

INDUSTRY AND INTERNATIONAL STANDARDS [Information Handling Services, Englewood, CO]
Business/Financial

INDUSTRY & MILITARY STANDARDS (CONCATENATED) [Information Handling Services, Englewood, CO]
Business/Financial

INDUSTRY DATA SOURCES [Information Access Co., Belmont, CA]
Business/Financial

INSPEC and backfile [INSPEC/IEEE, Piscataway, NJ]
Sciences/Medicine

INTERNATIONAL PHARMACEUTICAL ABSTRACTS [International Pharmaceutical Abstracts, American Society of Hospital Pharmacists, Bethesda, MD]
Sciences/Medicine

IRCS MEDICAL SCIENCE [IRCS Medical Science, Lancaster, England]
Sciences/Medicine

IRS PUBLICATIONS [Internal Revenue Service, Washington, DC]
Reference

KIRK-OTHMER ENCYCLOPEDIA OF CHEMICAL TECHNOLOGY [John Wiley & Sons, Inc., Electronic Publishing Division, New York, NY]
Sciences/Medicine

LANGUAGE AND LANGUAGE BEHAVIOR ABSTRACTS [Sociological Abstracts, San Diego, CA]
Social Sciences/Humanities

MANAGEMENT CONTENTS [Management Contents, Northbrook, IL]
Business/Financial

MATHFILE [American Mathematical Society, Providence, RI]
Sciences/Medicine

MEDLINE and backfiles [National Library of Medicine, Bethesda, MD]
Sciences/Medicine

MENTAL MEASUREMENTS YEARBOOK [Buros Institute of Mental Measurements, U. of Nebraska-Lincoln, Lincoln, NB]
Social Sciences/Humanities

MESH/PSYC PREVIEWS [BRS/Saunders, New York, NY]
Sciences/Medicine

MESSAGES (electronic message switching) [BRS, Latham, NY]
BRS Special Files

MILITARY AND FEDERAL SPECIFICATIONS AND STANDARDS [Information Handling Services, Englewood, CO]
Business/Financial

NATIONAL CLEARINGHOUSE FOR MENTAL HEALTH [National Clearinghouse for Mental Health Information, Rockville, MD]
Social Sciences/Humanities

NATIONAL COLLEGE DATABANK [Peterson's Guides, Inc., Princeton, NJ]
Education

NATIONAL REHABILITATION INFORMATION CENTER [National Rehabilitation Information Center, Catholic University of America, Washington, DC]
Social Sciences/Humanities

NATIONAL TECHNICAL INFORMATION SERVICE [National Technical Information Service (NTIS), Springfield, VA]
Sciences/Medicine

NEWS (system update file) [BRS, Latham, NY]
BRS Special Files

ONLINE MICROCOMPUTER SOFTWARE GUIDE AND DIRECTORY [Online, Inc., Georgetown, CT]
Sciences/Medicine

ONTARIO EDUCATION RESOURCES INFORMATION [Ontario Ministry of Education, Toronto, Ontario, Canada]
Education

PATDATA [BRS, Latham, NY]
Business/Financial

POLLUTION ABSTRACTS [Cambridge Scientific Abstracts, Bethesda, MD]
Sciences/Medicine

PREDICASTS ANNUAL REPORTS ABSTRACTS [Predicasts, Inc., Cleveland, OH]
Business/Financial

PREDICASTS CONCATENATED CURRENT BIBLIOGRAPHIC FILES [Predicasts, Inc., Cleveland, OH]
Business/Financial

PREDICASTS F & S INDEXES (and weekly update file) [Predicasts, Inc., Cleveland, OH]
Business/Financial

PREDICASTS FORECASTS [Predicasts, Inc., Cleveland, OH]
Business/Financial

PREDICASTS HISTORICAL TIME SERIES [Predicasts, Inc., Cleveland, OH]
Business/Financial

PREDICASTS PROMT (and weekly update file) [Predicasts, Inc., Cleveland, OH]
Business/Financial

PREDICASTS F & S INDEXES, PROMT CONCATENATED and backfile [Predicasts, Inc., Cleveland, OH]
Business/Financial

PSYCINFO [American Psychological Association, Washington, DC]
Social Sciences/Humanities

PUBLIC AFFAIRS INFORMATION SERVICE [Public Affairs Information
Service, Inc., New York, NY]
Social Sciences/Humanities

PUBLISHERS, DISTRIBUTORS & WHOLESALERS [R. R. Bowker Company, New York, NY]
Reference

RELIGION INDEX [American Theological Library Association, Chicago, IL]
Social Sciences/Humanities

RESOURCES IN COMPUTER EDUCATION [Northwest Regional Education Laboratory, Portland, OR]
Education

RESOURCES IN VOCATIONAL EDUCATION [The National Center for Research in Vocational Education, Ohio State University, Columbus, OH]
Education

RESOURCES, ORGANIZATIONS AND MEETINGS FOR EDUCATORS DATABASE [National Center for Research in Vocational Rehabilitation, Columbus, OH]
Education

ROBOTICS INFORMATION DATABASE [Cincinnati Milacron Industries, Inc., Corporate Information Center, Cincinnati, OH]
Sciences/Medicine

SCHOOL PRACTICES INFORMATION FILE [BRS, Latham, NY]
Education

SOCIAL SCIENCE CITATION INDEX (and backfile) [Institute for Scientific Information (ISI), Philadelphia, PA]
Social Sciences/Humanities

SOCIOLOGICAL ABSTRACTS [Sociological Abstracts, San Diego, CA]
Social Sciences/Humanities

SUPERINDEX [Superindex, Inc., Boca Raton, FL]
Sciences/Medicine

TERM (social science thesauri) [BRS, Latham, NY]
BRS Special Files

TEXAS EDUCATION COMPUTER COOPERATIVE [Texas Education Computer Cooperative (TECC), Statewide Microcomputer Courseware Evaluation Network, Region IV Education Service Center, Houston, TX]
Education

ULRICH'S PERIODICALS DIRECTORY [R. R. Bowker Company, New York, NY]
Reference

VENDOR INFORMATION DATABASE [Information Handling Services, Englewood, CO]
Sciences/Medicine

VOCATIONAL EDUCATION CURRICULUM MATERIALS [Curriculum Coordination Centers and The National Center for Vocational Education, Ohio State University, Columbus, OH]
Education

VOLUNTARY STANDARDS INFORMATION NETWORK [Information Handling Services, Englewood, CO]
Business/Financial

CHEMICAL ABSTRACTS SERVICE®

Chemical Abstracts Service®
2540 Olentangy River Road
P. O. Box 3012
Columbus, OH 43210
phone:
Information about CAS Online®
614-421-3600
Search Assistance Desk:
800-848-6533 (toll-free in continental U.S. outside OH)
800-848-6538 (toll-free in OH)
614-421-3698

International offices in England, France, Germany, and Japan.

Information services offering bibliographic and chemical structure searching on a wide range of terminals and microcomputers. Optional graphics input and display require Tektronix Plot 10 vector graphics compatibility. Telecommunications services are available through TELENET, TYMNET, and Datex-P (W. Germany).

CAS ONLINE® databases*:

CA File
    journal articles; patents; proceedings from meetings, symposia, and edited collections; technical reports; deposited documents; dissertations; books

Registry File
    registry of substances, including unique CAS registry number, molecular structure diagram, molecular formula, structurally descriptive CA index name, and synonyms

*Courtesy of Chemical Abstracts Service®, Columbus, OH.

DIALOG®

DIALOG® Information Services
3460 Hillview Avenue
Palo Alto, CA 94304
phone:
800-227-1927—Marketing

800-227-8282—Training
800-227-1960—Customer Services
(above numbers toll-free in continental U.S. outside CA)
800-982-5835 (toll-free in CA)
415-858-3785

Offices in Boston, MA; Chicago, IL; Houston, TX; Los Angeles, CA, New York, NY; Philadelphia, PA; and Washington, DC. International Representatives in Australia, Canada, England, and Japan.

Information services are available through a wide range of terminals and microcomputers. Telecommunications services are available through DIALNET, TELENET, TYMNET, and UNINET.

DIALOG® offers a private database service. DIALOG® databases with their suppliers (in brackets) followed by topical categories*:

ABI/INFORM [Data Courier, Inc., Louisville, KY]
Business/Economics—market research, industry, management

ACADEMIC AMERICAN ENCYCLOPEDIA [Grolier Electronic Publishing, New York, NY]
Multidisciplinary

ADTRACK [Corporate Intelligence, Inc., St. Paul, MN]
Business/Economics—industry specific

AGRICOLA [National Agriculture Library, Beltsville, MD]
Agriculture and Nutrition

AIM/ARM [The Center for Vocational Education, The Ohio State University, Columbus, OH]
Education

AMERICA: HISTORY AND LIFE [ABC–Clio Information Services, Santa Barbara, CA]
Social Sciences and Humanities

AMERICAN MEN AND WOMEN OF SCIENCE [R. R. Bowker, New York, NY]
Directories

APTIC (air pollution database) [Manpower and Technical Information Branch, U.S. Environmental Protection Agency, Research Triangle Park, NC]
Energy and Environment

AQUACULTURE [National Oceanic and Atmospheric Administration, Rockville, MD]
Energy and Environment

AQUALINE [Water Research Centre, Medmenham, Buckinghamshire, England]
Energy and Environment

*Courtesy of DIALOG® Information Services, Palo Alto, CA.

AQUATIC SCIENCES AND FISHERIES ABSTRACTS [NOAA/Cambridge Scientific Abstracts, Bethesda, MD]
Energy and Environment

ARTBIBLIOGRAPHIES MODERN [ABC–Clio Information Services, Santa Barbara, CA]
Social Sciences and Humanities

ARTHUR D. LITTLE/ONLINE [Arthur D. Little Decision Resources, Cambridge, MA]
Business/Economics—market research, industry, management

ASI (American Statistics Index) [Congressional Information Service, Inc., Washington, DC]
Law and Government

A–V ONLINE [National Information Center for Educational Media, Access Innovations, Inc., Albuquerque, NM]
Education

BI/DATA FORECASTS [Business International Corporation, New York, NY]
Business/Economics—statistical/demographic data

BI/DATA TIME SERIES [Business International Corporation, New York, NY]
Business/Economics—statistical/demographic data

BIOGRAPHY MASTER INDEX [Gale Research Company, Detroit, MI]
Directories

BIOSIS PREVIEWS [BioSciences Information Service, Philadelphia, PA]
Agriculture and Nutrition; Energy and Environment; Medicine and Biosciences

BLS CONSUMER PRICE INDEX [Bureau of Labor Statistics, U.S. Department of Labor, Washington, DC]
Business/Economics—statistical/demographic data

BLS EMPLOYMENT, HOURS, AND EARNINGS [Bureau of Labor Statistics, U.S. Department of Labor, Washington, DC]
Business/Economics—statistical/demographic data

BLS LABOR FORCE [Bureau of Labor Statistics, U.S. Department of Labor, Washington, DC]
Business/Economics—statistical/demographic data

BLS PRODUCER PRICE INDEX [Bureau of Labor Statistics, U.S. Department of Labor, Washington, DC]
Business/Economics—statistical/demographic data

BOOK REVIEW INDEX [Gale Research Company, Detroit, MI]
Bibliography—Books and Monographs

BOOKS IN PRINT [R. R. Bowker, New York, NY]
Bibliography—Books and Monographs

BUSINESS/PROFESSIONAL SOFTWARE DATABASE [Data Courier, Inc., Louisville, KY]
Computer Science

CA SEARCH [Chemical Abstracts Service, Columbus, OH]
Chemistry; Energy and Environment; Materials Sciences; Medicine and Biosciences; Patents and Trademarks

CAB ABSTRACTS [Commonwealth Agricultural Bureaux, Farnham Royal, Slough, England]
Agriculture and Nutrition

CANADIAN BUSINESS AND CURRENT AFFAIRS [Micromedia Ltd., Toronto, Ontario, Canada]
Business/Economics—market research, industry, management; Current Affairs

CAREER PLACEMENT REGISTRY/EXPERIENCED PERSONNEL [Career Placement Registry, Inc., Alexandria, VA]
Directories

CAREER PLACEMENT REGISTRY/STUDENT [Career Placement Registry, Inc., Alexandria, VA]
Directories

CHEMICAL EXPOSURE [Chemical Effects Information Center, Oak Ridge National Laboratory, Oak Ridge, TN]
Chemistry; Medicine and Biosciences

CHEMICAL INDUSTRY NOTES (CIN) [Chemical Abstracts Service and American Chemical Society, Columbus, OH]
Business/Economics—industry specific; Chemistry

CHEMICAL REGULATIONS AND GUIDELINES SYSTEM (CRGS) [U.S. Interagency Regulatory Liaison Group, CRC Systems, Inc., Fairfax, VA]
Chemistry; Law and Government

CHEMNAME [DIALOG Information Services, Inc., Palo Alto, CA; Chemical Abstracts Service, Columbus, OH]
Chemistry; Materials Sciences; Medicine and Biosciences

CHEMSEARCH [DIALOG Information Services, Inc., Palo Alto, CA; Chemical Abstracts Service, Columbus, OH]
Chemistry; Materials Sciences; Medicine and Biosciences

CHEMSIS (CHEM Singly Indexed Substances) [DIALOG Information Services, Inc., Palo Alto, CA; Chemical Abstracts Service, Columbus, OH]
Chemistry; Materials Sciences; Medicine and Biosciences

CHEMZERO [DIALOG Information Services, Inc., Palo Alto, CA; Chemical Abstracts Service, Columbus, OH]
Chemistry; Materials Sciences; Medicine and Biosciences

CHILD ABUSE AND NEGLECT [National Center on Child Abuse and Neglect, Children's Bureau, U.S. Department of Health and Human Services, Washington, DC]
Social Sciences and Humanities

CHRONOLOG NEWSLETTER [DIALOG Information Retrieval Service, Inc., Palo Alto, CA]
Current Affairs

CIS [Congressional Information Service, Inc., Washington, DC]
Law and Government

CLAIMS/CITATION [Search Check, Inc., Arlington, VA; IFI/Plenum Data Company, Alexandria, VA]
Patents and Trademarks

CLAIMS/CLASS [IFI/Plenum Data Company, Alexandria, VA]
Patents and Trademarks

CLAIMS COMPOUND REGISTRY [IFI/Plenum Data Company, Alexandria, VA]
Chemistry; Patents and Trademarks

CLAIMS/U.S. PATENT ABSTRACTS [IFI/Plenum Data Company, Alexandria, VA]
Patents and Trademarks

CLAIMS/U.S. PATENT ABSTRACTS WEEKLY [IFI/Plenum Data Company, Alexandria, VA]
Patents and Trademarks

CLAIMS/UNITERM [IFI/Plenum Data Company, Alexandria, VA]
Patents and Trademarks

COFFEELINE [International Coffee Organization, London, England]
Business/Economics—industry specific

COMMERCE BUSINESS DAILY [Commerce Business Daily, U.S. Department of Commerce, Chicago, IL]
Business/Economics—market research, industry, management; Law and Government

COMPENDEX [Engineering Information, Inc., New York, NY]
Computer Science; Science and Technology

COMPUTER DATABASE [Management Contents, Inc., Northbrook, IL]
Computer Science

CONFERENCE PAPERS INDEX [Cambridge Scientific Abstracts, Bethesda, MD]
Multidisciplinary

CONGRESSIONAL RECORD ABSTRACTS [Capitol Services, Inc., Washington, DC]
Law and Government

CRIMINAL JUSTICE PERIODICALS INDEX [University Microfilms International, Ann Arbor, MI]
Law and Government

CRIS/USDA (Current Research Information System/USDA) [U.S. Department of Agriculture, Washington, DC]
Agriculture and Nutrition

D & B—DUN'S MARKET IDENTIFIERS [Dun's Marketing Services, Parsippany, NJ]
Business/Economics—company and financial

D & B—MILLION DOLLAR DIRECTORY (MDD) [Dun's Marketing Services, Parsippany, NJ]
Business/Economics—company and financial

D & B PRINCIPAL INTERNATIONAL BUSINESSES [International Marketing Services, Dun & Bradstreet International, New York, NY]
Business/Economics—company and financial

DERWENT WORLD PATENTS INDEX [Derwent Publications Ltd., London, England]
Patents and Trademarks

DIALINDEX (cross-file searching) [DIALOG Information Services, Inc., Palo Alto, CA]
Multidisciplinary

DIALOG PUBLICATIONS [DIALOG Information Services, Inc., Palo Alto, CA]
Bibliography—Books and Monographs

DISCLOSURE II (U.S. Securities and Exchange Commission (SEC) reports) [Disclosure, Inc., Bethesda, MD]
Business/Economics—company and financial

DISCLOSURE/SPECTRUM OWNERSHIP [Disclosure, Inc., Bethesda, MD]
Business/Economics—company and financial

DISSERTATION ABSTRACTS ONLINE [University Microfilms International, Ann Arbor, MI]
Multidisciplinary

DOE ENERGY [U.S. Department of Energy, Washington, DC]
Energy and Environment

DONNELLEY DEMOGRAPHICS [Donnelley Marketing Information Services, a Company of the Dun & Bradstreet Corporation, Stamford, CT]
Business/Economics—statistical/demographic data

DRUG INFORMATION FULLTEXT [American Society of Hospital Pharmacists, Washington, DC]
Medicine and Biosciences

ECONOMIC LITERATURE INDEX [American Economic Association, Pittsburgh, PA]
Business/Economics—market research, industry, management

ECONOMICS ABSTRACTS INTERNATIONAL [Netherlands Foreign Trade Agency, The Hague, Netherlands]
Business/Economics—market research, industry, management

Ei ENGINEERING MEETINGS [Engineering Information, Inc., New York, NY]
Science and Technology

EIS INDUSTRIAL PLANTS [Economic Information Systems, Inc., New York, NY]
Business/Economics—company and financial

EIS NONMANUFACTURING ESTABLISHMENTS [Economic Information Systems, Inc., New York, NY]
Business/Economics—company and financial

ELECTRIC POWER DATABASE [Electric Power Research Institute (EPRI), Palo Alto, CA]
Energy and Environment

ELECTRONIC YELLOW PAGES—CONSTRUCTION DIRECTORY [Market Data Retrieval, Inc., Westport, CT]
Business/Economics—company and financial

ELECTRONIC YELLOW PAGES—FINANCIAL SERVICES DIRECTORY [Market Data Retrieval, Inc., Westport, CT]
Business/Economics—company and financial

ELECTRONIC YELLOW PAGES INDEX [DIALOG Information Services, Inc., Palo Alto, CA]
Business/Economics—company and financial

ELECTRONIC YELLOW PAGES—MANUFACTURERS DIRECTORY [Market Data Retrieval, Inc., Westport, CT]
Business/Economics—company and financial

ELECTRONIC YELLOW PAGES—PROFESSIONALS DIRECTORY [Market Data Retrieval, Inc., Westport, CT]
Business/Economics—company and financial

ELECTRONIC YELLOW PAGES—RETAILERS DIRECTORY [Market Data Retrieval, Inc., Westport, CT]
Business/Economics—company and financial

ELECTRONIC YELLOW PAGES—SERVICES DIRECTORY [Market Data Retrieval, Inc., Westport, CT]
Business/Economics—company and financial

ELECTRONIC YELLOW PAGES—WHOLESALERS DIRECTORY [Market Data Retrieval, Inc., Westport, CT]
Business/Economics—company and financial

EMBASE [Excerpta Medica, Amsterdam, Netherlands]
Medicine and Biosciences

ENCYCLOPEDIA OF ASSOCIATIONS [Gale Research Company, Detroit, MI]
Directories

ENERGYLINE [Environmental Information Center, Inc., New York, NY]
Energy and Environment

ENERGYNET [Environmental Information Center, Inc., New York, NY]
Energy and Environment

ENVIROLINE [Environmental Information Center, Inc., New York, NY]
Energy and Environment

ENVIRONMENTAL BIBLIOGRAPHY [Environmental Studies Institute, Santa Barbara, CA]
Energy and Environment

ERIC (Educational Resources Information Center) [National Institute of Education, Washington, DC; ERIC Processing and Reference Facility, Bethesda, MD]
Education

EXCEPTIONAL CHILD EDUCATION RESOURCES [The Council for Exceptional Children, Reston, VA]
Education

FACTS ON FILE [Facts on File, Inc., New York, NY]
Current Affairs

FAMILY RESOURCES [National Council on Family Relations, Minneapolis, MN; Inventory of Marriage and Family Literature Project, University of Minnesota, Minneapolis, MN]
Social Sciences and Humanities

FEDERAL INDEX [Capitol Services International, Washington, DC]
Law and Government

FEDERAL REGISTER ABSTRACTS [Capitol Services International, Washington, DC]
Law and Government

FEDERAL RESEARCH IN PROGRESS [National Technical Information Service (NTIS), U.S Department of Commerce, Springfield, VA]
Science and Technology

FIND/SVP REPORTS AND STUDIES INDEX [FIND/SVP, New York, NY]
Business/Economics—market research, industry, management

FLUIDEX [BHRA, The Fluid Engineering Centre, Cranfield, Bedford, England]
Science and Technology

FOOD SCIENCE AND TECHNOLOGY ABSTRACTS [International Food Information Service, Reading, Berkshire, England]
Agriculture and Nutrition

FOODS ADLIBRA [Foods Adlibra Publications, Minneapolis, MN]
Agriculture and Nutrition; Business/Economics—industry specific

FOREIGN TRADERS INDEX [U.S. Department of Commerce, Washington, DC]
Business/Economics—market research, industry, management

FOUNDATION DIRECTORY [The Foundation Center, New York, NY]
Foundations and Grants

FOUNDATION GRANTS INDEX [The Foundation Center, New York, NY]
Foundations and Grants

GEOARCHIVE [Geosystems, London, England]
Science and Technology

GEOREF [American Geological Institute, Falls Church, VA]
Science and Technology

GPO MONTHLY CATALOG [U.S. Government Printing Office, Washington, DC]
Bibliography—Books and Monographs; Law and Government

GPO PUBLICATIONS REFERENCE FILE [U.S. Government Printing Office, Washington, DC]
Bibliography—Books and Monographs; Law and Government

GRANTS [Oryx Press, Phoenix, AZ]
Foundations and Grants

HARFAX INDUSTRY DATA SOURCES [Harfax Database Publishing, Cambridge, MA]
Business/Economics—market research, industry, management

HARVARD BUSINESS REVIEW [John Wiley & Sons, Inc., New York, NY]
Business/Economics—market research, industry, management

HEALTH PLANNING AND ADMINISTRATION [U.S. National Library of Medicine, Bethesda, MD]
Medicine and Biosciences

HISTORICAL ABSTRACTS [ABC-Clio Information Services, Santa Barbara, CA]
Social Sciences and Humanities

ICC BRITISH COMPANY DIRECTORY [Inter Company Comparisons Ltd, London, England]
Business/Economics—company and financial

ICC BRITISH COMPANY FINANCIAL DATASHEETS [Inter Company Comparisons Ltd, London, England]
Business/Economics—company and financial

INFORMATION SCIENCE ABSTRACTS [IFI/Plenum Data Company, Alexandria, VA]
Social Sciences and Humanities

INSPEC [The Institution of Electrical Engineers, London, England]
Computer Science; Science and Technology

INSURANCE ABSTRACTS [University Microfilms International, Ann Arbor, MI]
Business/Economics—industry specific

INTERNATIONAL LISTING SERVICE [ILS-International Listing Service, McLean, VA]
Business/Economics—market research, industry, management

INTERNATIONAL PHARMACEUTICAL ABSTRACTS [American Society of Hospital Pharmacists, Washington, DC]
Medicine and Biosciences

INVESTEXT [Business Research Corporation, Boston, MA]
Business/Economics—company and financial

IRIS (Instructional Resources Information System) [U.S. Environmental Protection Agency Information Project, Ohio State University, Columbus, OH]
Education

ISMEC (Information Service in Mechanical Engineering) [Cambridge Scientific Abstracts, Bethesda, MD]
Science and Technology

LABORLAW [Bureau of National Affairs, Inc., Washington, DC]
Law and Government

LANGUAGE AND LANGUAGE BEHAVIOR ABSTRACTS (LLBA) [Sociological Abstracts, Inc., San Diego, CA]
Social Sciences and Humanities

LC MARC [U.S. Library of Congress, Washington, DC]
Bibliography—Books and Monographs

LEGAL RESOURCE INDEX [Information Access Company, Belmont, CA]
Law and Government

LIFE SCIENCES COLLECTION [Cambridge Scientific Abstracts, Bethesda, MD]
Medicine and Biosciences

LISA (LIBRARY AND INFORMATION SCIENCE ABSTRACTS) [Library Association Publishing, London, England]
Social Sciences and Humanities

MAGAZINE ASAP [Information Access Company, Belmont, CA]
Current Affairs

MAGAZINE INDEX [Information Access Company, Belmont, CA]
Current Affairs

MANAGEMENT CONTENTS [Management Contents, Inc., Northbrook, IL]
Business/Economics—market research, industry, management

MARQUIS WHO'S WHO [Marquis Who's Who, Inc., Chicago, IL]
Directories

MATHFILE [American Mathematical Society, Providence, RI]
Science and Technology

MEDIA GENERAL DATABANK [Media General Financial Services, Richmond, VA]
Business/Economics—company and financial

MEDLINE [U.S. National Library of Medicine, Bethesda, MD]
Medicine and Biosciences

MENTAL HEALTH ABSTRACTS [National Clearinghouse for Mental Health Information (NCMHI), National Institute of Mental Health, Rockville, MD, through 1982; IFI/Plenum Data Company, Alexandria, VA, from 1983 to present]
Medicine and Biosciences

MENU—THE INTERNATIONAL SOFTWARE DATABASE [International Software Database Corporation, Fort Collins, CO]
Computer Science

METADEX [American Society for Metals, Metals Park, OH; The Metals Society, London, England]
Materials Sciences

METEOROLOGICAL AND GEOASTROPHYSICAL ABSTRACTS [American Meteorological Society, Boston, MA]
Science and Technology

MICROCOMPUTER INDEX [Microcomputer Information Services, Santa Clara, CA]
Science and Technology

MIDDLE EAST; ABSTRACTS & INDEX [Northumberland Press, Pittsburgh, PA]
Current Affairs

MIDEAST FILE [Learned Information Ltd., Abingdon, Oxford, England; Shiloah Centre for Middle Eastern and African Studies, Tel Aviv University, Tel Aviv, Israel]
Current Affairs

MLA BIBLIOGRAPHY [Modern Language Association, New York, NY]
Social Sciences and Humanities

MOODY'S CORPORATE PROFILES [Moody's Investors Services, Inc., New York, NY]
Business/Economics—company and financial

NATIONAL FOUNDATIONS [The Foundation Center, New York, NY]
Foundations and Grants

NATIONAL NEWSPAPER INDEX [Information Access Company, Belmont, CA]
Current Affairs

NCJRS [National Criminal Justice Reference Service, Rockville, MD]
Law and Government

NEWSEARCH [Information Access Company, Belmont, CA]
Current Affairs

NICSEM/NIMIS (National Instructional Materials Information System) [National Information Center for Special Education Materials, University of Southern California, Los Angeles, CA]
Education

NONFERROUS METALS ABSTRACTS [British Non-Ferrous Metals Technology Centre, Wantage, Oxfordshire, England]
Materials Sciences

NTIS [National Technical Information Service (NTIS), U.S. Department of Commerce, Springfield, VA]
Law and Government; Multidisciplinary; Science and Technology

NURSING AND ALLIED HEALTH (CINAHL), [Cumulative Index to Nursing & Allied Health Literature (CINAHL), Glendale, CA]
Medicine and Biosciences

OCCUPATIONAL SAFETY AND HEALTH (NIOSH) [U.S. National Institute for Occupational Safety and Health Technical Information Center (NIOSHTIC), Cincinnati, OH]
Medicine and Biosciences

OCEANIC ABSTRACTS [Cambridge Scientific Abstracts, Bethesda, MD]
Energy and Environment

ONLINE CHRONICLE [Online, Inc., Weston, CT]
Current Affairs

ONTAP ABI/INFORM [Data Courier, Inc., Louisville, KY; DIALOG Information Services, Inc., Palo Alto, CA]
Online Training and Practice

ONTAP BIOSIS PREVIEWS [BioSciences Information Service, Philadelphia, PA; DIALOG Information Services, Inc., Palo Alto, CA]
Online Training and Practice

ONTAP CA SEARCH [Chemical Abstracts Service, Columbus, OH; DIALOG Information Services, Inc., Palo Alto, CA]
Online Training and Practice

ONTAP CAB ABSTRACTS [Commonwealth Agricultural Bureaux, Farnham Royal, Slough, England; DIALOG Information Services, Inc., Palo Alto, CA]
Online Training and Practice

ONTAP CHEMNAME [Chemical Abstracts Service, Columbus, OH; DIALOG Information Services, Inc., Palo Alto, CA]
Online Training and Practice

ONTAP COMPENDEX [Engineering Information, Inc., New York, NY; DIALOG Information Services, Inc., Palo Alto, CA]
Online Training and Practice

ONTAP DIALINDEX [DIALOG Information Services, Inc., Palo Alto, CA]
Online Training and Practice

ONTAP EMBASE [Excerpta Medica, Amsterdam, Netherlands; DIALOG Information Services, Inc., Palo Alto, CA]
Online Training and Practice

ONTAP ERIC (Educational Resources Information Center) [National Institute of Education, Washington, DC; ERIC Processing and Reference Facility, Bethesda, MD; DIALOG Information Services, Inc., Palo Alto, CA]
Online Training and Practice

ONTAP HARFAX INDUSTRY DATA SOURCES [Harfax Database Publishing, Cambridge, MA; DIALOG Information Services, Inc., Palo Alto, CA]
Online Training and Practice

ONTAP INSPEC [The Institution of Electrical Engineers, London, England; DIALOG Information Services, Inc., Palo Alto, CA]
Online Training and Practice

ONTAP MAGAZINE INDEX [Information Access Company, Belmont, CA; DIALOG Information Services, Inc., Palo Alto, CA]
Online Training and Practice

ONTAP MEDLINE [U.S. National Library of Medicine, Bethesda, MD; DIALOG Information Services, Inc., Palo Alto, CA]
Online Training and Practice

ONTAP PTS PROMT [Predicasts, Inc., Cleveland, OH; DIALOG Information Services, Inc., Palo Alto, CA]
Online Training and Practice

ONTAP TRADEMARKSCAN [Thomson and Thomson, Boston, MA; DIALOG Information Services, Inc., Palo Alto, CA]
Online Training and Practice

PAIS INTERNATIONAL [Public Affairs Information Service, Inc., New York, NY]
Current Affairs; Social Sciences and Humanities

PAPERCHEM [Institute of Paper Chemistry, Appleton, WI]
Chemistry; Materials Sciences

PATLAW [Bureau of National Affairs, Inc., Washington, DC]
Law and Government; Patents and Trademarks

PETERSON'S COLLEGE DATABASE [Peterson's Guides, Inc., Princeton, NJ]
Directories

PHARMACEUTICAL NEWS INDEX [Data Courier, Inc., Louisville, KY]
Business/Economics—industry specific; Medicine and Biosciences

PHILOSOPHER'S INDEX [Philosophy Documentation Center, Bowling Green State University, Bowling Green, OH]
Social Sciences and Humanities

POLLUTION ABSTRACTS [Cambridge Scientific Abstracts, Bethesda, MD]
Energy and Environment

POPULATION BIBLIOGRAPHY [Carolina Population Center, University of North Carolina, Chapel Hill, NC]
Social Sciences and Humanities

PsycALERT [American Psychological Association, Washington, DC]
Social Sciences and Humanities

PsycINFO [American Psychological Association, Washington, DC]
Social Sciences and Humanities

PTS ANNUAL REPORTS ABSTRACTS [Predicasts, Inc., Cleveland, OH]
Business/Economics—company and financial

PTS DEFENSE MARKETS AND TECHNOLOGY [Predicasts, Inc., Cleveland, OH]
Business/Economics—industry specific

PTS F&S INDEXES (FUNK & SCOTT) [Predicasts, Inc., Cleveland, OH]
Business/Economics—market research, industry, management

PTS INTERNATIONAL FORECASTS [Predicasts, Inc., Cleveland, OH]
Business/Economics—statistical/demographic data

PTS INTERNATIONAL TIME SERIES [Predicasts, Inc., Cleveland, OH]
Business/Economics—statistical/demographic data

PTS PROMT (Predicast Overview of Markets and Technology) [Predicasts, Inc., Cleveland, OH]
Business/Economics—market research, industry, management

PTS U.S. FORECASTS [Predicasts, Inc., Cleveland, OH]
Business/Economics—statistical/demographic data

PTS U.S. TIME SERIES [Predicasts, Inc., Cleveland, OH]
Business/Economics—statistical/demographic data

RELIGION INDEX [American Theological Library Association, Chicago, IL]
Social Sciences and Humanities

REMARC (U.S. Library of Congress catalog 1897–1980) [Carrollton Press, Arlington, VA]
Bibliography—Books and Monographs

RILM ABSTRACTS (Repertoire International de Litterature Musicale Abstracts) [International RILM Center, City University of New York, New York, NY]
Social Sciences and Humanities

SCISEARCH [Institute for Scientific Information, Philadelphia, PA]
Chemistry; Medicine and Biosciences; Science and Technology

SOCIAL SCISEARCH [Institute for Scientific Information, Philadelphia, PA]
Social Sciences and Humanities

SOCIOLOGICAL ABSTRACTS [Sociological Abstracts, Inc., San Diego, Ca]
Social Sciences and Humanities

SPIN (Searchable Physics Information Notices) [American Institute of Physics, New York, NY]
Science and Technology

SSIE CURRENT RESEARCH (Smithsonian Science Information Exchange Current Research) 1978-February 1982 [National Technical Information Service (NTIS), U.S. Department of Commerce, Springfield, VA]
Science and Technology

STANDARD & POOR'S CORPORATE DESCRIPTIONS [Standard & Poor's Corporation, New York, NY]
Business/Economics—company and financial

STANDARD & POOR'S NEWS [Standard & Poor's Corporation, New York, NY]
Business/Economics—company and financial; Current Affairs

STANDARDS AND SPECIFICATIONS [National Standards Association, Inc., Bethesda, MD]
Science and Technology

TELEGEN [Environment Information Center, Inc., New York, NY]
Medicine and Biosciences

TEXTILE TECHNOLOGY DIGEST [Institute of Textile Technology, Charlottesville, VA]
Science and Technology

TRADE AND INDUSTRY ASAP [Information Access Company, Belmont, CA]
Business/Economics—market research, industry, management

TRADE AND INDUSTRY INDEX [Information Access Company, Belmont, CA]
Business/Economics—market research, industry, management

TRADE OPPORTUNITIES [U.S. Department of Commerce, Washington, DC]
Business/Economics—market research, industry, management

TRADE OPPORTUNITIES WEEKLY [U.S. Department of Commerce, Washington, DC]
Business/Economics—market research, industry, management

TRADEMARKSCAN [Thomson and Thomson, Boston, MA]
Patents and Trademarks

TRIS (Transportation Research Information Service) [U.S. Department of Transportation and Transportation Research Board, Washington, DC]
Science and Technology

TSCA INITIAL INVENTORY (Toxic Substances Control Act Chemical Substance Inventory [DIALOG Information Services, Inc., Palo Alto, CA; Environmental Protection Agency, Office of Toxic Substances, Washington, DC]
Chemistry; Law and Government

ULRICH'S INTERNATIONAL PERIODICALS DIRECTORY [R. R. Bowker, New York, NY]
Directories

UNITED STATES POLITICAL SCIENCE DOCUMENTS [NASA Industrial Applications Center, University of Pittsburgh, Pittsburgh, PA]
Social Sciences and Humanities

UPI NEWS [United Press International, Inc., New York, NY]
Current Affairs

U.S. EXPORTS [U.S. Department of Commerce, Washington, DC]
Business/Economics—statistical/demographic data

U.S. PUBLIC SCHOOL DIRECTORY [National Center for Educational Statistics (NCES), Washington, DC]
Education

WASHINGTON POST INDEX [Research Publications, Inc., Woodbridge, CT]
Current Affairs

WATER RESOURCES ABSTRACTS [U.S. Department of the Interior, Washington, DC]
Energy and Environment

WATERNET [American Water Works Association, Denver, CO]
Energy and Environment

WELDASEARCH [The Welding Institute, Cambridge, England]
Science and Technology

WILEY CATALOG/ONLINE [John Wiley & Sons, Inc., New York, NY]
Bibliography—Books and Monographs

WORLD AFFAIRS REPORT [California Institute of International Affairs, Stanford, CA]
Current Affairs; Social Sciences and Humanities

WORLD ALUMINUM ABSTRACTS [American Society for Metals, Metals Park, OH]
Materials Sciences

WORLD TEXTILES [Shirley Institute, Manchester, England]
Science and Technology

ZOOLOGICAL RECORD [BioSciences Information Service, Philadelphia, PA; Zoological Society of London, London, England]
Medicine and Biosciences

MEAD DATA CENTRAL

Mead Data Central
P. O. Box 933
Dayton, OH 45401
phone:
800-227-4908 (toll-free in continental U.S.)

Sales offices in approximately 30 U.S. cities, London, and Paris.

Information services are available through a wide range of terminals and microcomputers. Telecommunications services are available through MeadNet, TELENET, or WATS.

MDC offers a private database service (see LEXTRACK™ below). Unless otherwise indicated, most MDC databases consist of full text information. Databases are classified into libraries, as follows*:

NEXIS® Library Contents
   15 newspapers
   38 magazines
   12 wire services
   48 newsletters
GOVERNMENT DOCUMENTS
   The Federal Register
   The Code of Federal Regulations
   Federal Reserve Bulletin
   Weekly Compilation of Presidential Documents
FORENSIC SERVICES DIRECTORY
INFOBANK
   The New York Times
   The Abstracts (of articles selected from the New York Times and 60+ other publications)
   Advertising and Marketing Intelligence (abstracts of selected stories from 60+ trade and professional publications)
   Deadline Data on World Affairs (geopolitical profiles of 250+ countries, states, territories, and organizations)
TODAY (summary of the day's morning and afternoon news from the New York Times)
ENCYCLOPAEDIA BRITANNICA
THE ASSOCIATED PRESS POLITICAL SERVICE
NATIONAL AUTOMATED ACCOUNTING RESEARCH SYSTEM (NAARS) [see entry]
LEXPAT™ [see entry]
EXCHANGE (financial library of reports from brokerage firms and SEC filings)
Four reference databases are now available, and a REFERENCES LIBRARY will be introduced late in 1984.

LEXIS® Library Contents
   General Federal Law Libraries

*Courtesy of Mead Data Central, Dayton, OH.

State Law Libraries
United Kingdom Law Libraries
French Law Libraries
Shepard's® Citations
Auto-Cite™ Service
Matthew Bender publications
LEXPAT™ [see entry]
American Bar Association Files
NEXIS® [see entry]
Forensic Services Directory (EXPERT)
INFOBANK and TODAY [see entry]
DIALOG (access to DIALOG® Information Services databases)
Accounting Information Library (NAARS) [see entry]
Encyclopaedia Britannica
Library of Law Reviews
Special libraries in: tax; securities; trade regulations;
international trade; patent, trademark, and copyright;
communications; labor; bankruptcy; energy; public contracts;
admiralty; military justice; Delaware corporations; Baldwin
Bankruptcy case.

NAARS™/LEXIS® LIBRARY
  NAARS™ (National Automated Accounting Research System) LIBRARY
    ANNUAL REPORT FILE (corporation reports)
    LITERATURE FILE (accounting literature)
    PROXY FILE—NAARS
  LEXIS® LIBRARY [see entry]

LEXPAT™ FILES
  ALL (All Patents)
  UTL (Utility Patents)
  DESIGN (Design Patents)
  PLANT (Plant Patents)
  CLASS (Original and Cross Reference Classifications for patents issued
  prior to the period covered by the ALLUTL file)
  INDEX (Index to the U.S. Patent Classification)
  CLMNL (Manual of Classification of the U.S. Patent and Trademark Of-
  fice)

LEXTRACK™
  Private libraries services (for litigation support, work product, etc.)

National Library of Medicine
MEDLARS® Management Section
8600 Rockville Pike
Bethesda, MD 20209
phone:
800-638-8480—Customer Service (toll-free in continental U.S. outside MD)
301-496-6193—Noncustomer Inquiries

**NATIONAL
LIBRARY OF
MEDICINE**

Information services are available through a wide range of terminals and microcomputers. Telecommunications services are available through TELENET, TYMNET, and UNINET.

NLM databases*:
  AVLINE (Audiovisuals Online)
  BIOETHICSLINE (Bioethics Online)
  CANCEREXPRESS (Current Awareness Cancer Literature)
  CANCERLIT (Cancer Literature)
  CANCERPROJ (Cancer Research Projects)
  CATLINE (Catalog Online)
  CHEMLINE (Chemical Dictionary Online)
  CLINPROT (Clinical Cancer Protocols)
  DIRLINE (Directory of Information Sources Online)
  HEALTH PLANNING AND ADMIN (Health Planning and Administration)
  HISTLINE (History of Medicine Online)
  INFORM (Information—NLM System/Databases News and Explanations)
  MEDLINE (MEDLARS Online)
  MeSH VOCABULARY FILE
  NAME AUTHORITY FILE
  POPLINE (Population Information Online)
  RTECS (Registry of Toxic Effects of Chemical Substances)
  SERLINE (Serials Online)
  TDB (Toxicology Data Bank)
  TOXLINE (Toxicology Information Online)

*Courtesy of National Library of Medicine, Bethesda, MD.

NEWSNET®

NewsNet®
945 Haverford Road
Bryn Mawr, PA 19010
phone:
800-345-1301 (toll-free in continental U.S. outside PA)
215-527-8030

Information services are available through a wide range of terminals and microcomputers. Telecommunications services are available through TELENET, TYMNET, and UNINET.

Databases are full text newsletters, PR (Press Release) Newswire, and UPI (United Press International) Newswire, although UPI is not available for interactive searching. NewsFlash, an electronic clipping service, allows you to specify up to 10 words or phrases for constant monitoring of all incoming information, including from UPI. Successful matches result in storage and displays of headlines for you the next time you sign on, at which point you may read, delete, or save them.

NewsNet® offers a private database service known as Closed User Groups (CUG). NewsNet® databases with their suppliers (in brackets) followed by topical categories*:

ACCESS REPORTS/FREEDOM OF INFORMATION [The Washington Monitor]
Government and Regulatory

ADVANCED OFFICE CONCEPTS [Advanced Office Concepts]
Office

AFRICA NEWS [Africa News Service]
International

AGRI-MARKETS DATA SERVICE [Capitol Publications, Inc.]
Farming and Food

AGRICULTURAL RESEARCH REVIEW [Lloyd Dinkins]
Farming and Food

AIR/WATER POLLUTION REPORT [Business Publishers, Inc.]
Environment

ALTMAN & WEIL REPORT TO LEGAL MANAGEMENT [Altman & Weil Publications, Inc.]
Management

ANNEX COMPUTER REPORT [Annex Holdings Corporation]
Electronics and Computers

BANK NETWORK NEWS [Bario Communications Corp.]
Finance and Accounting

BANKING REGULATOR [Reports, Inc.]
Finance and Accounting

BEHAVIOR TODAY [Atcom, Inc.]
Social Sciences

BIOTECHNOLOGY INVESTMENT OPPORTUNITIES [High Tech Publishing Company]
Investment

THE BUSINESS COMPUTER [Pik Associates, Inc.]
Electronics and Computers

BUSINESS OPPORTUNITIES AUSTRALIA [Chronicle Publications Pty, Ltd.]
International

CABLE HOTLINE [Larimi Communications Associates, Ltd.]
Public Relations

CABLENEWS [Phillips Publishing, Inc.]
Telecommunications

*Courtesy of NewsNet®, Bryn Mawr, PA.

CELLULAR RADIO NEWS [FutureComm Publications, Inc.]
Telecommunications

CHARITABLE GIVING [Walter S. Bristow III, P.C.]
Taxation

CHURCH NEWS INTERNATIONAL [Resources for Communication]
Social Sciences

COMMUNICATIONS & DISTRIBUTED RESOURCES REPORT [International Corporation]
Electronics and Computers

COMMUNICATIONS DAILY [Television Digest, Inc.]
Telecommunications

THE COMPUTER COOKBOOK [William Bates]
Electronics and Computers

THE COMPUTER COOKBOOK UPDATE [William Bates]
Electronics and Computers

COMPUTER FARMING NEWSLETTER [Lloyd Dinkins]
Farming and Food

COMPUTER MARKET OBSERVER [Auerbach Publishers, Inc.]
Electronics and Computers

CONTACTS DAILY REPORT [Larimi Communications Associates, Ltd.]
Public Relations

CONTACTS WEEKLY [Larimi Communications Associates, Ltd.]
Public Relations

CORPORATE ACQUISITIONS & DISPOSITIONS [Mark A. Stephens, Ltd.]
Taxation

CREDIT UNION REGULATOR [Reports, Inc.]
Finance and Accounting

CRITTENDEN BULLETIN [Crittenden Financing, Inc.]
Real Estate

CRITTENDEN REPORT [Crittenden Financing, Inc.]
Real Estate

DAILY INDUSTRIAL INDEX ANALYZER [News-a-tron]
Investment

DAILY METALS REPORT [News-a-tron]
Metals and Mining

DAILY PETRO FUTURES [News-a-tron]
Energy

DATA CHANNELS [Phillips Publishing, Inc.]
Telecommunications

DATACABLE NEWS [TeleStrategies Publishing, Inc.]
Telecommunications

DBS NEWS [Phillips Publishing, Inc.]
Telecommunications

DIACK NEWSLETTER [Diack, Inc.]
Health and Hospitals

EDITORS ONLY [Editors Only]
Publishing and Broadcasting

EMPLOYEE RETIREMENT PLANS [Mark A. Stephens, Ltd.]
Taxation

ENERGIES, TRENDS, CYCLES [Pat Esclavon]
Investment

ENERGY & MINERALS RESOURCES [Business Publishers, Inc.]
Energy

THE ENTREPRENEURIAL MANAGER [The Center for Entrepreneurial
Management, Inc.]
Management

EXECUTIVE INVESTING [Gryphon Asset Management Corp.]
Investment

EXECUTIVE PRODUCTIVITY [Newsletter Management Corp.]
Management

THE EXPORTER [Trade Date Reports]
International

F&S POLITICAL RISK LETTER [Frost & Sullivan, Inc.]
Politics

FARM EXPORTS [Lloyd Dinkins]
Farming and Food

FARM SOFTWARE DEVELOPMENTS [Lloyd Dinkins]
Farming and Food

THE FEARLESS TASTER [Resources for Communication]
Entertainment and Leisure

FEDERAL RESEARCH REPORT [Business Publishers, Inc.]
Research and Development

FEDERAL RESERVE WEEK [Business Publishers, Inc.]
Finance and Accounting

FEDWATCH [Money Market Services, Inc.]
Investment

FIBER/LASER NEWS [Phillips Publishing, Inc.]
Telecommunications

FIBER OPTICS AND COMMUNICATIONS NEWSLETTER [Information Gatekeepers]
Telecommunications

FIBER OPTICS AND COMMUNICATIONS WEEKLY NEWSLETTER [Information Gatekeepers]
Telecommunications

FINANCIAL MANAGEMENT ADVISOR [Newsletter Management Corp.]
Finance and Accounting

FINTEX ALL-DAY FOREIGN EXCHANGE MONITOR [Fintex, Inc.]
Finance and Accounting

FINTEX ALL-DAY U.S. MONEY MARKET MONITOR [Fintex, Inc.]
Finance and Accounting

FINTEX INTERNATIONAL ECONOMIC SUMMARIES [Fintex, Inc.]
International

FORD INVESTMENT REVIEW [Ford Investor Services]
Investment

FRAUD AND THEFT NEWSLETTER [LPS Marketing, Inc.]
Retailing

THE GOLD SHEET [National-Wide Sports Publications]
Entertainment and Leisure

GRANTS AND CONTRACTS ALERT [Capitol Publications, Inc.]
Government and Regulatory

GRANTS AND CONTRACTS WEEKLY [Capitol Publications, Inc.]
Government and Regulatory

HEALTH BENEFIT COST CONTAINMENT NEWSLETTER [Health Information Services]
Health and Hospitals

HI TECH PATENTS: DATA COMMUNICATIONS [Communications Publishing Group]
Research and Development

HI TECH PATENTS: FIBER OPTICS TECHNOLOGY [Communications Publishing Group]
Research and Development

HI TECH PATENTS: LASER TECHNOLOGY [Communications Publishing Group]
Research and Development

HI TECH PATENTS: TELEPHONY [Communications Publishing Group]
Research and Development

HOLLYWOOD HOTLINE [Eliot Stein]
Entertainment and Leisure

HOME COMPUTER NEWS [Phillips Publishing, Inc.]
Telecommunications

HOWARD RUFF'S FINANCIAL SURVIVAL REPORT [Target, Inc.]
Investment

IBM WATCH [Enterprise Information Systems, Inc.]
Electronics and Computers

IIA FRIDAY MEMO [Information Industry Association]
Publishing and Broadcasting

INSIGHT [Money Market Services, Inc.]
Investment

INTERACTIVE VIDEO TECHNOLOGY [Heartland Communications]
Electronics and Computers

INTERNATIONAL INTERTRADE INDEX [International Intertrade Index]
General Business

INTERNATIONAL PETROLEUM FINANCE [Petroleum Analysis, Ltd.]
Energy

IRS PRACTICES AND PROCEDURES [Mark A. Stephens, Ltd.]
Taxation

LAN [Information Gatekeepers]
Telecommunications

LAND USE PLANNING REPORT [Business Publishers, Inc.]
Environment

LATIN AMERICAN ENERGY REPORT [Business Publishers, Inc.]
International

LEGISLATIVE INTELLIGENCE WEEK [Communications Services, Inc.]
Politics

LINK NEWS BRIEFS [Link Resources Corp.]
Publishing and Broadcasting

LOW-PRICED STOCK ALERT [Idea Publishing Corporation]
Investment

MANAGEMENT CONTENTS PREVIEW [Management Contents]
Management

MARKET CONSENSUS ALERT [Idea Publishing Corporation]
Investment

MARKET DIGEST [Gryphon Asset Management Corp.]
Investment

MARRIAGE AND DIVORCE TODAY [Atcom, Inc.]
Social Sciences

MICRO MOONLIGHTER [J. Normal Goode]
Electronics and Computers

MINI/MICRO BULLETIN [Auerbach Publishers, Inc.]
Electronics and Computers

MODEM NOTES [Modem Notes, Inc.]
Electronics and Computers

NA HOTLINE [The Newsletter Association]
Publishing and Broadcasting

NEWSNET ACTION LETTER [NewsNet, Inc.]
Publishing and Broadcasting

NEWSNET'S ONLINE BULLETIN [NewsNet, Inc.]
Publishing and Broadcasting

NUCLEAR WASTE NEWS [Business Publishers, Inc.]
Environment

OFFICE AUTOMATION UPDATE [Newsletter Management Corp.]
Management

ON-LINE COMPUTER TELEPHONE DIRECTORY [J. A. Cambron Co., Inc.]
Telecommunications

ONLINE DATABASE REPORT [Link Resources Corp.]
Publishing and Broadcasting

PACS & LOBBIES [Amward Publications, Inc.]
Government and Regulatory

PENNY STOCK PREVIEW [Idea Publishing Corporation]
Investment

PERSONAL COMPUTERS TODAY [Phillips Publishing, Inc.]
Electronics and Computers

PETROLEUM INFORMATION INTERNATIONAL [Petroleum Information Corporation]
Energy

THE PHOTOLETTER [Photosearch International]
Publishing and Broadcasting

PR NEWSWIRE [PR Newswire Association, Inc.]
Public Relations

PUBLIC BROADCASTING REPORT [Television Digest, Inc.]
Publishing and Broadcasting

RADIONEWS [Television Digest, Inc.]
Publishing and Broadcasting

REAL ESTATE INVESTING LETTER [HBJ Newsletter Bureau]
Real Estate

RESEARCH MONITOR NEWS [National Information Service]
Research and Development

RFC NEWS SERVICE [Resources for Communication]
Social Sciences

RIA EXECUTIVE ALERT [The Research Institute of America, Inc.]
Management

ROBOTRONICS AGE NEWSLETTER [Twenty-First Century Media Communications, Inc.]
Electronics and Computers

S. KLEIN NEWSLETTER ON COMPUTER GRAPHICS [Technology & Business Communications, Inc.]
Electronics and Computers

SATELLITE NEWS [Phillips Publishing, Inc.]
Telecommunications

SATELLITE NEWS BULLETIN SERVICE [Phillips Publishing, Inc.]
Telecommunications

SEXUALITY TODAY [Atcom, Inc.]
Social Sciences

THE SEYBOLD REPORT ON OFFICE SYSTEMS [Seybold Publications, Inc.]
Office

THE SEYBOLD REPORT ON PROFESSIONAL COMPUTING [Seybold Publications, Inc.]
Electronics and Computers

THE SEYBOLD REPORT ON PUBLISHING SYSTEMS [Seybold Publications, Inc.]
Publishing and Broadcasting

THE SMALL BUSINESS TAX REVIEW [Hooksett Publishing, Inc.]
Taxation

SMR NEWS [FutureComm Publications, Inc.]
Telecommunications

SOLAR ENERGY INTELLIGENCE REPORT [Business Publishers, Inc.]
Energy

THE STANGER REPORT [Robert A. Stanger and Co.]
Investment

STOCK ADVISORS' ALERT [Idea Publishing Corporation]
Investment

TAX NOTES BULLETIN SERVICE [Tax Analysts]
Taxation

TAX NOTES INTERNATIONAL [Tax Analysts]
International

TAX NOTES TODAY [Tax Analysts]
Taxation

TAX SHELTER INSIDER [Newsletter Management Corp.]
Investment

TELECOMMUNICATIONS COUNSELOR [Voice & Data Resources, Inc.]
Telecommunications

TELEPHONE ANGLES [Telephone Angles]
Telecommunications

TELEPHONE BYPASS NEWS [TeleStrategies Publishing, Inc.]
Telecommunications

TELEPHONE NEWS [Phillips Publishing, Inc.]
Telecommunications

TELEPOINTS [Telecomputer Research]
Telecommunications

TELEVISION DIGEST [Television Digest, Inc.]
Publishing and Broadcasting

TRADE MEDIA NEWS [Larimi Communications Associates, Ltd.]
Public Relations

TRAVELWRITER MARKETLETTER [Robert Scott Milne]
Publishing and Broadcasting

TRUDE LATIMER'S STOCK TRADERS' HOTLINE [Trude Latimer]
Investment

TWO/SIXTEEN MAGAZINE [Richard H. Young]
Electronics and Computers

UNIQUE: YOUR INDEPENDENT UNIX/C ADVISOR [InfoPro Systems]
Electronics and Computers

UNITED METHODIST INFORMATION [United Methodist Communications]
Social Sciences

UPDATE/THE AMERICAN STATES [Tower Consultants Int'l, Inc.]
General Business

U.S. CENSUS REPORT [Business Publishers, Inc.]
Government and Regulatory

VIDEO WEEK [Television Digest, Inc.]
Entertainment and Leisure

VIDEONEWS [Phillips Publishing, Inc.]
Telecommunications

VIEWDATA/VIDEOTEX REPORT [Link Resources Corp.]
Publishing and Broadcasting

VIEWTEXT [Phillips Publishing, Inc.]
Telecommunications

WALL ST. MONITOR: WEEKLY MARKET DIGEST [Karen Lazarovic Publications, Inc.]
Investment

WASHINGTON CREDIT LETTER [Business Publishers, Inc.]
Finance and Accounting

WEEKLY MARKETEER [Insurance Marketing Services, Inc.]
Insurance

THE WEEKLY REGULATORY MONITOR [The Washington Monitor, Inc.]
Government and Regulatory

WILEY BOOK NEWS [John Wiley & Sons, Inc.]
Publishing and Broadcasting

WORLD ENVIRONMENT REPORT [Alexander Research & Communications, Inc.]
Environment

WORLDWIDE VIDEOTEX UPDATE [Worldwide Videotex]
Publishing and Broadcasting

SDC® Information Services
2500 Colorado Avenue
Santa Monica, CA 90406
phone:
800-421-7729 (toll-free in continental U.S. outside CA)
800-352-6689 (toll-free in CA)
213-453-6194 or
213-820-4111 x6194

Other U.S. offices:

SDC® Information Services
7929 Westpark Drive
McLean, VA 22101
phone:
800-336-3313 (toll-free in continental U.S. outside VA)
(703) 790-9850

SDC® Information Services
Suite 300 East
4801 Woodway Drive
Houston, TX 77056
phone:
(713) 840-8093

SDC®

SDC® Information Services
Burroughs Corporation
605 Third Avenue
New York, NY 10158
phone:
(212) 883-7952

Other associate offices in Australia, England, and Japan. Representative in Brazil.

Information services are available through a wide range of terminals and microcomputers. Telecommunications services are available through TELENET and TYMNET.

ORBIT® offers a private database service. ORBIT® Search Service databases with their suppliers (in brackets) followed by topical categories*:

ACCOUNTANTS [American Institute of Certified Public Accountants]
Business & Economics; Government & Legislation

APILIT [Central Abstracting & Indexing Service of the American Petroleum Institute]
Chemistry; Energy & Environment; Engineering & Electronics; Industry-Specific; Science & Technology

APIPAT [Central Abstracting & Indexing Service of the American Petroleum Institute]
Chemistry; Energy & Environment; Engineering & Electronics; Industry-Specific; Patents; Science & Technology

ASI (American Statistics Index) [Congressional Information Service, Inc.]
Government & Legislation; Multidisciplinary; Social Sciences

BANKER [Bell & Howell]
Business & Economics; Government & Legislation; Industry-Specific

BIOTECHNOLOGY [Derwent Publications, Ltd.]
Industry-Specific; Life Science; Science & Technology

CAS82/CAS77/CAS72/CAS67 [Chemical Abstracts Service of the American Chemical Society]
Chemistry; Energy & Environment; Engineering & Electronics; Patents; Science & Technology

CASSI (Chemical Abstracts Source Index) [Chemical Abstracts Service of the American Chemical Society]
Chemistry; Life Science; Science & Technology

CEH-ONLINE (Chemical Economics Handbook-Online) [SRI International]
Business & Economics; Chemistry; Science & Technology

*Courtesy of SDC Information Services, Santa Monica, CA.

CHEMDEX/CHEMDEX2/CHEMDEX3 [Chemical Abstracts Service of the American Chemical Society]
Chemistry; Science & Technology

CIN (Chemical Industry Notes) [Chemical Abstracts Service of the American Chemical Society]
Business & Economics; Chemistry; Industry-Specific

CIS [Congressional Information Service, Inc.]
Government & Legislation; Multidisciplinary; Social Sciences

COLD [Cold Regions Research and Engineering Laboratory of the U.S. Army Corps of Engineers]
Engineering & Electronics; Patents

COMPENDEX [Engineering Information, Inc]
Energy & Environment; Engineering & Electronics; Multidisciplinary; Science & Technology

CORROSION [Marcel Dekker]
Engineering & Electronics; Industry-Specific; Science & Technology

CRDS (Chemical Reactions Documentation Service) [Derwent Publications, Ltd.]
Chemistry

CRECORD (Congressional Record abstracts) [Capitol Services International]
Government & Legislation; Multidisciplinary; Social Sciences

DBI (Data Base Index) [SDC Information Services]
Multidisciplinary

EBIB (Energy Bibliography) [Gulf Publishing Company; Texas A & M University Library]
Chemistry; Energy & Environment; Science & Technology

EDB (Energy Data Base) [U.S. Department of Energy]
Chemistry; Energy & Environment; Patents; Science & Technology

EIMET (EI Engineering Meetings) [Engineering Information, Inc.]
Engineering & Electronics; Energy & Environment; Science & Technology

ENERGYLINE [EIC/Intelligence]
Energy & Environment; Science & Technology

ENVIROLINE [EIC/Intelligence]
Energy & Environment; Life Science; Social Sciences; Science & Technology

EPIA (Electric Power Industry Abstracts) [Edison Electric Institute]
Energy & Environment; Industry-Specific; Science & Technology

ERIC (Educational Resources Information Center) [ERIC Processing & Reference Facility of the National Institute of Education]
Social Sciences

FEDREG (Federal Register abstracts) [Capitol Services International]
Government & Legislation; Multidisciplinary; Social Sciences

FOREST [Forest Products Research Society]
Engineering & Electronics; Industry-Specific; Patents; Science & Technology

FSTA (Food Science and Technology Abstracts) [International Food Information Service]
Engineering & Electronics; Industry-Specific; Life Science; Patents; Science & Technology

GeoRef (Geological Reference) [The American Geological Institute]
Energy & Environment; Science & Technology

GRANTS [The Oryx Press]
Multidisciplinary; Social Sciences

INFORM [Data Courier, Inc.]
Business & Economics; Social Sciences

INSPEC [Institution of Electrical Engineers]
Engineering & Electronics; Patents; Science & Technology

LABORDOC [The International Labour Organization]
Business & Economics; Social Sciences

LC/LINE (Library of Congress catalog) [SDC Information Services]
Multidisciplinary

LISA (Library and Information Science Abstracts) [Library Association Publishing, Ltd.]
Social Sciences

MANAGEMENT [Management Contents, Inc.]
Business & Economics; Social Sciences

MDF/I (Metals Information Designations and Specifications Datafile) [American Society for Metals]
Engineering & Electronics; Industry-Specific; Science & Technology

METADEX [American Society for Metals]
Engineering & Electronics; Industry-Specific; Science & Technology

MICROSEARCH [Information, Inc.]
Business & Economics; Engineering & Electronics; Science & Technology

MONITOR (Christian Science Monitor Index) [Bell & Howell]
Business & Economics; Government & Legislation; Multidisciplinary

NDEX (Newspaper Index) [Bell & Howell]
Business & Economics; Government & Legislation; Multidisciplinary

NTIS/NTIS6469 [National Technical Information Service (NTIS) of the U.S. Department of Commerce]
Energy & Environment; Engineering & Electronics; Government & Legislation; Multidisciplinary; Patents; Science & Technology

NUC/CODES (names, addresses, and National Union Catalog Codes for libraries cited in CASSI) [SDC Information Services]
Chemistry; Engineering & Electronics; Life Science; Multidisciplinary; Science & Technology

ORBIT (ORBIT maintenance and housekeeping database) [SDC Information Services]

ORBCHEM/ORBPAT (ORBIT housekeeping database to assist searching of chemical and patent databases) [SDC Information Services]

PAPERCHEM [The Institute of Paper Chemistry]
Chemistry; Industry-Specific; Patents; Science & Technology

P/E NEWS (Petroleum/Energy Business News Index) [The Central Abstracting & Indexing Service of the American Petroleum Institute]
Business & Economics; Energy & Environment; Industry-Specific

PESTDOC/PESTDOC-II [Derwent Publications, Ltd.]
Chemistry; Energy & Environment; Industry-Specific; Life Science; Science & Technology

PIE (Pacific Islands Ecosystems) [Office of Biological Services of the U.S. Fish and Wildlife Service]
Life Science; Multidisciplinary; Social Sciences; Science & Technology

POWER [Energy Library, U.S. Department of Energy]
Energy & Environment; Engineering & Electronics; Industry-Specific; Science & Technology

PSYCINFO [The American Psychological Association, Inc.]
Life Science; Social Sciences

RINGDOC UDB/RINGDOC/RING6475 [Derwent Publications, Ltd.]
Chemistry; Industry-Specific; Life Science; Science & Technology

SAE [Society of Automotive Engineers, Inc.]
Engineering & Electronics; Industry-Specific; Science & Technology

SDF (Standard Drug File) [Derwent Publications, Ltd.]
Chemistry; Science & Technology

SPORT [Sport Information Resource Centre (SIRC)]
Life Science; Social Sciences

TROPAG [Koninklijk Instituut voor den Tropen (Royal Tropical Institute)]
Life Science; Science & Technology

TSCA PLUS (Toxic Substances Control Act file) [Office of Toxic Substances, U.S. Environmental Protection Agency]
Chemistry; Science & Technology

TULSA (petroleum abstracts) [University of Tulsa, Information Services Department]
Energy & Environment; Engineering & Electronics; Industry-Specific; Patents; Science & Technology

USCLASS (U.S. Classifications for patents) [Derwent Publications, Ltd]
Engineering & Electronics; Patents; Science & Technology

USGCA (U.S. Government Contract Awards) [Washington Representative Services]
Business & Economics; Government & Legislation; Multidisciplinary

USPA/USP77/USP70 (U.S. Patent Office files) [Derwent, Inc.]
Chemistry; Engineering & Electronics; Government & Legislation; Life Science; Multidisciplinary; Patents; Science & Technology

VETDOC UDB/VETDOC [Derwent Publications, Ltd.]
Industry-Specific; Life Science; Science & Technology

WPI/WPIL (World Patents Index) [Derwent Publications, Ltd.]
Chemistry; Engineering & Electronics; Life Science; Multidisciplinary; Patents; Science & Technology

WILSONLINEˢᴹ

WILSONLINEˢᴹ
The H. W. Wilson Company
950 University Avenue
Bronx, NY 10452
phone:
1-800-622-4002 (toll-free in continental U.S. outside NY)
212-588-8998 (collect calls accepted from NY)

Information services are available through a wide range of terminals and microcomputers. Telecommunications services are available from TELENET and TYMNET.

WILSONLINEˢᴹ databases*:

Applied Science & Technology Index
Art Index
Bibliographic Index
Biography Index
Biological & Agriculture Index
Business Periodicals Index
Book Review Digest
Cumulative Book Index
Education Index
General Science Index
Humanities Index
Index to Legal Periodicals
Library Liteature
LC MARC Database
Readers' Guide to Periodical Literature
Social Sciences Index
Subject file associated with each of the preceding databases
Journal Directory
Publishers Directory
Name Authority File

*Courtesy of H. W. Wilson Company, Bronx, NY.

Selected Sources

B

This appendix provides sources for further information on computerized retrieval. It is divided into sections, corresponding to types of sources, as follows: Textbooks and Other Monographs, Dictionaries, Periodicals, Directories, Comprehensive Database User Service, Membership Organizations, Conferences and Proceedings, and Graduate Schools of Information/Library Science. The emphasis is on sources relevant to computerized database retrieval in the United States.

Sources provided by database retrieval services and database suppliers are not listed here. In general, however, they include the following: database catalogs and guides; manuals, thesauruses and other authority lists; newsletters; training packages (beginners' manuals, workbooks, audiocassettes, computer-assisted instruction programs); courses (introductory, beginner, advanced); and low-cost practice files for training and self-assessment. Database guides, authority lists, and newsletters may be available as computerized files as well as publications. There are continuous updates for materials needed for keeping up with database and retrieval capability changes.

Sources produced by database suppliers are frequently announced in news, update, and review columns from the periodical literature (see the "Periodicals" section), while those produced by database retrieval services are more likely to be announced in their promotional literature available on request or at presentations of their products and services at conference exhibits and sessions.

Christine L. Borgman, Dineh Moghdam, and Patti K. Corbett
Effective online searching
New York, NY: Dekker, 1984

Everett H. Brenner, editor
NFAIS indexing in perspective education kit, second edition Philadelphia, PA:
National Federation of Abstracting and Information Services, 1984

**TEXTBOOKS
AND OTHER
MONOGRAPHS**

Ching-Chih Chen and Susanne Schweizer
Online bibliographic searching: a learning manual
New York, NY: Neal-Schuman Publishers, 1981

Kenneth Z. Dowlin
The electronic library: the promise and the process
New York, NY: Neal-Schuman Publishers, 1984

Emily Gallup Fayen
The online catalog: improving public access to libary materials
White Plains, NY: Knowledge Industry Publications, 1983

Emily Gallup Fayen
The era of online public access catalogs
White Plains, NY: Knowledge Industry Publications, 1983

Alfred Glossbrenner
*The complete handbook of personal computer communications: everything
you need to know to go online with the world*
New York, NY: St. Martin's Press, 1983

Carol H. Fenichel and Thomas H. Hogan
Online searching: a primer, second edition
Medford, NJ: Learned Information, 1984

Brenda Gerrie
*Online information systems: use and operating characteristics, limitations,
and design alternatives*
Arlington, VA: Information Resources Press, 1983

Elizabeth P. Hartner
An introduction to automated literature searching
New York, NY: Dekker, 1981

H. S. Heaps
Information retrieval: computational and theoretical aspects
New York, NY: Academic, 1978

W. M. Henry, J. A. Leigh, L. A. Tedd, and P. W. Williams
Online searching: an introduction
Boston, MA: Butterworth, 1980

Charles R. Hildreth
Online public access catalogs: the user interface
Dublin, OH: OCLC, 1982

Ryan E. Hoover, editor
The library and information manager's guide to online services
White Plains, NY: Knowledge Industry Publications, 1980

Ryan E. Hoover, editor
Online search strategies
White Plains, NY: Knowledge Industry Publications, 1982

Ryan E. Hoover
The executive's guide to information services
White Plains, NY: Knowledge Industry Publications, 1984

Bernard Houghton and John Convey
Online information retrieval systems: an introductory manual to principles and practices, second edition
London, England: Clive Bingley, 1984
Distributors: The Shoe String Press, Hamden, CT

Doran Howitt and Marvin I. Weinberger
Inc. Magazine's databasics: your guide to online business information
New York, NY: Garland Publishing, Aug. 1984

Bill Katz and Ruth A. Fraley, editors
Video to online reference services and the new technology
New York, NY: Haworth Press, 1983
or
same editors, title, in the following journal issue:
The Reference Librarian 1982 Fall/Winter;1(5/6)

Bill Katz and Anne Clifford, editors
Reference and online services handbook
New York, NY: Neal-Schuman Publishers, 1982

F. W. Lancaster
Information retrieval systems: characteristics, testing, and evaluation, second edition
New York, NY: John Wiley & Sons, 1979

F. W. Lancaster
Libraries and librarians in an age of electronics
Arlington, VA: Information Resources Press, 1982

F. Wilfrid Lancaster
Vocabulary control for information retrieval, second edition
Arlington, VA: Information Resources, 1985

Joann Lee
Online searching: the basics, settings, and management
Littleton, CO: Libraries Unlimited, 1983

Hugh Evison Look, editor
Electronic publishing—a snapshot of the early 1980s
Medford, NJ: Learned Information, 1983

James J. Maloney, editor
Online searching technique and management
Chicago, IL: American Library Association, 1983

Joseph R. Matthews
Public access to online catalogs: a planning guide for managers
Weston, CT: Online, 1982

Joseph R. Matthews, Gary S. Lawrence, and Douglas K. Ferguson, editors
Using online catalogs: a nationwide survey
New York, NY: Neal-Schuman, 1983

Marsha Hamilton McClintock, compiler and editor
Training users of online public access catalogs: report of a conference spon-

sored by Trinity University and the Council on Library Resources, San Antonio, Texas, January 12–14, 1983
Washington, DC: Council on Library Resources, 1983

Charles T. Meadow and Pauline Atherton Cochrane
Basics of online searching
New York, NY: John Wiley & Sons, 1981

M. Lynn Neufeld, Martha Cornog, and Inez L. Sperr, editors
Abstracting and indexing services in perspective: Miles Conrad Memorial Lectures 1969–1983
Arlington, VA: Information Resources Press, 1983

Barbara Newlin
Answers online: your guide to informational data bases
Berkeley, CA: Osborne McGraw-Hill, 1985

Roger C. Palmer
Online reference and information retrieval
Littleton, CO: Libraries Unlimited, 1983

David Raitt, editor
Introduction to online information systems
Medford, NJ: Learned Information, 1984

G. Salton and M. J. McGill
Introduction to modern information retrieval
New York, NY: McGraw-Hill, 1983

Bonnie Snow, editor
Database search aids—health sciences
Weston, CT: Online, 1982
The Search Aids series is listed in the "Directories" section

C. J. Van Rijsbergen
Information retrieval, second edition
Boston, MA: Butterworth, 1979

DICTIONARIES

Greg Byerly
Online searching: a dictionary and bibliographic guide
Littleton, CO: Libraries Unlimited, 1983

Anthony Chandor with John Graham and Robin Williamson
The Penguin dictionary of computers, second edition
Harmondsworth, England: Penguin Books, 1977

Allen Kent, Harold Lancour (Vols. 1–32), and Jay E. Dailey (Vols. 9–35), editors
Encyclopedia of library and information science, 35 vols.
New York, NY: Dekker, 1968–83

D. Longley and M. Shain
Dictionary of information technology
London: Macmillan Press, 1982

A. J. Meadows, M. Gordon, and A. Singleton
The Random House dictionary of new information technology
New York, NY: Vintage, 1982
or
A dictionary of new information technology
London, England: Kogan Page, 1982

Robert Wedgworth, editor
ALA world encyclopedia of library and information services
Chicago, IL: American Library Association, 1980

Heartsill Young, editor
The ALA glossary of library and information science
Chicago, IL: American Library Association, 1983

This section consists of periodicals (published or computerized journals, newsletters, reports, and newspapers) exhibiting significant coverage of the computerized database retrieval literature. The list is arranged by publisher.

PERIODICALS

RQ
Chicago, IL: American Library Association
Quarterly
Column:
    Databases (critical reviews of databases and software packages), edited by
    Danuta A. Nitecki

Journal of the American Society for Information Science (JASIS)
Washington, DC: American Society for Information Science
Bimonthly

Library Journal
New York, NY: R. R. Bowker
20 issues/year
Columns:
    Letters
    Calendar
    News
    News In Review (annual review of previous years' news)
    Professional Reading
    Online Data Bases (monthly), by Carol Tenopir
    Online Information & Public Libraries (5 times/year), by Tina Roose
    Reports covering major annual conferences

Journal of Fee-Based Information Services
Houston, TX: Burwell Enterprises
Bi-monthly
Provides updates for *The Directory of Fee-Based Information Services* (listed
in the "Directories" section)

Medical Reference Services Quarterly
New York, NY: Haworth Press
Quarterly
Columns:
   Online Updates: A Column for Search Analysts, by Patti K. Corbett
   Online News (section of Online Updates)

Online Hotline
Phoenix, AZ: Information Intelligence
24 issues/year
Daily updated editions online free to subscribers through the publisher
Categories:
   newsfront; people; telecommunications; library and information networks;
   new equipment and developments; new and forthcoming databases; forthcoming meetings; publications and user aids; bits, bytes, and nibbles

Online Newsletter
Phoenix, AZ: Information Intelligence
10 issues/year

Data Base Alert (See Data Base User Service in the "Comprehensive Database
User Service" section.)

IDP Report: Information and Data Base Publishing Report
White Plains, NY: Knowledge Industry Publications
Biweekly

*Electronic Publishing Review: The International Journal of the Transfer of
Published Information via Videotex and Online Media*
Medford, NJ: Learned Information
Quarterly

Online Review
Medford, NJ: Learned Information
Bimonthly
Columns:
   News (including Databases section and Information Retrieval section)
   Calendar
   Book Reviews
   Online Information Retrieval Bibliography (annually), by Donald T. Haw-
   kins
   International Comparative Price Guide to Databases Online (February and
   August issues)

Information Today [newspaper]
Medford, NJ: Learned Information
10 issues/year
Features:
   Company Profiles
   Telecommunications Hardware & Software Reviews
   Microcomputers in the Information World
   Electronic Publishing Technology & Markets

Training Course Calendar
Book Reviews
Online Services Buyers' Guide
Employment Opportunities

Online Database Report
New York, NY: LINK Resources
Available online via NewsNet®
Monthly

NFAIS Newsletter
Philadelphia, PA: National Federation of Abstracting and Information Services
Bimonthly
Sections:
NewVIEWS (opinion column)
NewPHASES (brief reports on topics of common interest)
NewPUBS (announcements of new publications)
NewDATES (calendar of national information-oriented meetings)
Product development and educational activities of NFAIS member organizations

NFAIS Trainers' Circuit Newsletter
Philadelphia, PA: National Federation of Abstracting and Information Services
Quarterly
Content:
articles, news, and "tricks of the trade" aimed at those who train users to do online searching.

Database Update
Boca Raton, FL: Newsletter Management Corporation
Monthly
Sections:
Special Report
Database Update Briefs
Media Scan (bibliography of articles in small computer popular literature)

Database: The Magazine of Database Reference and Review
Weston, CT: Online
Quarterly
Columns:
Feature articles
The Friendly User, by Lucinda D. Conger
The Linear File (a column by the publisher), by Jeff Pemberton
Chemcorner, by Ronald R. Dweitgen
Offlines, by Donna R. Dolan
Letters to the Editor (a column by the readers)
Database Search Aids Review
SDI (The Database News Section), including Database Updates, Hard-

ware/Software (by Helen A. Gordon), Peopleware, and Search Aids & Publications

Online: The Magazine of Online Information Systems
Weston, CT: Online
Bimonthly
Columns:
  Feature articles
  The Inverted File (a column by the publisher), by Jeff Pemberton
  Document Delivery, by Antoinette Walton Colbert
  Hard Copy—Reviews of Recent Writings, by Jean-Paul Emard and Helen A. Gordon
  Letters to the Editor (a column by the readers)
  Circuit News (news of local online user groups), by current chairperson of National Online Circuit (listed in the "Membership Organizations" section)
  The Printout (news from around the world of online information), including Database Updates, Hardware/Software (by Helen A. Gordon), Peopleware, and Search Aids & Publications
  New Trends and Tech, by Douglas B. Seba
  Management Focus, by Jack Borbely
  European Notes, by L. J. Anthony and Jacky Deunette

Online Chronicle
Weston, CT: Online
Available online via DIALOG® Information Retrieval Services
Updated first and third Monday each month, cumulated
Categories:
  major and general news; database updates; information utilities; education and training; search aids and publications; book reviews; meetings and conferences; classified ads; feature stories; hardware; software; tips and techniques; "Have you read . . . ?"; letters to the editor; speakers bureau

Library Hi Tech
Ann Arbor, MI: Pierian Press
Quarterly
Columns
  Printout (announcements of conferences, workshops, seminars, and academic courses)
  Conference Reports
  Book Reviews/Books Received
  Search Strategy Index (annotated bibliography of articles containing hints on searching databases and vendor systems), by Steven C. Smith
  Software Review Index (bibliography of reviews of software), by Suzana Lisanti and Rebecca Dunkle
  Database Review Index (annotated bibliography of articles on databases), by Irene Perry

Library Hi Tech News
Ann Arbor, MI: Pierian Press
11 issues/year

Sections:
New & Noteworthy
Vendor Highlights
Cooperative Networks
Vendor Watch
Printout (announcements of conferences, workshops, seminars, and academic courses)
Periodicals
New Products
Book Notes
Books Received

The following list is arranged by title. Information on publicly available databases also appears regularly in certain periodicals (see content details in the ''Periodicals'' section).

DIRECTORIES

Martha E. Williams, Laurence Lannon, and Carolyn G. Robins, compilers
Computer-Readable Databases: A Directory and Data Sourcebook
Chicago, IL: American Library Association, 1984
Annual updates

Data Base Directory (See Data Base User Service in the ''Comprehensive Database User Service'' section.)

Data Base Online Access (See Data Base User Service in the ''Comprehensive Database User Service'' section.)

Database Search Aids
Weston, CT: Online
Search aids in following areas available individually or as a set: Business & Management; Education; Electronics, Computers & Communications; Government Documents; Health Sciences; Patents
The Health Sciences search aid is listed in the ''Textbooks and Other Monographs'' section under Bonnie Snow.

Van Mayros and D. Michael Werner
Databases for Business: Profiles and Applications
Radnor, PA: Chilton Book Co., 1982

Datapro Directory of On-Line Services
Delran, NJ: Datapro Research Corporation, 1984
Monthly updates and newsletter

Helen P. Burwell, editor
The Directory of Fee-Based Information Services, second edition
Houston, TX: Burwell Enterprises, 1985
Annual, with bimonthly updates in the *Journal of Fee-Based Information Services* (listed in the ''Periodicals'' section) [directory of information brokers, many of whom search computerized databases for their clients]

David M. Abels, Kenneth R. Duzy, Rebecca G. Alden, Ruth N. Cuadra, and Judith Wanger
Directory of Online Databases
Santa Monica, CA: Cuadra Associates, Spring 1983 (complete directory), Summer 1983 (update)
Quarterly: 2 complete directories, 2 update supplements

Janet Kubalak, editor
Directory of Online Information Resources
Kensington, MD: CSG Press, 1982
Semiannual updates

Barry W. Champany and Sharon Modrick Hotz, editors
Document Retrieval: Resources and Services
San Francisco, CA: The Information Store, 1982 [directory of document suppliers]

John Schmittroth, Jr., editor
Encyclopedia of Information Systems and Services, sixth edition
Detroit, MI: Gale, 1985

Sharon Zarozny and Monica Horner
The Federal Data Base Finder: A Directory of Free and Fee-Based Data Bases and Files Available from the Federal Government
Potomac, MD: Information USA, 1984

Guide to Online Databases
Boca Raton, FL: Newsletter Management Corporation, 1983 [replaced by Database Update—listed in the "Periodicals" section under Newsletter Management Corporation]

Information Industry Market Place: An International Directory of Information Products and Services
New York, NY: R. R. Bowker, 1982
Annual

International Comparative Price Guide to Databases Online
Online Review 1984 Feb;8(1):105–12
Updates in February and August issues of *Online Review* (listed in the "Periodicals" section)

Mike Edelhard and Owen Davies
Omni Online Database Directory
New York, NY: Macmillan, 1983

James L. Hall and Marjorie J. Brown
Online Bibliographic Databases: A Directory and Sourcebook, third edition
London, England: Aslib, 1983
Distributors in U. S. and Canada: Gale Research Company, Detroit, MI.

J. B. Deunette and L. C. Dibb, editors
Online Database
London, England: Aslib, 1983
Distributors in U. S. and Canada: Gale Research Company, Detroit, MI.

John Schmittroth, Jr., and Doris Morris Maxfield, editors
Online Database Search Services Directory, first edition
Detroit, MI: Gale, 1984

R&D Database Handbook: A Worldwide Guide to Key Scientific and Technical Databases
Englewood, NJ: Technical Insights, Nov. 1984
Annual updates

Jay M. Shafritz and Louise Alexander
*The Reston Dictionary of On-Line Databases: Your Computer's Phone Book
(A Travel Guide to the World of Information that can be Called Up on any
Computer)*
Reston, VA: Reston, 1984

*UNINET the Right Connection: A Directory of On-Line
Databases 1984*
Santa Monica, CA: Cuadra Associates, 1983

COMPREHENSIVE DATABASE USER SERVICE

Data Base User Service
White Plains, NY: Knowledge Industry Publications
Administered in cooperation with American Society for Information Science
Service components:
    Data Base Directory (annual publication)—Louise Moore, executive ed.,
    and Terry Mollo, managing ed.
    Data Base Alert (monthly newsletter with semiannual index and binder)
    Data Base Online Access (online directory)
    Data Base Hotline (toll-free hotline to editors of the service)

MEMBERSHIP ORGANIZATIONS

Organizations in this section are concerned with information retrieval, as well as other aspects of information processing such as computerization, library services, and databases.

The following organizations offering individual memberships are listed in this section (each has local area chapters located throughout the United States):

American Association of Law Libraries (AALL)

American Library Association (ALA)

American Society for Information Science (ASIS)

Association for Computing Machinery (ACM)

Medical Library Association (MLA)

Special Libraries Association (SLA)

online user groups (see National Online Circuit in the next list)

The following organizations offering institutional memberships are listed in this section:

Bibliographic Center for Research (BCR), Rocky Mountain Region

Cooperative Library Agency for Systems and Services (CLASS)

National Online Circuit (NOC)

National Federation of Abstracting and Information Services (NFAIS)

BCR and CLASS are library networks whose membership consists of libraries in certain geographic regions of the United States, and which exist primarily to facilitate resource-sharing. Through participation in networks, libraries are able to offer broader and more economical services than each could offer separately. By contracting for retrieval services through these nonprofit networks, libraries can take advantage of group rates and discounts. BCR and CLASS are authorized by major retrieval services to conduct seminars and workshops throughout their regions, and provide consultation on their use.

American Association of Law Libraries (AALL)
53 West Jackson Blvd.
Chicago, IL 60604
312-939-4764

Membership Classification:
    Individual Active
    Institutional
    Individual Associate
    Institutional Associate
    Sustaining
    Student

Publications initiated or sponsored by AALL (*indicates publication included in membership benefits):
    *AALL Newsletter
    AALL Publications Series
    Biographical Directory of Law Librarians
    Current Law Index (in cooperation with Information Access Corp.)
    Current Publications in Legal and Related Fields
    *Directory of Law Libraries
    Index to Foreign Legal Periodicals
    *Law Library Journal
    Recruitment Checklist

Special Interest Sections:
    Academic Law Libraries
    Automation and Scientific Development
    Contemporary Social Problems
    Government Documents
    Micrographics and Audio/Visual

On-Line Bibliographic Services
Private Law Libraries
Readers' Services
State, Court and County Law Libraries
Technical Services

American Library Association (ALA)
50 East Huron St.
Chicago, IL 60611
312-944-6780

Membership Classification:
Regular First Year
Regular Renewing
Student
Non-Salaried, Inactive, or Retired Librarians, or Librarians with Salary of
Less than $6000 Per Annum
Foreign Librarians
Trustee and Associate

Publications (*indicates publication included in membership benefits):
*American Libraries (11 issues per year)
*ALA Handbook of Organization
Computer-Readable Databases: a Directory and Data Sourcebook (annual updates)—listed in the "Directories" section
Publications of special interest to practitioners, scholars, teachers, and students of library and information science in categories of public services, children's services and literature, technical services, library history, administration and management, and reference (ALA publication listed in the "Textbooks and Other Monographs" section under Maloney; ALA publications listed in the "Dictionaries" section under Wedgworth and Young)

Divisions (followed by publications included in respective division membership benefits):
Public Library Association (PLA)
Public Libraries (quarterly journal)
Association of College and Research Libraries (ACRL)
College & Research Libraries (bimonthly journal)
C&RL News (11 issues per year)
Association of Specialized and Cooperative Library Agencies (ASCLA)
Interface (quarterly newsletter)
American Association of School Librarians (AASL)
School Library Media Quarterly (journal)
Young Adult Services Division (YASD)
Top of the News (quarterly journal)
Association for Library Service to Children (ALSC)
Top of the News (quarterly journal)
ALSC Newsletter (semiannual)
Resources and Technical Services Division (RTSD)
Library Resources & Technical Services (quarterly journal)

RTSD Newsletter (bimonthly)
Library Administration and Management Association (LAMA)
LAMA Newsletter (quarterly)
Reference and Adult Services Division (RASD)
RQ (quarterly journal)—listed in the "Periodicals" section
RASD Update (issued periodically)
American Library Trustee Association (ALTA)
The Public Library Trustee (issued periodically)
Library and Information Technology Association (LITA)
Information Technology and Libraries (quarterly)
LITA Newsletter (3 issues per year)

American Society for Information Science
(ASIS [pronounced aiśis])
1010 Sixteenth St., N.W.
Washington, DC 20036
202–659–3644

Membership Classification:
  Regular
  Student receiving ASIS Bulletin
  Student receiving ASIS Journal
  Student receiving both ASIS publications

Publications (*indicates publication included in membership benefits):
  Annual Review of Information Science and Technology (ARIST)
  *ASIS Handbook & Directory (annually)
  *ASIS News (monthly)
  *Bulletin of the American Society for Information Science (bimonthly)
  Data Base Alert (monthly)—published in cooperation with ASIS; listed in
  the "Comprehensive Database User Service" section
  Data Base Directory (annually)—published in cooperation with ASIS;
  listed in the "Comprehensive Database User Service" section
  Information Science Abstracts (ISA) (bimonthly)
  *Journal of the American Society for Information Science (bimonthly)—
  listed in the "Periodicals" section
  *Proceedings of ASIS Annual Meetings
Data Base User Service—administered in cooperation with ASIS; listed in the
"Comprehensive Database User Service" section
Special Interest Groups (SIGs) (SIG newsletter included in respective SIG
membership benefits):
  Arts and Humanities (AH)
  Automated Language Processing (ALP)
  Automated Office of the Future (AOF)
  Behavioral and Social Sciences (BSS)
  Biological and Chemical Information Systems (BC)
  Classification Research (CR)
  Community Information Services (CIS)
  Computerized Retrieval Services (CRS)

Education for Information Science (ED)
Energy and Environment Information (EEI)
Foundations of Information Science (FIS)
Information Analysis and Evaluation (IAE)
Information Generation and Publishing (PUB)
Information Services to Education (ISE)
International Information Issues (III)
Law and Information Technology (LAW)
Library Automation and Networks (LAN)
Management (MGT)
Medical Records (MED)
Numeric Data Bases (NDB)
Public-Private Interface (PPI)
Storage and Retrieval Technology (SRT)
Technology, Information, and Society (TIS)
User Online Interaction (UOI)

Association for Computing Machinery (ACM)
P.O. Box 12115
Church Street Station
New York, NY 10249
or
11 West 42nd Street
New York, NY 10036
212–869–7440

Membership Classification:
  Voting
  Associate
  Student
  Other special categories

Publications (*indicates publication included in membership benefits):
   Journal of the ACM (quarterly)
   Computing Surveys (quarterly)
   Computing Reviews (monthly)
   **Communications of the ACM* (monthly)
   Mathematical Software (quarterly)
   Database Systems (quarterly)
   Programming Languages and Systems (quarterly)
   Graphics (quarterly)
   Office Information Systems (quarterly)
   Computer Systems (quarterly)

Special Interest Groups (SIGs) (SIG newsletter included in respective SIG
membership benefits):

  Automata and Computability Theory (SIGACT)
  APL (SIGAPL)
  Computer Architecture (SIGARCH)

Artificial Intelligence (SIGART)
Business Data Processing and Management (SIGBDP)
Biomedical Computing (SIGBIO)
Computers and the Physically Handicapped (SIGCAPH) (newsletter includes print, cassette, or both print and cassette editions)
Computers and Society (SIGCAS)
Computer and Human Interaction (SIGCHI)
Data Communication (SIGCOMM)
Computer Personnel Research (SIGCPR)
Computer Science Education (SIGCSE)
Computer Uses in Education (SIGCUE)
Design Automation (SIGDA)
Documentation (SIGDOC)
Computer Graphics (SIGGRAPH)
Information Retrieval (SIGIR)
Mathematical Programming (SIGMAP)
Measurement & Evaluation (SIGMETRICS)
Microprogramming (SIGMICRO)
Management of Data (SIGMOD)
Numerical Mathematics (SIGNUM)
Office Automation (SIGOA)
Operating Systems (SIGOPS)
Personal Computing (SIGPC)
Programming Languages (SIGPLAN)
    SIGPLAN Tech. Comm. on Ada (SIGPLAN-AdaTEC)
    SIGPLAN Tech. Comm. on Fortran (SIGPLAN-FORTEC)
Security, Audit and Control (SIGSAC)
Symbolic & Algebraic Manipulation (SIGSAM)
Simulation (SIGSIM)
Small Computing Systems and Applications (SIGSMALL)
Software Engineering (SIGSOFT)
University and College Computing Services (SIGUCCS)

Bibliographic Center for Research (BCR), Rocky Mountain Region
1777 South Bellaire
Suite G-150
Denver, CO 80222
303–691–0550

BCR is a library network (see introduction to this section)

Cooperative Library Agency for Systems and Services (CLASS)
1415 Koll Circle
Suite 101
San Jose, CA 95112
408–289–1756

CLASS is a library network (see introduction to this section)

Medical Library Association (MLA)
919 N. Michigan Ave., Suite 3208
Chicago, IL 60611
312–266–2456

Membership Classification:
  Regular
  Associate
  Emeritus
  Student
  Life
  Sustaining
  Institutional
  Elective (Honorary, Fellows)

Publications (*indicates publication included in membership benefits)
  *Bulletin of the Medical Library Association (quarterly)
  Bulletin Cumulative Indexes
  Current Catalog Proof Sheets (weekly)
  *Directory of the Medical Library Association (annually)
  Index to Audiovisual Serials in the Health Sciences (quarterly)
  *MLA News (10 per year, Jun./Jul. and Nov./Dec. combined issues)
  MLA Annual Conference Proceedings
  Individual publications pertaining to medical librarianship

National Federation of Abstracting and Information Services
(NFAIS [pronounced enface])
112 South 16th St.
Philadelphia, PA 19102
215–563–2406

Institutional Membership only (institutional members include retrieval services, database suppliers, and membership organizations)

Publications:
  NFAIS Newsletter (bimonthly)—listed in the "Periodicals" section
  NFAIS Trainers' Circuit Newsletter (quarterly)—listed in the "Periodicals" section
  NFAIS Membership Directory (biannually)
  Proceedings of NFAIS Annual Conferences
  Individual research reports and other publications, including compilations of key papers, special reports, education kits, information resource guides, and career guides (NFAIS publication listed in the "Textbook and Other Monographs" section under Brenner)

National Online Circuit (NOC)
No official standing headquarters. Chairperson of NOC
appointed for yearly term. For information, contact:
Online, Inc. (publisher of journals Online and Database)
11 Tannery Lane
Weston, CT 06883

Institutional Members only (local online user groups in the United States)
Publications:

> *National Online Circuit Directory,* fourth revised edition, September 1984
> (lists 75 local user groups within seven U.S. regions)

Special Libraries Association (SLA)
235 Park Avenue South
New York, NY 10003
212-477-9250

Membership Classification:
  Member
  Associate
  Student
  Retired

Publications (*indicates publication included in membership benefits)
  Special Libraries (quarterly)
  SpeciaList (monthly newsletter)
  Who's Who in Special Libraries
  Publications in the areas of management techniques, library technology,
  bibliographies and directories, and theories and practices of special librar-
  ianship

Divisions (bulletin or newsletter included in respective Division membership
benefits):
  Advertising & Marketing
  Aerospace
  Biological Sciences
  Business and Finance
  Chemistry
  Education
  Engineering
  Environmental Information
  Food & Nutrition
  Geography and Map
  Information Technology
  Insurance and Employee Benefits
  Library Management
  Metals/Materials
  Military Librarians
  Museums, Arts & Humanities
  Natural Resources
  Newspaper
  Nuclear Science
  Petroleum & Energy Resources
  Pharmaceutical
  Physics-Astronomy-Mathematics
  Picture
  Public Utilities

Publishing
Science-Technology
Social Science
Telecommunications
Transportation

Most of the preceding organizations hold national conferences, conferences sponsored by SIGs (Special Interest Groups) of these organizations, and local and regional conferences. They announce their conferences through their publications and publish or arrange to publish the proceedings.

CONFERENCES AND PROCEEDINGS

Annual conferences sponsored by publications:

National Online Meeting
Sponsored by the journal *Online Review*
The publisher, Learned Information (Medford, NJ), publishes proceedings titled: *National online meeting proceedings—1983* [*1984, 1985,* and so on]

Online '83 ['84, '85, and so on]
Sponsored by Online, publisher of the journals *Database* and *Online*
The publisher, Online (Weston, CT), publishes executive briefs to the proceedings titled: *Online '83* [*'84, '85,* and so on] conference proceedings

References to published proceedings, including references to selected papers, of five 1983 annual conferences are listed in the "Recent Readings" section under American Society for Information Science, Association for Computing Machinery Special Interest Group on Information Retrieval, National Federation of Abstracting and Information Services, National Online Meeting, and Online '83.

The following are graduate information/library science schools in the United States accredited by the American Library Association, Chicago, IL, March 1984. The list is arranged alphabetically by state.

GRADUATE SCHOOLS OF INFORMATION/ LIBRARY SCIENCE

University of Alabama
Graduate School of Library Service
University, AL 35486
(205) 348-4610

University of Arizona
Graduate Library School
Tucson, AZ 85721
(602) 626-3565

University of California, Berkeley
School of Library and Information Studies
Berkeley, CA 94720
(415) 642-1464

University of California, Los Angeles
Graduate School of Library and Information Science
Los Angeles, CA 90024
(213) 825-4351

San Jose State University
Division of Library Service
San Jose, CA 95192
(408) 277-2292

University of Southern California
School of Library and Information Management
Los Angeles, CA 90089-0031
(213) 743-2548

University of Denver
Graduate School of Librarianship and Information Management
Denver, CO 80208
(303) 753-2557

Southern Connecticut State University
School of Library Science and Instructional Technology
New Haven, CT 06515
(203) 397-4532

Catholic University of America
School of Library and Information Science
Washington, DC 20064
(202) 635-5085

Florida State University
School of Library and Information Studies
Tallahassee, FL 32306
(904) 644-5775

University of South Florida
Graduate Department of Library, Media and Information Studies
Tampa, FL 33620
(813) 974-3520

Atlanta University
School of Library and Information Studies
Atlanta, GA 30314
(404) 681-0251, ext. 230

Emory University
Division of Library and Information Management
Atlanta, GA 30322
(404) 329-6840

University of Hawaii
Graduate School of Library Studies
Honolulu, HA 96822
(808) 948-7321

University of Chicago
Graduate Library School
Chicago, IL 60637
(312) 962-8272

University of Illinois
Graduate School of Library and Information Science
1407 West Gregory, 410 DKH
Urbana, IL 61801
(217) 333-3280

Northern Illinois University
Department of Library Science
DeKalb, IL 60115
(815) 753-1733

Rosary College
Graduate School of Library and Information Science
River Forest, IL 60305
(312) 366-2490

Ball State University
Department of Library and Information Science
Muncie, IN 47306
(317) 285-5900 or 5901

Indiana University
School of Library and Information Science
Bloomington, IN 47405
(812) 335-2848

University of Iowa
School of Library and Information Science
Iowa City, IA 52242
(319) 353-3644

University of Kentucky
College of Library and Information Science
Lexington, KY 40506-0027
(606) 257-8876

Louisiana State University
School of Library and Information Science
Baton Rouge, LA 70803
(504) 388-3158

University of Maryland
College of Library and Information Services
College Park, MD 20742
(301) 454-5441

Simmons College
Graduate School of Library and Information Science
Boston, MA 02115
(617) 738-2225

University of Michigan
School of Library Science
Ann Arbor, MI 48109-1346
(313) 764-9376

Wayne State University
Division of Library Science
Detroit, MI 48202
(313) 577-1825

University of Minnesota
Library School
117 Pleasant St., S.E.
Minneapolis, MN 55455
(612) 373-6100

University of Mississippi
Graduate School of Library and Information Science
University, MS 38677
(601) 232-7440

University of Southern Mississippi
School of Library Service
Hattiesburg, MS 39406
(601) 266-4228

University of Missouri, Columbia
School of Library and Informational Science
Columbia, MO 65211
(314) 882-4546

Rutgers University
School of Communication, Information and Library Studies
New Brunswick, NJ 08903
(201) 932-7917

Columbia University
School of Library Service
New York, NY 10027
(212) 280-2291

Long Island University, C.W. Post Center
Palmer School of Library and Information Science
Greenvale, NY 11548
(516) 299-2855 or 2856

State University of New York, Albany
School of Library and Information Science
Albany, NY 12222
(518) 455-6288

State University of New York at Buffalo
School of Information and Library Studies
Buffalo, NY 14260
(716) 636-2411

Pratt Institute
Graduate School of Library and Information Science
Brooklyn, NY 11205
(212) 636-3702

Queens College, City University of New York
Graduate School of Library and Information Studies
Flushing, NY 11367
(212) 520-7194

St. John's University
Division of Library and Information Science
Jamaica, NY 11439
(212) 990-6161, ext. 6200

Syracuse University
School of Information Studies
Syracuse, NY 13210
(315) 423-2911

University of North Carolina
School of Library Science
Chapel Hill, NC 27514
(919) 962-8366

University of North Carolina at Greensboro
Department of Library Science/Educational Technology
Greensboro, NC 27412
(919) 379-5100

North Carolina Central University
School of Library Science
Durham, NC 27707
(919) 683-6485

Case Western Reserve University
Matthew A. Baxter School of Information and Library Science
Cleveland, OH 44106
(216) 368-3500

Kent State University
School of Library Science
Kent, OH 44242
(216) 672-2782

University of Oklahoma
School of Library Science
Norman, OK 73019
(405) 325-3921

Clarion University
College of Library Science
Clarion, PA 16214
(814) 226-2271

Drexel University
College of Information Studies
Philadelphia, PA 19104
(215) 895-2474

University of Pittsburgh
School of Library and Information Science
Pittsburgh, PA 15260
(412) 624-5230

University of Rhode Island
Graduate Library School
Kingston, RI 02881
(401) 792-2947

University of South Carolina
College of Library and Information Science
Columbia, SC 29208
(803) 777-3858

University of Tennessee, Knoxville
Graduate School of Library and Information Science
Knoxville, TN 37996-4330
(615) 974-2148

Vanderbilt University, George Peabody College for Teachers
Department of Library and Information Science
Nashville, TN 37203
(615) 322-8050

North Texas State University
School of Library and Information Sciences
Denton, TX 76203
(817) 565-2445

University of Texas at Austin
Graduate School of Library and Information Science
Austin, TX 78712-7576
(512) 471-3821

Texas Woman's University
School of Library Science
Denton, TX 76204
(817) 387-2418

Brigham Young University
School of Library and Information Sciences
Provo, UT 84602
(801) 378-2977

University of Washington
Graduate School of Library and Information Science
Seattle, WA 98195
(206) 543-1794

University of Wisconsin-Madison
Library School
Madison, WI 53706
(608) 263–2900

University of Wisconsin-Milwaukee
School of Library and Information Science
Milwaukee, WI 53201
(414) 963–4707

Selected Readings

C

This appendix contains references to selected feature articles and opinion papers from the periodical literature and selected papers from four conferences. Periodical sources include those listed in the "Periodicals" and "Organizations" sections of Appendix B, as well as additional sources covering the library, computer, scientific, technical, medical, legal, and business literature. References are arranged by first author except for references to conference papers, which are arranged primarily by conference organization and secondarily by first author. If the cited document contains end-references, the number of references is given.

References to news items, announcements of products and services, book reviews, conference reports, database and software package reviews, and ongoing bibliographies are too numerous to be cited here. These appear in newsletters, reports, newspapers, and journal columns (cited in the "Periodicals" section of Appendix B), issues of which may be scanned for items of interest.

American Society for Information Science
Raymond T. Vondran, Anne Caputo, Carol Wasserman, and Richard A. V. Diener, editors
Edmond J. Sawyer, conference chairman
Productivity in the information age
Proceedings of the 46th ASIS Annual Meeting, 1983, Volume 20, Washington, DC, October 2–6, 1983
White Plains, NY: Knowledge Industry Publications, 1983
95 papers
Selected Papers:
   Mary E. Bongiorno. *On the way to an online catalog.* Pp. 172-6. [4 references]

Christine L. Borgman. *Performance effects of a user's mental model of an information retrieval system.* Pp. 121-4. [12 references]

Charles E. Hansen and Wesley L. Tennant. *Integrating multiple numeric data sources into a single online system: the Energy Data and Projections System.* Pp. 69-75.

Donald L. Layman. *Information literature and educational productivity.* Pp. 309-12. [13 references]

Richard S. Marcus. *Computer-assisted search planning and evaluation.* Pp. 19-21. [7 references]

Karen Markey. *Favorable experiences with online catalog features from the perspective of library patrons and staff.* Pp. 161-6 [11 references]

Roberta Maxwell. *Measured benefits of an SDI program in a corporate environment.* Pp. 99-100.

Charles T. Meadow. *Cost-benefit of some computer aided training systems.* Pp. 303-7. [8 references]

Barbara Meiser. *The challenge of relevant service—information professionals in the era of productivity.* Pp. 76-9. [4 references]

Lawrence G. Mondschein. *Factors involved in the enhancement of the SDI.* Pp. 92-8. [4 references]

Klaus Obermeier. *Expert systems—enhancement of productivity?* Pp. 9-13. [23 references]

John H. Schneider and Dianne E. Tingley. *Use of group SDI (CANCER-GRAMS) and a current-awareness database (CANCEREXPRESS) as model information systems designed to increase productivity of technical staff.* Pp. 101-4.

Jacque-Lynne A. Schulman. *Automated patent searching—application of technology.* Pp. 252-4. [1 reference]

Bruce A. Shuman. *Interactive availability: DIALOG, ORBIT, and BRS under scrutiny.* Pp. 136-8.

Peter J. Vigil. *Psychological factors for online education and productivity.* Pp. 129-31. [14 references]

Cathleen M. Anderson
BRS comments on "After Dark" and "Knowledge Index" [letter]
Online 1984 Jan;8(1):64

Verl A. Anderson
Simultaneous remote searching: the system and the reality.
Library Hi Tech 1984;2(2):61-4. [7 references]

David Andrews
Legal information retrieval: have they got it right?
American Bar Association Journal 1983 Dec;69:1865-7

Arthur A. Antony
Registry numbers on CA SEARCH: four vendor interpretations.
Database 1983 Aug;6(3):76-80. [13 references]

Margaret Armstrong and Betty Costa
Computer cat at Mountain View Elementary School.
Library Hi Tech 1983 Winter;1(3):47–52. [10 references]

Linda Arret
Can online catalogs be too easy?
American Libraries 1985 Feb;16(2):118–20. [4 references]

Association for Computing Machinery Special Interest Group on Information
    Retrieval, in cooperation with: American Society for Information Science,
    Gesellschaft für Informatik, and British Computer Society-Information
    Retrieval Group
Jennifer J. Kuehn, editor
Michael J. McGill, chairperson
Research and development in information retrieval
Sixth Annual International ACM SIGIR Conference, a publication of the
    Special Interest Group on Information Retrieval, 1983 Summer, Vol. 17,
    No. 4, hosted by: National Library of Medicine, Bethesda, MD, June
    6–8, 1983
New York, NY: Association for Computing Machinery, 1983
28 papers
Selected Papers:
    Madeleine Bates and Robert J. Bobrow. *Information retrieval using a
        transportable natural language interface.* Pp. 81–6. [20 references]

    Gerald DeJong. *Artificial intelligence implications for information re-
        trieval.* Pp. 10–7. [37 references]

    V. J. Geller and M. E. Lesk. *User interfaces to information systems: choices
        vs. commands.* Pp. 130–5. [14 references]

    Jose-Marie Griffiths and Donald W. King. *An approach to enhancement
        of statistical survey databases.* Pp. 239–45. [5 references]

    Karen Kukich. *Knowledge-based report generation: a technique for auto-
        matically generating natural language reports from databases.* Pp. 246–
        50. [15 references]

    Michael Lebowitz. *Intelligent information systems.* Pp. 25–30. [18 refer-
        ences]

    A. S. Pollitt. *End user touch searching for cancer therapy literature—a rule
        based approach.* Pp. 136–45. [24 references]

    G. Salton. *Some research problems in automatic information retrieval.* Pp.
        252–65. [48 references]

Linda Arret
Can online catalogs be too easy?
American Libraries 1985 Feb; 16(2): 118–20. [4 references]

Steven D. Atkinson
Paragraph qualification: a search approach with BRS/Search system features.
Online 1983 Jan;7(1):39–47

Steven D. Atkinson and Donna R. Dolan
A search of research studies in online databases.
Online 1983 Mar;7(2):51–63. [3 references]

Steve Atkinson
New royalty charges penalize database browsers says writer [letter]
Online 1984 May;8(3):4,73

Ethel Auster and Stephen B. Lawton
Search interview techniques and information gain as antecedents of user sat-
    isfaction with online bibliographic retrieval.
Journal of the American Society for Information Science 1984 Mar;35(2):90–
    103. [27 references]

Ethel Auster
User satisfaction with the online negotiation interview: contemporary concern
    in traditional perspective.
RQ 1983 Fall;23(1):47–56. [91 references]

Roger S. Bagnall and John B. Hench
Man versus machine: are we prepared for the technological revolution in
    scholarly research?
Change 1983 Jul/Aug;15(5):38–42

Alberta S. Bailey
Save time and money with a consolidated database update file.
Online 1983 Mar;7(2):65–7

Carole A. Baker
COLLEAGUE: a comprehensive online medical library for the end user.
Medical Reference Services Quarterly 1984 Winter;3(4):13–26

John M. Barnard, Michael F. Lynch, and Stephen M. Welford
Computer storage and retrieval of generic chemical structures in patents. 6.
    An interpreter program for the generic description language GENSAL.
Journal of Chemical Information and Computer Science 1984 May;24(2):66–
    71. [24 references]

Marcia J. Bates
The fallacy of the perfect thirty-item online search.
RQ 1984 Fall;24(1):43–50. [11 references]

Christopher A. Bean
Softerm and its use in online searching.
Online 1984 Sep;8(5):52–6. [2 references]

Alison M. Belna, Jeanne L. Spala, and Richard W. Stark
Olympic Information in the SPORT database.
Database 1984 Aug;7(3):20–6

Lionel M. Bernstein and Robert E. Williamson
Testing of a natural language retrieval system for a full text knowledge base.

Journal of the American Society for Information Science 1984 Jul;35(4):235–47. [5 references]

John Berry
Intermediaries: our tough new job [editorial]
Library Journal 1984 May 1;109(8):834

Phil Bertoni
Nothing artificial please [artificial intelligence]
Popular Computing 1984 Jan;3(3):107–8,110

David C. Blair and M. E. Maron
An evaluation of retrieval effectiveness for a full-text document-retrieval system
Communications of the ACM 1985 Mar; 28(3):289–99. [9 references]

Richard W. Blood
Evaluation of online searches.
RQ 1983 Spring;22(3):266–77. [11 references]

Jeff Blyskal
Technology for technology's sake?
Forbes 1983 May 9;131(10):196,200,203–4

Margaret J. Bodley
Family Resources Database: a system design to meet information needs in an emerging discipline
Online Review 1984 Feb;8(1):41–56

Christine L. Borgman
Psychological research in human-computer interaction.
Annual Review of Information Science and Technology 1984;19:34–64. [168 references]

Jak Boumans
Dutch treat for U.S. database producers.
Online 1984 Nov;8(6):32–5. [4 references]

Bert R. Boyce, David Martin, Barbara Francis, and MaryEllen Sievert
A drill and practice program for online retrieval.
Journal of the American Society for Information Science 1984 Mar;35(2):129–34. [3 references]

Bert R. Boyce and Beth Carlin
Online and offline print costs in MEDLINE.
Bulletin of the Medical Library Association 1984 Apr;72(2):177–9. [8 references]

Alice A. Brand and Lenora A. Kinzie
A comparison of online access to psychoanalytic literature.
Database 1984 Feb;7(1):54–63. [13 references]

Fern Brody and Maureen Lambert
Alternative databases for anthropology searching.
Database 1984 Feb;7(1):28–33

Robert E. Buntrock
Graphics files, personal computers, endusers, pot pourri . . .
Database 1984 Feb;7(1):99–100

Robert E. Buntrock
Cost effectiveness of on-line searching of chemical information: an industrial
  viewpoint.
Journal of Chemical Information and Computer Science 1984 May;24(2):54–
  7. [16 references]

Nancy Calabretta
Educating the online search requester: a checklist.
Medical Reference Services Quarterly 1983 Winter;2(4):31–9. [12 references]

Susan Casbon
Online searching with a microcomputer—getting started.
Online 1983 Nov;7(6):42–6. [16 references]

John Chambers
A scientist's view of print versus online.
Aslib Proceedings 1984 Jul/Aug;36(7/8):309–16. [1 reference]

Janet Chisman and William Treat
An online reference system.
RQ 1984 Summer;23(4):438–45. [2 references]

Anne Clarke and Blaise Cronin
Expert systems and library/information work.
Journal of Librarianship 1983 Oct;15(4):277–92. [24 references]

James W. Clasper
Robotics information.
Database 1984 Dec;7(4):39–42

Cyril Cleverdon.
Optimizing convenient online access to bibliographic databases.
Information Services & Use 1984 Apr;4(1/2):37–47. [13 references]

Pauline A. Cochrane
Can a standard for an online common command language be developed?
Online 1983 Jan;7(1):36–7.

Pauline Atherton Cochrane
Modern subject access in the online age [American Libraries' first continuing
  education course]
American Libraries 1984 Feb;15(2):80–3. [5 references]

Pauline Atherton Cochrane
Modern subject access in the online age [American Libraries' first continuing
   education course: lesson two]
American Libraries 1984 Mar;15(3):145–50. [8 references]

Pauline Atherton Cochrane
Modern subject access in the online age [American Libraries' first continuing
   education course: lesson three]
American Libraries 1984 Apr;15(4):250–5. [4 references]

Pauline Atherton Cochrane
Modern subject access in the online age [American Libraries' first continuing
   education course: lesson four]
American Libraries 1984 May;15(5):336–9.

Pauline Atherton Cochrane, with Charles Bourne, Tamas Doczkocs, Jeffrey
   C. Griffith, F. Wilfrid Lancaster, William R. Nugent, and Barbara M.
   Preschel
Modern subject access in the online age [American Libraries' first continuing
   education course: lesson five]
American Libraries 1984 Jun;15(6):438–43. [2 references]

Pauline Atherton Cochrane
Modern subject access in the online age [American Libraries' first continuing
   education course: lesson six]
American Libraries 1984 Jul/Aug;15(7):527–9. [8 references]

Antoinette Walton Colbert
Payment methods for documents can make a difference in delivery times.
Online 1983 Jul;7(4):78–79

Lucinda D. Conger
Keeping up.
Database 1983 Feb;6(1):69–76

Lucinda D. Conger
Limiting to major [searching weighted terms]
Database 1984 Aug;6(3):72–5

Lucinda D. Conger
Date searching.
Database 1983 Dec;6(4):86–93

Lucinda D. Conger
Types of databases—some definitions.
Database 1984 Feb;7(1):94–5

Lucinda D. Conger
Review of the year online: 1983.
Database 1984 Jun;7(2):89–92

Lucinda D. Conger
Parlez-vous online: language searching on BRS, DIALOG, and ORBIT.
Database 1984 Aug;7(3):86–92

Peter R. Cook
Electronic encyclopedias.
Byte 1984 Jul;9(7):151–2,154,157–8,160,162,164,168,170

Rick Cook
Seeing is retrieving. [optical disk storage]
PC World 1984 Jul; 90–5

Michael D. Cooper
Usage patterns of an online search system.
Journal of the American Society for Information Science 1983 Sep;34(5):343–
    9. [17 references]

William S. Cooper
Exploiting the maximum entropy principle to increase retrieval effectiveness.
Journal of the American Society for Information Science 1983 Jan;34(1):31–
    9. [22 references]

Elaine Coppola
Who trains the trainer? Library staff are OPAC [Online Public Access Cat-
    alog] users, too.
Library Hi Tech 1983 Winter;1(3):36–8. [12 references]

Patti K. Corbett
Vendor-based private files: building your own database.
Medical Reference Services Quarterly 1983 Spring;2(1):67–9

Patti K. Corbett and Steven L. Ifshin
Online retrieval of environmental and occupational health literature: a com-
    parative study.
Medical Reference Services Quarterly 1983 Fall;2(3):25–36

Patti K. Corbett
Mastering an online database.
Medical Reference Services Quarterly 1984 Spring;3(1):75–7

Maureen Corcoran
Mead Data Central and "all the news that's fit to print."
Online 1983 Jul;7(4):32–5. [1 reference]

Betty Costa
An online catalog for an elementary school library media center.
School Library Media Quarterly 1982 Summer;10(4):337–40,345–6. [5 refer-
    ences]

Betty Costa and Marie Costa
"Card" catalog on a microcomputer—so easy a child can use it.
Catholic Library World 1982 Nov;54(4):166–9

Lela Beth Criswell
Serials on optical disks: a Library of Congress pilot program.
Library Hi Tech 1983 Winter;1(3):17–21

Carlos A. Cuadra
Commentary on the opinion paper "Downloading or downusing?"
NFAIS Newsletter 1983 Oct;25(5):2

Richard L. Currier
Interactive videodisc learning systems.
High Technology 1983 Nov; 3(11):51–9,87. [7 references]

Eva M. Dadlez
Catalyst resources for women on BRS.
Database 1983 Dec;6(4):32–43

Eva M. Dadlez
Full-text files: the operators and the operand.
Database 1984 Feb;7(1):102–4

Eva M. Dadlez
Orwell's 1984: natural language searching and the contemporary metaphor.
Database 1984 Jun;7(2):98–104

Eva M. Dadlez
The flipside of full-text: Superindex and the Harvard Business Review/On-
line.
Online 1984 Nov;8(6):38–45

Prudence W. Dalrymple
Closing the gap: the role of the librarian in online searching.
RQ 1984 Winter;24(2):177–95. [43 references]

Bruce D'Ambrosio
Expert systems—myth or reality?
Byte 1985 Jan;10(1):275–6,278,280,282. [3 references]

Craig E. Daniels
Online information retrieval: an underutilized educational tool.
Information Services & Use 1984 Aug;4(4):229–43. [3 references]

Susan David
More reasons why a search may go wrong [letter]
Online 1984 Mar;8(2):86

Roy Davies
Documents, information or knowledge? Choices for librarians.
Journal of Librarianship 1983 Jan;15(1):47–65. [59 references]

Dwight B. Davis
English: the newest computer language.
High Technology 1984 Feb;4(2):59–63,79. [6 references]

M. W. de Jong-Hofman and H. H. Siebers
Experiences with online literature searching in a water-related subject field:
    Aqualine, Biosis, CA Search and Pascal, compared using the ESA/Infor-
    mation Retrieval System.
Online Review 1984 Feb;8(1):59–73. [6 references]

Tim Dempsey
Dow Jones News/Retrieval—an indepth look.
Database 1984 Jun;7(2):44–64

Virgil Diodato
Modern algebra and information science.
Journal of the American Society for Information Science 1983 Jul;34(4):257–
    61. [10 references]

Virgil Diodata
Population magazines discuss online information retrieval
[appendix of 55 references to articles in popular magazines]
Online 1984 May;8(3):24–9. [1 reference]

Jane Dodd and Vicki Anders
Free online searches for undergraduates: a research project on use, costs, and
    projections.
Library Hi Tech 1984 Spring;1(4):43–50. [10 references]

Donna R. Dolan
Conceptualizing online search requests.
Database 1983 Feb 6(1):77–8. [3 references]

Donna R. Dolan
Staying on top of database documentation.
Database 1983 Aug;6(3):84–6. [9 references]

Donna R. Dolan
Databases for everyman.
Database 1983 Dec;6(4):101–4. [2 references]

Donna R. Dolan and Laura J. Hoffman
Careers in online: second in a series. Want ads in the online industry.
Online 1984 Jan;8(1):54–64. [1 reference]

Donna R. Dolan
Non-technical literature: getting it out of databases: 1. BRS/AFTER DARK.
Database 1984 Aug;7(3):94–103. [3 references]

Donna R. Dolan
Careers in online . . . fourth in a series: planning and research & development
    jobs in the online industry.
Online 1984 Jul;8(4):28–33. [2 references]

Georgia Fox Donati
Free online searching in a public library system: An unscientific study.
Online 1983 Mar;7(2):12–9

Tamas E. Doszkocs
CITE NLM: natural-language searching in an online catalog.
Information Technology and Libraries 1983 Dec;2(4):364–80. [9 references]

Karen Dowling
Online searching and the school media program.
School Library Media Annual 1984;2:425–35. [17 references]

Joanne C. Drozdoski
DISCLOSURE/SPECTRUM OWNERSHIP online.
Online 1984 Sep;8(5):74–82

Ronald G. Dunn
Why secondary services will survive and thrive.
Online Review 1983 Oct;7(5):399–403. [2 references]

Ronald G. Dunn and Harry F. Boyle
On-line searching: costly or cost effective? A marketing perspective.
Journal of Chemical Information and Computer Science 1984 May;24(2):51–
    4. [2 references]

Jane Eisenberg and Jeffrey Hill
Using natural-language systems on personal computers: your computer may
    speak English in 1984.
Byte 1984 Jan;9(1):226–38. [5 references]

Arthur W. Elias and John C. Blair, Jr.
Behind the scenes at BIOSIS: a wide ranging interview with Art Elias on new
    products . . . database economics . . . relations with online services . . .
    the hardships of the ''training gypsies'' . . .
Online 1983 Jan;7(1):11–7

Philip Elmer-DeWitt
Terminals among the stacks: public libraries are moving into the electronic
    age.
Time 1985 Feb 25;125(8):92

Pat Ensor and Richard A. Curtis
Search Helper: low-cost online searching in an academic library.
RQ 1984 Spring;23(3):327–31

Barbara A. Epstein
The terminology of psychiatry: DSM-III, Medical Subject Headings and the
    Thesaurus of Psychological Index Terms.
Medical Reference Services Quarterly 1984 Spring;3(1):49–66. [15 references]

Leigh Estabrook
The human dimension of the catalog: concepts and constraints in information
    seeking.
Library Resources & Technical Services 1984 Jan/Mar;27(1):68–75. [3 refer-
    ences]

Emily Fabiano
Testing 1...2...3... additional files available for test information online.
Online 1984 Sep;8(5):59–74

Joyce Duncan Falk
America: history and life online: history and much more.
Database 1983 Jun;6(2):14–25

Deborah R. Farrell and Anne W. Compton
POPLINE: an overview for searchers.
Medical Reference Services Quarterly 1983 Winter;2(4):1–20. [14 references]

Emily Fayen
Dartmouth College: the BRS link.
Library Hi Tech 1983 Summer;1(1):55–8

Emily Gallup Fayen
An online catalog for the Dartmouth College Library: the experiment continues.
Catholic Library World 1983 Mar;54(8):307–9. [3 references]

Mary J. Feeney and Ruth Miller
Downloading: piracy or panacea?
Journal of Information Science 1984 Feb;8(1):7–11. [14 references]

Susan J. Feinglos
MEDLINE at BRS, DIALOG, and NLM: is there a choice?
Bulletin of the Medical Library Association 1983 Jan;71(1):6–12. [6 references]

S. Norman Feingold and Tom Suprenant
Information industry careers in 2000: an interview with S. Norman Feingold.
Library Hi Tech 1983 Winter;1(3):5–8

Anne Conway Fernald
First look: TRADEMARKSCAN database.
Online 1984 Sep;8(5):36–40

Elizabeth M. Ferrarini
All the data you will ever need.
Business Computer Systems 1983 Oct;51–3

Elizabeth M. Ferrarini
Bulletin board preview: the After Dark connection.
Link-Up 1983 Oct;1(2):54–6

Elizabeth Ferrarini
The know-it-all connection.
Link-Up 1983/1984 Dec/Jan;1(4):20–6

Elizabeth M. Ferrarini
Online newsletters.
Link-Up 1984 Feb;1(5):42–3

Elizabeth M. Ferrarini
Fingertip power.
Micro Communications 1984 Feb;52–65

Raya Fidel and Dagobert Soergel
Factors affecting online bibliographic retrieval: a conceptual framework for
  research.
Journal of the American Society for Information Science 1983 May;34(3):163–
  80. [21 references]

Raya Fidel
Online searching types: a case-study-based model of searching behavior.
Journal of the American Society for Information Science 1984 Jul;35(4):211–
  21. [13 references]

Raya Fidel
Moves in online searching
Online Review 1985 Feb;9(1):61–74. [7 references]

Steven E. Fisher
The AMA/GTE medical information network.
The Journal of the Florida Medical Association 1983 Nov;70(11):1017–8

Donald Frazier
A dialog with Dialog.
Digital Review 1984 Mar;88–93

John Free
Computerized encyclopedias.
Popular Science 1983 Jun;222(6):138–9

Gary A. Freiburger
The online catalog: more than a catalog online.
Catholic Library World 1983 Dec;55(5):213–5

Bernard Friedman
Pharmaceutical riches on-line.
PC Magazine 1985 Feb 5;4(3):291,292,295

Mark E. Funk, Carolyn Anne Reid, and Leon S. McGoogan
Indexing consistency in MEDLINE.
Bulletin of the Medical Library Association 1983 Apr;71(2):176–83. [12 ref-
  erences]

Larry Fujitani
Laser optical disk: the coming revolution in on-line storage.
Communications of the ACM 1984 Jun;27(6):546–54

June Glaser
Index to Dental Literature and MEDLINE: a guide to searching the dental
  literature.
Medical Reference Services Quarterly 1984 Summer;3(2):1–16. [6 references]

Alfred Glossbrenner
Personal computers: passport to the electronic universe.
Technology Review 1983 May/Jun;86(4):62–71

Charles M. Goldstein
Computer-based information storage technologies.
Annual Review of Information Science and Technology 1984;19:65–96. [160
    references]

Morris Goldstein, Jeffery K. Pemberton, and Jean-Paul Emard
What's new at Information Access Corp.: an interview with Morris Goldstein,
    President.
Database 1984 Aug;7(3):12–8

Katherine A. Golomb and Sydelle S. Reisman
Using DIALOG for ready reference.
Library Journal 1984 Apr 15;109(7):786–8

Rebecca A. Gonzales
Regional online user group update.
Online 1983 Jan;7(1):70–1

Dena W. Gordon
A guide to searching ONTAP ABI/INFORM: a behind-the-scenes look at the
    development of a new training manual.
Online 1984 Mar;8(2):66–9. [4 references]

Dana M. Grabiner
Abracadabra—computerization of the libraries!
Precis: Faculty/Staff Newsletter of the University of Maryland, College Park
    Campus 1983 Dec 5;14(14):(unnumbered)

Peter S. Graham
Technology and the online catalog.
Library Resources & Technical Services 1983 Jan/Mar;27(1):18–35. [29 ref-
    erences]

John O. Green
Making computers smarter: a look at the controversial field of artificial in-
    telligence.
Popular Computing 1984 Jan;3(3):96–100,102–4. [9 references]

Robert T. Grieves
Short circuiting reference books: students are beginning to tap into on-screen
    encyclopedias.
Time 1983 Jun 13;121(24):76

Susan J. Grodsky
Searching the TELEGEN and BIOTECHNOLOGY files: genetic information
    online.
Medical Reference Services Quarterly 1983 Spring;2(1):7–21

Clyde W. Grotophorst
Another method for editing downloaded files.
Online 1984 Sep;8(5):85–93

Richard Gruner and Carol E. Heron
New resources for computer-aided legal research: an assessment of the use-
    fulness of the DIALOG system in securities regulation studies.
Database 1984 Dec;7(4):13–29. [26 footnotes (including 29 references)]

Judith S. Haines
Experiences in training end-user searchers.
Online 1982 Nov;6(6):14–23 [3 references]

Michael Halperin
Free "do-it-yourself" online searching . . . what to expect.
Online 1985 Mar;9(2):82–4. [1 reference]

Peter Halpin
Transferring a national information system from the public sector to the pri-
    vate sector—how the Administration on Aging did it.
Journal of the American Society for Information Science 1985 Jan;36(1):53–
    5. [4 references]

Michael Ham
Playing by the rules [artificial intelligence expert systems]
PC World 1984 Jan;34–41. [3 references]

Kathryn A. Hammell
Regional online union catalog of the Greater Midwest Regional Medical Li-
    brary Network: development and operation.
Bulletin of the Medical Library Association 1984 Apr;72(2):155–61. [12 ref-
    erences]

Stephen P. Harter
Scientific inquiry: a model for online searching.
Journal of the American Society for Information Science 1984 Mar;35(2):110–
    7. [25 references]

Gardner Haskell
How videotaped online searches can supplement the teaching of online search
    strategy.
Online Review 1984 Dec;8(6):561–8. [4 references]

Donald T. Hawkins
Information retrieval bibliography: sixth update [572 references]
Online Review 1983 Apr;7(2):127–87. [2 references]

Donald T. Hawkins
The literature of online information retrieval: an update.
Online Review 1984 Apr;8(2):153–64. [3 references]

Donald T. Hawkins
Online information retrieval bibliography: seventh update. Part I [931 references]
Online Review 1984 Jun;8(3):247–77

Donald T. Hawkins
Online information retrieval bibliography: seventh update. Part II [931 references]
Online Review 1984 Aug;8(3):325–81

Sylvia Helm
On-line information: closer than you think
Medicine & Computer 1983 Oct/Nov;1(1):28–34

Jeremy Joan Hewes
DIALOG: the ultimate on-line library.
PC World 1983 Sep;74–88

Nancy S. Hewison
The veteran MEDLINE searcher's encounter with other databases.
Medical Reference Services Quarterly 1983 Summer;2(2):75–80

Nancy S. Hewison
Whatever shall we do about user-friendly online?
Medical Reference Services Quarterly 1983 Winter;2(4):67–70. [1 reference]

Nancy S. Hewison
The reflective practice of online searching.
Medical Reference Services Quarterly 1984 Summer;3(2):69–71

Jack E. Hibbs, Ronald F. Bobner, Isadore Newman, Charles M. Dye, and
    Carolyn R. Benz
How to use online databases to perform trend analysis in research.
Online 1984 Mar;8(2):59–64. [5 references]

Theodore C. Hines and Lois Winkel
A new information access tool for children's media.
Library Resources & Technical Services 1983 Jan/Mar;27(1):94–104. [15 references]

Eileen Hitchingham, Elizabeth Titus, and Richard Pettengill
A survey of database use at the reference desk.
Online 1984 Mar;8(2):44–50. [8 references]

Laura Hoffman and Donna R. Dolan
Careers in online: first in a series. Headhunters and related species: professional assistance for job seekers.
Online 1983 Nov;7(6):12–7

Laura J. Hoffman and Donna R. Dolan
Careers in online: third in a series.
Online 1984 Mar;8(2):23–8. [6 references]

Sara Anne Hook
Tailoring MEDLINE searches [letter]
Bulletin of the Medical Library Association 1983 Oct;71(4):441.

Gary L. Horowitz, Jerome D. Jackson, and Howard L. Bleich.
PaperChase: self-service bibliographic retrieval.
Journal of the American Medical Association 1983 Nov 11;250(18):2494-9.
   [15 references]

G. L. Horowitz, J. D. Jackson, and H. L. Bleich
PaperChase: computerized bibliographic retrieval to answer clinical questions.
Methods of Information in Medicine 1983 Oct;22(4):183-8 [25 references]

Forest Woody Horton, Jr.
Information literacy vs. computer literacy.
Bulletin of the American Society for Information Science 1983 Apr;9(4):
   14-6

Elisabeth Horwitt
Natural languages improve the user-computer dialogue.
Business Computer Systems 1984 Nov;32-4,38-40,42

Raymond C. Houghton, Jr.
Online help systems: a conspectus.
Communications of the ACM 1984 Feb;27(2):126-33. [28 references]

Susanne M. Humphrey
File maintenance of MeSH headings in MEDLINE.
Journal of the American Society for Information Science 1984 Jan;35(1):34-
   44. [16 references]

Susanne M. Humphrey
Current awareness in biomedical computing by searching MEDLINE at NLM.
[ACM] SIGBIO Newsletter 1984 Mar;6(4):21-32

Susanne M. Humphrey
We need to bridge the gap between computer science and information science
Bulletin of the American Society for Information Science 1984 Dec;11(2):
   25-7

Janne A. Hunter
When your patrons want to search—the library as advisor to endusers . . . a
   compendium of advice and tips.
Online 1984 May;8(3):36-41. [9 references]

Peter Ingwersen
A cognitive view of three selected online search facilities.
Online Review 1984 Oct;8(5):465-92. [32 references]

Cynthia W. Isaacs
Documents "derti dada" [letter]
Database 1984 Jun;7(2):5.

Robert F. Jack
EROS main image file: a picture perfect database for Landsat imagery and aerial photography.
Database 1984 Feb;7(1):35-52. [4 backnotes (3 are references)]

Robert F. Jack
Searching LOGIN, the local government information network.
Database 1984 Jun;7(2):35-43. [3 backnotes (2 are references)]

Robert F. Jack
Cost considerations in database selection: a comparison of DIALOG and ESA/IRS.
Online 1984 Jul;8(4):51-4

Angela R. Haygarth Jackson
Online information handling—the user perspective.
Online Review 1983 Jan;7(1):25-32. [8 references]

Richard V. Janke
Business on BRS: focus on Predicasts.
Database 1983 Aug;6(3):33-50. [3 references]

Richard V. Janke
BRS/After Dark: the birth of online self-service.
Online 1983 Sep;7(5):12-29. [9 references]

Richard Janke
Online after six: end user searching comes of age.
Online 1984 Nov;8(6):15-29. [79 references]

Eric Wm. Johnson
Full text vs. abstracts.
NFAIS Newsletter 1983 Oct;25(5):3-4

Dolores Zegar Judkins
Searching hints: a chronic disease hedge for us on MEDLINE.
Medical Reference Services Quarterly 1984 Summer;3(2):72-3

Tamar Joy Kahn and Cecily Orr
BIOETHICSLINE: an overview for searchers.
Medical Reference Services Quarterly 1984 Fall;3(3):1-21 [5 references]

Ron Kaminecki
Cleaning up dirty data: an awesome task [letter]
Database 1984 Feb;7(1):5

Howard Karten
Getting smart: public databases
Management Technology 1983 Aug;49-53

Howard Karten
Getting Smart: public databases II.
Management Technology 1983 Sep;34-9

David Keith
The databases of I.P. Sharp . . . and how they are accessed with a program
    called MAGIC.
Database 1983 Aug;6(3):52–61

Elizabeth A. Kelly and Cynthia Fedders
Instructional support for an online catalog.
Medical Reference Services Quarterly 1983 Winter;2(4):73–7. [2 references]

Sue Kennedy
First look: The MARQUIS WHO'S WHO database.
Online 1984 Mar;8(2):31–5

David Kenton
The development of a more equitable method of billing for online services.
Online 1984 Sep;8(5):13–7

Terry Kepner
Databasing.
The Color Computer Magazine 1984 Mar;2(1):18–25

Cheryl Kern-Simirenko
OPAC [Online Public Access Catalog] user logs: implications for biblio-
    graphic instruction.
Library Hi Tech 1983 Winter;1(3):27–35. [3 references]

Debra S. Ketchell
Online searching by microcomputer.
Bulletin of the Medical Library Association 1984 Oct;72(4):370–2. [2 refer-
    ences]

Paul Kimmelman
GOTO school.
The Color Computer Magazine 1984 Mar;2(1):52–3

Paul Kinnucan
Artificial intelligence: making computers smarter.
High Technology 1982 Nov/Dec;2(6):60–3,66,68–70,113. [5 references]

Paul Kinnucan
Computers that think like experts.
High Technology 1984 Jan;4(1):30–7,40–2,71. [9 references]

Paul Kinnucan
Software tools speed expert system development.
High Technology, 1985 Mar;5(3):16–20,82. [2 references]

Henry M. Kissman and Philip Wexler
Toxicologic information.
Annual Review of Information Science and Technology 1983;18:185–230. [276
    references]

Simone Klugman
Online trends in the 80s: dispersal or convergence? [guest editorial]
Online 1983 Mar;7(2):6–7.

Simone Klugman
Online humor . . . a lighthearted look at present trends.
Online 1984 May;8(3):50–1

Sara D. Knapp
Free text searching of online databases.
The Reference Librarian 1982 Fall/Winter (5/6):143–53. [8 references]

Sara D. Knapp
Title-descriptor royalties held "counterproductive" [letter]
Online 1984 Mar;8(2):88

Sara D. Knapp
Cocitation searching: some useful strategies.
Online 1984 Jul;8(4):43–8. [8 references]

Sara D. Knapp
Creating BRS/TERM, a vocabulary database for searchers.
Database 1984 Dec;7(4):70–5. [3 references]

Leroy C. Knodel and Nancy F. Bierschenk
Selective use of online literature searching by a drug information service.
American Journal of Hospital Pharmacy 1983 Feb;40(2):257–9 [4 references]

Stuart J. Kolner
The IBM PC as an online search machine—Part I: Anatomy for searchers.
Online 1985 Jan;9(1):37–42

Stuart J. Kolner
The IBM PC as an online search machine. Part II: Physiology for searchers.
Online 1985 Mar;9(2):39–46

Kathryn W. Kruse
Online searching of the pharmaceutical literature.
American Journal of Hospital Pharmacy 1983 Feb;40(2):240–53. [18 references]

Carol S. Kulp
Patent databases . . . a survey of what is available from DIALOG, Questel, SDC, Pergamon and INPADOC.
Database 1984 Aug;7(3):56–72

Myer Kutz
John Wiley comments on HBRO status and features [letter]
Database 1983 Dec;6(4):49

J. A. Large and C. J. Armstrong
The microcomputer as a training aid for online searching.
Online Review 1983 Jan;7(1):51–9. [7 references]

Paul Lasbo
Upload on a micro application.
Online 1984 Jan;8(1):12–7

Gary S. Lawrence, Joseph R. Matthews, and Charles E. Miller
Costs and features of online catalogs: the state of the art.
Information Technology and Libraries 1983 Dec;2(4):409–49. [45 references
and notes]

Gerri G. Lawrence
Electronic legislative search system.
Database 1983 Aug;6(3):23–31

Ray Lester
User education in the online age.
Aslib Proceedings 1984 Feb;36(2):96–112. [28 references]

Louise R. Levy
Gateway software: is it for you?
Online 1984 Nov;8(6):67–79. [6 references]

Eugene Linden
Intellicorp: the selling of artificial intelligence.
High Technology 1985 Mar;5(3)22,25

Anne Lipow
Practical considerations of subject access in online public catalogs.
Library Resources & Technical Services 1983 Jan-Mar;27(1):81–7. [1 refer-
ence]

Frank Lowenstein
The plastic library
Technology Review 1983 Aug/Sep;86(6):80–1

Sally Lyon
The 1983 National Online Meeting.
Library Hi Tech 1983 Fall;1(2):92–4

Sally Lyon
End-user searching on online databases: a selective annotated bibliography
[26 references]
Library Hi Tech 1984;2(2):47–50

Stephen C. Lucchetti
CAS Online: access via lower cost Tektronix terminal look-alikes.
Online 1984 Jan;8(1):44–9. [3 references]

Barry Mahon
7th International Online Information Meeting—a personal view—warts and
all!
Online Review 1984 Feb;8(1):5–8.

Richard S. Marcus
An experimental comparison of the effectiveness of computers and humans as search intermediaries.
Journal of the American Society for Information Science 1983 Nov;34(6):381–404. [76 references]

Karen Markey
Thus spake the OPAC user [Online Public Access Catalog]
Information Technology and Libraries 1983 Dec;2(4):381–7. [8 references]

Karen Markey
Offline and online user assistance for online catalog searchers.
Online 1984 May;8(3):54–66

William Marovitz, Jean-Paul Emard, and Jeff Pemberton
Future online systems: an interview with BRS' William Marovitz.
Online 1983 May;7(3):15–9

Sharon G. Marsh
Strategic planning information online: a step-by-step guide through major checkpoints . . . what database to use when.
Database 1984 Jun;7(2):20–5.

V. Mathur
SDI (Selective Dissemination of Information)—a need for special facilities in commercial systems.
Online Review 1983 Aug;7(4):321–7.

Christine A. Matthews
Supplemental training program for MEDLARS searchers.
Medical Reference Services Quarterly 1983 Winter;2(4):21–30. [12 references]

Joseph R. Matthews and Joan Frye Williams
The User Friendly Index: a new tool.
Online 1984 May;8(3):31–4. [7 references]

Priscilla Mayden and Carol Tenopir
The library connection—information retrieval.
Update: Computers in Medicine 1984 Jul/Aug:24–37

Daniel E. Mayer, David W. Mehlman, Ellen S. Reeves, Regina B. Origoni, Delores Evans, and Douglas W. Sellers
Comparison study of overlap among 21 scientific databases in searching pesticide information.
Online Review 1983 Jan;7(1):33–43. [9 references]

William J. Mayer
Do magazine readers get the most out of their reading? Here's how information professionals cap use databases to fine tune their patrons' reading "profiles."
Database 1983 Aug;6(3):18–21

Davis B. McCarn and Grace H. McCarn
BEACON: H. W. Wilson's computerized information system.
Information Technology and Libraries 1983 Jun;2(2):142–50. [2 references]

W. J. McDowell and Barbara B. Corey
A new approach to information retrieval problems in separations science.
Journal of Chemical Information and Computer Science 1984 May;24(2):108–12. [2 references]

Emma Jean McKinin and E. Diane Johnson
Techniques of online citation verification in NLM databases.
Medical Reference Services Quarterly 1983 Fall;2(3):1–23. [32 references]

Charles T. Meadow
User adaptation in interactive information retrieval.
Journal of the American Society for Information Science 1983 Jul;34(4):289–91. [2 references]

Charles T. Meadow
End user searching [letter]
Library Journal 1983 Sep 1;108(15):1622–3. [2 references]

Charles T. Meadow
Charles Meadow comments on the enduser editorial [letter]
Database 1983 Dec;6(4):49–50

Henry N. Mendelsohn
Social work online.
Database 1984 Aug;7(3):36–49. [5 references]

S. V. Meschel
Numeric databases in the sciences.
Online Review 1984 Feb;8(1):77–103. [76 references]

Daniel E. Meyer, David W. Mehlman, Ellen S. Reeves, Regina B. Origoni, Delores Evans, and Douglas W. Sellers
Comparison study of overlap among 21 scientific databases in searching pesticide information.
Online Review 1983 Feb;7(1):33–43. [9 references]

Daniel E. Meyer and Timothy S. Pinegar
Updating in Excerpta Medica . . . how to deal with its inconsistencies.
Database 1983 Dec;6(4):67. [2 references]

Ralph Miller
How novices may be misled by front-end programs [letter]
Online 1985 Mar;9(2):5

Ralph Miller
Designing your own low-cost front-end software.
Online 1985 Mar;9(2):94–8

Anne P. Mintz
Information practice and malpractice . . . do we need malpractice insurance.
Online 1984 Jul;8(4):20–6. [10 references]

Michael Morgan
A short essay on database language problems.
Online 1983 Mar;7(2):49

Carol M. Moss
Online encyclopedias.
Link-Up 1984 Feb;1(5):38–41

Gretchen V. Naisawald
Your computer puts the literature at your fingertips.
MeDcomp 1983 Oct;34–8,72. [1 reference]
[This issue is premier issue. Starting with first regular issue (1983 Jan) name
   of journal changed to *M.D. Computing.*]

National Federation of Abstracting and Information Services
M. Lynne Neufeld, Inez L. Sperr, Russel J. Rowlett, Jr., and Maryanne A.
   Miller, editors
Information transfer: incentives for innovation
Proceedings of the 25th Annual Conference of the National Federation of
   Abstracting and Information Services, February 27-March 2, 1983, Ar-
   lington, VA
Philadelphia, PA: National Federation of Abstracting and Information Ser-
   vices, 1984
27 papers
Selected Papers:
   Marilyn C. Bracken. *The next era of the information age.* Pp. 153–5.
   Everett H. Brenner [session leader] and Betty Miller [author of synopsis].
      Update—vocabularies and vocabulary control [session]. Pp. 4–5.
   Everett H. Brenner. *The end users.* Pp. 48–51. [2 references]
   John E. Creps, Jr. *STI—a psychohistorical evaluation 1983: "chimo"*
      [Miles Conrad Memorial Lecture]. Pp. 165–74. [4 references]
   Melvin S. Day. *The next era of the information age.* Pp. 156–60.
   E. K. Gannett. *Changing roles in the production and distribution of in-
      formation.* Pp. 52–5.
   Dena W. Gordon. *Training information consumers: today's challenge.* Pp.
      143–52. [27 references]
   Stella Keenan. *Update—indexing formats and systems.* Pp. 6–8.
   H. William Koch. *Blurring of distinction between primary, secondary, and
      tertiary forms of information.* Pp. 56–63.
   Robert Taylor. *Report on value-added processes project.* Pp. 132–42.

National Online Meeting Proceedings—1983, New York, April 12-4, 1983
Online Review, sponsor
Martha E. Williams and Thomas H. Hogan, compilers

Martha E. Williams, program chairman

Medford, NJ: Learned Information, 1983

73 papers

Selected Papers:

Steven D. Atkinson. *Searchforms: worksheets for online searchers.* Pp. 11–6. [7 references]

Bernard Bayer. *A role for batch systems in the world of online searching.* Pp. 17–20. [9 references]

William A. Benjamin, Kathleen C. Jamieson, and James P. Rutt. *The design of a full-text company information database for multi-vendor delivery.* Pp. 33–7.

Mike Beyer and Katharina Klemperer. *The teaching function of the online library catalog: an analysis of current catalogs and prospects for the future.* Pp. 39–44. [10 references]

Alice Bodtke-Roberts. *Faculty end-user searching of BIOSIS.* Pp. 45–53.

David K. Bond and Dena W. Gordon. *Revision and correction of the ABI/INFORM backfile.* Pp. 57–66.

Janet Bruman. *Smart terminal software packages for microcomputers.* Pp. 75–81.

Marilyn Carr. *Build your own database: using database management systems for custom applications.* Pp. 87–91. [5 references]

Tamas Doszkocs and John Ulmschneider. *A practical stemming algorithm for online search assistance.* Pp. 93–105. [10 references]

Valerie Geller and Michael Lesk. *An on-line library catalog offering menu and keyword user interfaces.* Pp. 159–65. [6 references]

Richard K. Hunt, H. Leonard Fisher, Viktor E. Hampel, Richard A. Kawin, and Neil A. Lann. *The "T15" intelligent gateway computer, an alternative to the "doomsday scenario."* Pp. 211–22. [17 references]

Janne A. Hunter. *What did you say the end-user was going to do at the terminal, and how much is it going to cost?* Pp. 223–9.

C. D. Hurt. *Intermediaries, self-searching and satisfaction.* Pp. 231–7. [4 references]

Michael C. Kremin. *The development of a checklist for the evaluation of computer documentation—a case study of current online vendor documentation.* Pp. 267–70. [7 references]

Nancy Leipzig, Marlene Galante Kozak, and Ronald A. Schwartz. *Experiences with end-user searching at a pharmaceutical company.* Pp. 325–32. [8 references]

Lois F. Lipsett, Lois F. Lunin, and Ruthann Bates. *The integration of multiple health-related data bases to increase ease of access.* Pp. 339–45.

Michael J. McGill, Gerhard E. Brown, and Sidney Siegel. *The Chemical Substances Information Network: its evaluation and evolution.* Pp. 367–76 [11 references]

Ellen M. Poler. *The impact of electronics on publishing*. Pp. 429-37. [6 references]

Nina M. Ross. *Newspaper databases update, 1982*. Pp. 463-73. [5 references]

Bruce A. Shuman. *"Who's user-friendly? A comparative appraisal of DIALOG, ORBIT, and BRS."* Pp. 491-8. [1 reference]

Steven K. Sieck. *Database publishing applications of optical videodiscs.* Pp. 499-502.

Elliot R. Siegel, Karen Kameen, Sally K. Sinn, and Frieda O. Weise. *Research strategy and methods used to conduct a comparative evaluation of two prototype online catalog systems.* Pp. 503-11. [6 references]

Seldon W. Terrant, Lorrin R. Garson, Stanley M. Cohen, and Barbara E. Meyers. *ACS primary journal online database.* P. 551.

Martha E. Williams. *Highlights of the online database field—statistics, downloading and microcomputers.* Pp. 1-3.

Philip W. Williams. *A microcomputer system to improve the recall performance of skilled searchers.* Pp. 581-90. [6 references]

M. Lynne Neufeld
Future of secondary services.
Online Review 1983 Oct;7(5):421-6. [7 references]

M. Lynne Neufeld and Martha Cornog
Secondary information systems and services.
Annual Review of Information Science and Technology 1983;18:151-83. [142 references]

Brian Nielsen
An unfolding, not an unveiling: creating an online public library.
Library Journal 1984 Jun 15;109(11):1214-8. [5 references]

Patty Noukas
First look: CQ Washington Alert Service . . . Congress at your fingertips.
Database 1984 Dec;7(4):44-7

Julie Blume Nye and Ellen C. Brassil
Online searching on selected business databases for management aspects of health care.
Medical Reference Services Quarterly 1984 Spring;3(1):33-48. [3 references]

Marydee Ojala
Knowledge Index: a review
Online 1983 Sep;7(5):31-4

Marydee Ojala
Online pricing: some analogies [letter]
Online 1984 Jul;8(4):4-5

B. K. Oldroyd
Study of strategies used in online searching 5: differences between the experienced and the inexperienced searcher.
Online Review 1984 Jun;8(3):233–44. [8 references]

Online '83 Conference Proceedings, October 10, 11, 12
Jean-Paul Emard, conference chairman
Weston, CT: Online, 1983
64 papers

Selected Papers:

Boyd Childress. *Ethics in database searching*. Pp. 11–4.

Lucinda D. Conger. *1983 database review: current affairs, government affairs, public affairs, and legal affairs*. Pp. 15–20.

Alan B. Davidson. *TRADEMARKSCAN DIALOG file 226*. Pp. 35–7.

Debra A. Dawson. *The Electronic Yellow Pages*. Pp. 38–42.

Ronald R. Dueltgen. *Database reviews. . . science and technology*. Pp. 49–57.

Helen A. Gordon. *SOFT: a microcomputer software database review*. Pp. 74–6.

Jeffrey C. Griffith. *Why can't I do it? Emerging training concerns of end users and online professionals*. Pp. 77–81. [3 references]

Nancy F. Hardy. *Enhancing the grant-seeking process: using the Foundation Center's databases online*. Pp. 87–9.

Laura Hoffman and Donna R. Dolan. *Careers in the online business*. Pp. 117.

Richard V. Janke. *Online after six at the University of Ottawa*. Pp. 124–9. [6 references]

William A. Jenkins. *Predicasts, Inc.—Online '83*. Pp. 130–4.

Steve Kahofer. *Dun's Marketing Services*. Pp. 148–51.

David Keith. *Online databases and interactive analysis*. Pp. 152–8.

Sara D. Knapp. *BRS/TERM, a database for searchers*. Pp. 162–6.

Stuart J. Kolner. *Life sciences bibliographic databases: the year in review*. Pp. 167–71.

Katherine Konopasek. *An update on computer literature searching in education*. Pp. 172–6.

John Lucey. *A proposal for simplifying access to controlled vocabulary files*. Pp. 177–82.

Katherine Markee. *Data base review—arts, humanities, social sciences*. Pp. 186–8.

Meri Meredith. *Non-bibliographic/numeric databases*. Pp. 203–9.

Marydee Ojala. *The dark side of database searching: negative productivity*. Pp. 226–30.

Mary Ann S. Palma. *Reloaded substance files provide substructure keys*. Pp. 231–8. [3 references]

Ann Pfaffenberger. *Telefacsimile transmission: the technology and its uses.* Pp. 239–43. [5 references]

Barbara Quint. *Cross database/cross system searching or when are 35 databases and 5 search services enough?* Pp. 244–50.

Marilyn J. Rea. *NEXIS—bringing precision to full-text searching.* Pp. 251–3.

David Rouse. *Databases in review: an analysis of developments in 1983 business and finance.* Pp. 255–7.

Jane N. Ryland. *Optical storage of digital data on video discs for distributed reference information.* Pp. 258–61.

Jacque-Lynne Schulman. *Dirty data and the online user.* Pp. 262–5. [5 references]

Celeste Silvers. *The how-to's on Standard & Poor's News Online database.* Pp. 271–3.

Frances G. Spigai. *Downloading: tempest in a teapot?* Pp. 278–9.

Carol Tenopir. *End user search services: a comparison.* Pp. 280–5.

Rodes Trautman. *Interactive simultaneous remote searching (ISRS): implementing a reliable operation.* Pp. 286–8.

Robert Wagers. *Subject ready reference searching.* Pp. 296–301. [9 references]

Raymond A. Palmer
Medical Library Association position on the National Library of Medicine's pricing policy [editorial]
Bulletin of the Medical Library Association 1984 Oct;72(4):397–9. [2 references]

Jeff Pemberton
A backward and forward look at the New York Times Information Bank—a tale of ironies compounded . . . and an analysis of the Mead deal.
Online 1983 Jul;7(4):7–17.

Jeff Pemberton
Full text retrieval . . . can either primary or secondary publishers survive it?
Database 1983 Feb;6(1):6–8

Jeff Pemberton
Faults and failures—25 ways that online searching can let you down.
Online 1983 Sep;7(5):6–7

Jeff Pemberton
The dark side of online information—dirty data.
Database 1983 Dec;6(4):6–7

Jeff Pemberton
An essay on nomenclature . . . what should we call an online search service?
Database 1984 Feb;7(1):6–7

Jeff Pemberton
Database distribution . . . the controversy over Chemical Abstracts.
Online 1984 Mar;8(2):6–7

Jeff Pemberton
Some thoughts for marketers of online products.
Online 1984 May;8(3):6–7

Jeff Pemberton
Public relations in the online industry.
Database 1984 Jun;7(2):6–7

Jeff Pemberton
Some observations on the pricing of online services.
Online 1984 Jul;8(4):6–7

Jeff Pemberton
An essay on standards (or why we think we would like a uniform retrieval
    language but might not be so happy if we actually got one).
Database 1984 Aug;7(3):6–7

Jeff Pemberton
Is information a commodity . . . yet? Should databanks produce their own
    databases . . . or just distribute other people's? . . . The dilemma of charg-
    ing for downloading . . . and other questions raised at the BRS Database
    producers Meeting.
Database 1984 Dec;7(4):6–7

Pirkko Pietiläinen
Possibility for intelligent feedback in online searching.
Online Review 1983 Oct;7(5):391–6. [8 references]

Deborah Pietro and Michael Kremin
The School Practices Information Network and File
(Spin/Spif): information services for education.
Online 1983 Jan;7(1):51–7

Anne B. Piternick
Searching vocabularies: a developing category of online search tools.
Online Review 1984 (Oct;8(5):441–9 [8 references]

A. S. Pollitt
A 'front end' system: an expert system as an online search intermediary.
Aslib Proceedings 1984 May;36(5):229–34. [10 references]

Charles J. Popovich
A methodology for categorizing international business literature through on-
    line bibliographic searching.
Online Review 1983 Aug;7(4):341–55. [28 references]

Steven Prowse
Software for producing library keyword catalogues: a description of selected
    packages.
Elsevier International Bulletins 1983 Feb (EIB Report Series No. 1)

Ellen Pruitt and Karen Dowling
Searching for current information online . . . how high school library media
    centers in Montgomery County, Maryland are solving an information prob-
    lem by using DIALOG.
Online 1985 Mar;9(1):47-60

H. Rudy Ramsey and Jack D. Grimes
Human factors in interactive computer dialog.
Annual Review of Information Science and Technology 1983;18:29-59. [161
    references]

Judith P. Reid
Searching for genealogies in the Library of Congress computer catalog.
RQ 1983 Winter;23(2):195-201. [1 reference]

Betsy Reifsnyder
Disclosure II and Predicasts Annual Reports Abstract: a preliminary com-
    parison.
Database 1984 Feb;7(1):65-72

Fred Reneau and Richard Patterson
Comparison of online agricultural information services.
Online Review 1984 Aug;8(4):313-22. [3 references]

Phyllis A. Richmond
Futuristic aspects of subject access.
Library Resources & Technical Services 1983 Jan/Mar;27(1):88-93. [17 ref-
    erences]

Steven K. Roberts
On-line information retrieval: a new business tool.
Today 1983 Oct;2(10):14-20,48
[This is a magazine for CompuServe users (CompuServe, Inc., Columbus,
    OH). In 1984 its name was changed to *Online Today.*]

Steven K. Roberts
Online: a smorgasbord of services.
Today 1983 Nov;2(11):24-9,48
[See note at end of preceding entry.]

Judith Schiek Robinson and Rao Aluri
Federal government Research in Progress: information retrieval for science
    and technology.
Database 1983 Feb;6(1):36-43. [17 references]

Stephen Rollins
Chemical Abstracts' document delivery service.
Online Review 1984 Apr;8(2):183-91

Tina Roose
Online database searching in smaller public libraries.
Library Journal 1983 Sep 15;108(16):1769-70. [3 references]

Tina Roose
Who are the consumers? What are the questions?
Library Journal 1984 Feb 1;109(2):154-5

Tina Roose
Online searches & interlibrary loan.
Library Journal 1984 Apr 1;109(6):633-4

Tina Roose
Online searching: keys to success.
Library Journal 1984 May 15;109(9):958-9

Tina Roose
Going online: the ten most-asked questions.
Library Journal 1984 Sep 1;109(14):1614-5

Tina Roose
Online searching for kids
Library Journal 1984 Nov 1;109(18):2010-1

Dana L. Roth
Search mediation makes sense [letter]
Library Journal 1984 Apr 1;109(67):610

Gladys E. Rowe
Microform informing: use of DIALOG SDI to produce a microfiche announcement bulletin.
Online 1984 Mar;8(2):70-5. [2 references]

Peter P. Rowell and Nancy Utterback
Scientific literature currency and organization using a microcomputer.
Online 1984 Jan;8(1):18-21

Stephen R. Salmon
Characteristics of online public catalogs.
Library Resources & Technical Services 1983 Jan/Mar;27(1):36-67. [6 references]

Kristine Salomon and Curt Burgess
Patron presence during the online search: attitudes of university librarians.
Online Review 1984 Dec;8(6):549-58. [11 references]

G. Salton, C. Buckley, and E. A. Fox
Automatic query formulations in information retrieval.
Journal of the American Society for Information Science 1983 Jul;34(4):262–
80. [15 references]

Fred Schneiweiss
Use and cost analysis of online literature in a university-based drug information center.
American Journal of Hospital Pharmacy 1983 Feb;40(2):254-6. [21 refer-
ences]

J. J. Schröder
Study of strategies used in online searching: 3. Query refining.
Online Review 1983 Jun;7(3):229-36. [4 references]

J. J. Schröder
Study of strategies used in online searching: 4. Acronyms—the missing ele-
ment in your search?
Online Review 1983 Dec;7(6):475-84. [4 references]

Michael A. Shepherd and Carolyn Watters
PSI: a portable self-contained intermediary for access to bibliographic
database systems.
Online Review 1984 Oct;8(5):451-63. [21 references]

Rachel R. Shorthill
Unexpected online sources for business information.
Online 1985 Jan;9(1):68–78

Jacque-Lynne Shulman
Exclusive databases & more search services . . . the argument in favor.
Online 1984 Mar;8(2):54-7

MaryEllen Sievert and Bert R. Toyce
Hedge trimming and the resurrection of the controlled vocabulary in online
searching.
Online Review 1983 Dec;7(6):489-94. [9 references]

MaryEllen Sievert and Alison F. Verbeck
Online databases in physics—an overview of what is available in the U.S.
. . . both core databases and those containing a specialized area of ori-
entation.
Database 1984 Dec;7(4):54-63. [10 references]

I. Silbergeld and P. Kutok
Information retrieval using ADABAS-NATURAL (with applications for tele-
vision and radio).
Online Review 1984 Apr;8(2):165-81. [2 references]

Jack W. Simpson, Paul F. Nezi, Jeffery K. Pemberton, and Jean-Paul Emard
What's happening at Mead Data Central . . . an interview with Jack W. Simp-
   son, President, and Paul F. Nezi, Vice President–marketing operations.
Online 1984 Jul;8(4):13–9

Jack W. Simpson
Mean Data Central: positioned for the future.
Online Review 1984 Oct;8(5):413–20

Jack W. Simpson
Information megatrends [guest editorial]
Online 1985 Mar;9(2):6–7

Sana Siwolop
Touching all the data bases.
Discover 1983 Mar;4(3):68–71

Molly M. Skeen
Legislative databases—a review and evaluation of what is available.
Database 1984 Jun;7(2):13–9. [5 references]

Robert E. Skinner
Searching the history of science online.
Database 1983 Jun;6(2):54–61. [2 references]

Linda C. Smith and Amy J. Warner
A taxonomy of representations in information retrieval system design.
Journal of Information Science 1984 Apr;8(3):113–21. [40 references]

Stephen C. Smith
Online current-events retrieval services: developments and trends.
Library Hi Tech 1984 Spring;1(4):59–64. [12 references]

Bonnie Snow
Online database coverage of pharmaceutical journals.
Database 1984 Feb;7(1):12–26. [8 references]

Bonnie Snow and Steven L. Ifshin
Online database coverage of forensic medicine.
Online 1984 Mar;8(2):37–43. [2 references]

Bonnie Snow
Online searching for information on medical devices.
Medical Reference Services Quarterly 1984 Spring;3(1):19–32. [13 references]

Bonnie Snow
Making the rough places plain: designing MEDLINE end user training.
Medical Reference Services Quarterly 1984 Winter;3(4):1–11. [3 references]

Inez L. Sperr
Online searching and the print product: impact or interaction?
Online Review 1983 Oct;7(5):413–20. [11 references]

Fran Spigai
Databases: should they be vendor produced or delivered?
NFAIS Newsletter 1983 Dec;25(6):3–4

Suzanne St.-Jacques and Richard Janke
Online staff resources: Canadian university libraries.
Library Hi Tech 1983 Winter;1(3):55–61. [3 references]

Catheryne Stout and Thomas Marcinko
Sci-Mate: a menu-driven universal online searcher and personal data man-
ager.
Online 1983 Sep;7(5):112–6

Roger K. Summit, Jeffery K. Pemberton, and Jean-Paul Emard
DIALOG in 1984: an interview with Roger K. Summit.
Online 1984 Mar;8(2):13–20

Joan M. Sustik and Terrence A. Brooks
Retrieving information with interactive videodiscs.
Journal of the American Society for Information Science 1983 Nov;34(6):424–
32. [6 references]

Elaine Svenonius
Use of classification in online retrieval.
Library Resources & Technical Services 1983 Jan/Mar;27(1):76–80. [7 refer-
ences]

James H. Sweetland
America: history and life—a wide ranging database.
Database 1983 Dec;6(4):15–29

Robert S. Tannehill, Jr.
Bibliographic and information-processing standards.
Annual Review of Information Science and Technology 1983;18:61–94. [127
references]

Carol Tenopir
Databases: catching up & keeping up.
Library Journal 1983 Feb 1;108(3):180–2

Carol Tenopir
Dialog's Knowledge Index and BRS/After Dark: database searching on per-
sonal computers.
Library Journal 1983 Mar 1;108(5):471–4

Carol Tenopir
Full-text, downloading, & other issues.
Library Journal 1983 Jun 1;108(11):2140–1

Carol Tenopir
The online future at ASIS.
Library Journal 1983 Jul;108(13):332–3

Carol Tenopir
Online information in the health sciences.
Library Journal 1983 Oct 15;108(18):1932–3

Carol Tenopir
More publications about databases.
Library Journal 1983 Nov 15;108(20):2140–1

Carol Tenopir
Online '83 in Chicago.
Library Journal 1983 Dec 15;108(22):2310–2

Carol Tenopir
The database industry today: some vendors' perspectives.
Library Journal 1984 Feb 1;109(2):156–7

Carol Tenopir
Newspapers online.
Library Journal 1984 Mar 1;109(4):452–3

Carol Tenopir
To err is human: seven common searching mistakes.
Library Journal 1984 Apr 1;109(6):635–6

Carol Tenopir
In-house training & staff development.
Library Journal 1984 May 1;109(8):870–1. [11 references]

Carol Tenopir
IAC's document delivery and more.
Library Journal 1984 Jun 1;109(10):1104–5

Carol Tenopir
Pricing policies.
Library Journal 1984 Jul;109(12):1300–1

Carol Tenopir
H. W. Wilson: online at last!
Library Journal 1984 Sep 1;109(14):1616–7

Carol Tenopir
Database access software.
Library Journal 1984 Oct 1;109(16):1828–9. [4 references]

Carol Tenopir
Full-text databases.
Annual Review of Information Science and Technology 1984;19:215–46. [116 references]

Carol Tenopir
"Other" bibliographic systems.
Library Journal 1984 Nov 1;109(18):2008–9

Carol Tenopir
Online searching in the popular literature.
Library Journal 1984 Dec;109(20):2242–3

Carol Tenopir
Conferences for online professionals.
Library Journal 1985 Jan;110(1):62–3

Carol Tenopir
Searching Harvard Business Review Online . . . lessons in searching a full
   text database.
Online 1985 Mar;9(2):71–8

Jane I. Thesing
Online searching in perspective advantages and limitations.
Catholic Library World 1983 Feb;54(8):258–60. [5 references]

Benna Brodsky Thompson
Future direct users of sci-tech electronic databases [guest editorial]
Database 1983 Jun 6(2):6–9. [6 references]

Dwight R. Tousignaut
Online literature retrieval systems: how to get started.
American Journal of Hospital Pharmacy 1983 Feb;40(2):230–9. [6 references]

Rodes Trautman
Storage media for microcomputers.
Online 1983 Nov;7(6):19–28. [3 references]

Libby Trudell
Communicating in the online industry: how an information broker uses elec-
   tronic mail.
Online 1983 Nov;7(6):60–4

Elaine Trzebiatowski
End user study on BRS/After Dark.
RQ 1984 Summer;23(4):446–50. [4 references]

Carol Tschudi
The online searcher: education and training.
Library Hi Tech 1983 Summer;1(1):85–7. [11 references]

Daniel Uchitelle
RLIN and Avery: the online Index to Architectural Periodicals.
   [Eighteenth Century Short Title Catalog]
Database 1984 Aug;7(3):30–3

Daniel Uchitelle
RLIN and Avery: the Online Index to Architectural Periodicals.
Database 1984 Dec;7(4):66–9.

Nancy E. Van Buskirk
The review article in MEDLINE: ambiguity of definition and implications for
   online searchers.

Bulletin of the Medical Library Association 1984 Oct;72(4):349–52. [5 references]

Ann J. Van Camp and Catherine Seeley
A comparison of the currency of the BRS Pre-Med database with MED-LINE, SciSearch and ISI/BIOMED.
Database 1983 Feb;6(1):28–35. [4 references]

Ann J. Van Camp
The MeSH vocabulary file and CHEMLINE: online sources of chemical nomenclature.
Medical Reference Services Quarterly 1984 Spring;3(1):1–17. [19 references]

Linda J. VanHorn
A hedge for searching nutrition and disease on MEDLINE.
Medical Reference Services Quarterly 1984 Summer;3(2):31–42. [18 references]

Peter J. Vigil
The psychology of online searching.
Journal of the American Society for Information Science 1983 Jul;34(4):281–7. [25 references]

Peter J. Vigil
Analytical methods for online searching.
Online Review 1983 Dec;7(6):497–514. [2 references]

Kenneth R. Walton and Patricia L. Dedert
Experiences at Exxon in training end-users to search technical databases online.
Online 1983 Sep;7(5):42–50. [4 references]

Thomas S. Warrick
Large databases, small computers and fast modems . . . an attorney looks at the legal ramifications of downloading.
Online 1984 Jul;8(4):58–70. [59 backnotes (46 are references)]

Peter G. Watson
Touch-screen versus keyboard terminals for online catalogs.
Information Technology and Libraries 1983 Jun;2(2):182–4

Sylvia P. Webb
Using commercial databases online.
Aslib Proceedings 1984 Oct;36(10):393–400. [7 references]

Stephen M. Welford, Michael F. Lynch, and John M. Barnard
Towards simplified access to chemical structure information in the patent literature.
Journal of Information Science 1983 Mar;6(1):3–10. [16 references]

Stephen M. Welford, Michael F. Lynch, and John M. Barnard
Computer storage and retrieval of generic chemical structures in patents. 5. Algorithmic generation of fragment descriptors for generic structure screening.

Journal of Chemical Information and Computer Science 1984 May;24(2):57–66. [21 references]

Hans H. Wellisch
Capital games: the problem of compatibility of bibliographic citations in the databases and in printed publications.
Database 1983 Feb;6(1):54–7. [9 references]

Christine A. Wells
Quick reference command languages chart.
Online Review 1983 Jan;7(1):45–50, folded chart (unnumbered) [22 references]

Martin S. White
Private files—a comparative review of services offered by online vendors.
Online Review 1983 Apr;7(2):113–22. [3 references]

Donna Willman
First look: VU/TEXT databases.
Online 1985 Mar;9(2):61–8

Patrick Wilson
The catalog as access mechanism: background and concepts.
Library Resources & Technical Services 1983 Jan/Mar;27(1):4–17. [7 references]

Donald Wismer
Labels from the Electronic Yellow Pages: a BASIC routine.
Online 1984 Jul;8(4):36–40

Lucy Anne Wozny
Online bibliographic searching and student use of information: an innovative teaching approach.
School Library Media Quarterly 1982 Fall;11(1):35–42. [6 references]

Craig Zarley
Dialing into data bases.
Personal Computing 1983 Dec;7(12):135–7,139,234

A budding mass market for databases.
Business Week 1983 Jan 17;(2773):128,131

Can an electronic publisher be its own delivery boy?
Business Week 1983 Mar 7;(2780):83,86

An electronic key to the patent office.
Business Week 1983 Apr 4;(2784):38

International comparative price guide to databases online.
Online Review 1984 Feb;8(1):105–12

International comparative price guide to databases online.
Online Review 1984 Aug;8(4):385–92

Glossary

The entries in this glossary are defined in the context of computerized information retrieval.

abstract An abbreviated natural-language representation of the contents of a document.

accession number A numeric or alphanumeric code assigned to records as they enter the file, where the number is assigned to the records sequentially.

acoustic coupler A special type of modem that uses ordinary telephone handsets as part of the connection between terminals and telecommunications lines for accessing host computers. See also **modem.**

address, computer A number that identifies a location in the computer's memory.

adjacency operator See **positional operator.**

alphanumeric characters The set of characters consisting of numeric and alphabetic characters and special symbols such as punctuation and mathematical symbols.

AND logical operator See **intersection of search terms.**

arithmetic relational operator See **relational operator.**

artificial intelligence (AI) The study and implementation of techniques for programming computers to perform activities that are considered to require intelligence when performed by people; for example, symbolic reasoning, problem solving, language understanding, and learning. Applications include intelligent computer retrieval and indexing.

authority file A file of established forms of terms used for intellectual subject indexing or providing other controlled terminology, such as names of organizations or serial (journal) titles.

automatic search term completion See **search term completion, automatic.**

batch process A computer process for performing functions not in immediate response to the message requesting the process. The request is scheduled for processing at a later time.

bibliographic database A referral database consisting of references to documents.

bibliographic record A unit of related information in a bibliographic database, representing all the stored information related to a document.

Boolean operator See **logical operator.**

cathode ray tube display unit See **visual display unit.**

character A symbol from a set of elementary symbols, such as a single-digit number (0–9), an alphabetic letter (A–Z, a–z), or a special symbol (punctuation or mathematical symbol), as well as a blank space that could contain a symbol (blank character). A set of specific symbols is defined as a character set; for example, the numeric, alphabetic, or alphanumeric character set.

character string A sequence of characters.

class maintenance File maintenance that entails applying a single modification to a set of records. Usually performed as a batch process. May be performed against a retrieval file as a result of changes to an authority file (for example, a controlled indexing vocabulary) to ensure that authority-based terms in the retrieval file match the terms in the revised version of the authority file.

command language
The set of standard terms, abbreviations, and symbols for use in interactive information retrieval. Usually specific to the retrieval program of a particular retrieval service.

common command language
A set of standard terms, abbreviations, and symbols for use in interactive information retrieval proposed for reducing the existing diversity in command languages.

complement of search term
A logical relationship that would result in a positive retrieval only if a search term were not successfully matched against a set of records.

computer
A device that accepts information in a prescribed form, processes the information under the direction of a stored program, and supplies the results of the processing in a prescribed form.

computer program
A set of steps, stored in the computer, that instruct the computer to perform functions in order to solve a problem.

computer-readable information
Information recorded in a form that the computer can read and process.

connect time
The amount of time the terminal is connected to a host computer from the time of logon to the time of logoff.

controlled subject indexing term
An assigned subject indexing term from a controlled indexing vocabulary.

controlled subject indexing vocabulary
A set of predetermined words or phrases created and maintained specifically for representing the subject content of a collection of records, and assigned to records during the process of intellectual subject indexing.

conversational mode
See **interactive mode.**

CRT display unit
See **visual display unit.**

cumulative database
A database produced either by merging updates, as they occur, with the current database, usually for a designated number of updates; or

merging several updates, at designated intervals, with the initial database. An index to such a database is a cumulative index.

current awareness service

A service that alerts users to new information likely to be of interest to them. See also **selective dissemination of information.**

cursor

A movable position indicator that appears on a terminal or microcomputer screen to indicate a character to be corrected or a position where a character is to be entered. May be moved by cursor-moving commands, function keys known as cursor keys, or pointing devices.

cursor-moving command

A command for moving the cursor entered on a terminal or microcomputer by using the character keys on the keyboard.

database

A file or set of related files as provided by a database supplier designed for computerized retrieval.

database management

Creating, updating, and maintaining databases for retrieval. A system that performs these operations is known as a database management system (DBMS).

database supplier

An organization that provides one or more databases to a retrieval service.

DBMS

Acronym for database management system. See **database management.**

default

A value or category automatically assigned or a process automatically performed by the computer unless another is specified.

dialup

Telecommunications between terminals and the host computer over telephone lines, whether by direct dial or using a telecommunications network; in contrast to hardwire.

direct dial

Telecommunications between terminals and the host computer by telephone lines without using a telecommunications network.

dirty data

Errors in databases that are errors in form. May be one-time careless errors or system errors caused by absent, inadequate, or inoperative validation of information entered into the database.

distributed database

A database stored on a medium, such as magnetic tape, floppy disk, or optical disk, which may be marketed for localized information retrieval.

document delivery	A systematic method for supplying users with documents in response to requests, which frequently consist of references from a bibliographic database. Users may transmit requests by computer or manually. Documents may be distributed manually, or the user may be referred to a full text database for retrieving them by computer. Transmission of documents to users by computer in direct response to requests (electronic document delivery) may occur in the near future.
down	Inoperative status of the computer, or unavailability of a computer program or database for current use.
downloading	Electronic copying of retrieval sets on the host computer into local computer storage devices, either temporarily or permanently, for further computer-based manipulation or re-use.
electronic document delivery	See **document delivery.**
electronic journal	See **electronic publishing.**
electronic mail	Computerized transmission of messages, which includes storing messages in computers in order to delay them, to allow received messages to be read at the convenience of the recipient, or to retain them in computerized files.
electronic publishing	Computerized production and storage of documents for subsequent computerized distribution or access.
end-user	An individual who applies the information being sought from a retrieval service.
enter key	A key on a terminal or microcomputer keyboard that, when activated, transfers the current line of input to the computer for processing.
entry date	A computer-generated date automatically assigned to a record at the time it enters the file.
error message	A message from the computer when the user has entered a command that is misspelled, improperly formatted, or inappropriate to the situation and therefore cannot be processed.

execution of saved search
Instruction to the computer to locate and process a saved search.

explosion (hierarchical searching)
See **hierarchical searching of controlled vocabulary.**

field
A category of information in the record. A field may be further categorized into subfields. See also **indexed field.**

field value
Specific information that is an instance of a field. A field value appears in a location in the record reserved for that field.

file
A collection of related records, treated as a unit. See also **inverted file.**

file maintenance
Modifying the contents of a file to keep the information accurate and current, including modifying or regenerating the index to reflect the revised version. See also **class maintenance** and **individual record maintenance.**

file updating
Merging an update file with a master file, including modifying or regenerating the index to reflect the resulting newly updated master file.

floppy disk
A flexible disk that functions as a portable medium for magnetically recording and providing access to stored information. Commonly used with microcomputers and minicomputers.

free subject indexing term
An assigned subject indexing term that does not come from a controlled subject indexing vocabulary.

free text searching
Searching text as it occurs naturally in the record rather than as structured units of compound words, such as assigned indexing terms. See also **stringsearching** and **textword.**

function key
A special key on a terminal or microcomputer keyboard for moving the cursor or activating frequently used commands.

gateway
1. A microcomputer software package that connects to several retrieval services and provides features such as automatic dialup and logon, a substitute command language, uploading locally prepared or stored search formulations, and text editing of downloaded information. 2. A path for electronic access to a database retrieval service

from other computerized services, such as another database retrieval service or a home computer service.

graphics, computer   Generation and display by computer of pictorial representations of information.

graphics plotter   An output device for displaying graphics that is part of a visual display unit.

hard copy   Output printed on paper, in contrast to output displayed on the screen of a visual display terminal.

hardwire   Direct electrical communications (not via telephone lines) between terminals and the host computer. In contrast to dial-up.

hedge   A comprehensive collection of search terms pertaining to all facets of a specific subject. Usually developed by an individual through experience in searching the subject. Hedges may be distributed informally or published, or made available as computerized files accessible to others.

help message   A message from the computer in response to the user's request for help. May be contextual (provide information specific to the immediate situation) or addressable (provide information on a requested topic at any point during the session).

heuristic   An aid to problem solving that is likely, but not guaranteed, to lead to success. Often referred to as a "rule of thumb."

hierarchical classification of controlled vocabulary   A conceptual arrangement of subject terms according to a specified system of rankings, usually as tree-like structures with the most general concepts at the top leading down to more specific concepts. May refer to the classification of the complete vocabulary or of a segment.

hierarchical display of controlled vocabulary   Display of a hierarchical classification. May be tree-like or incorporated into an alphabetic display using the subdivisions "Narrower Term," for more general concepts, and "Broader Term," for more specific concepts. Examples of hierarchical displays are provided in Chapter 8.

hierarchical searching of controlled vocabulary   Searching a hierarchical classification as a union of search terms corresponding to the terms in the classification, usually employing right-handed truncation.

host computer   A computer operated by a retrieval service.

index   A collection of search key values and associated locations of records that correspond to these values. Usually includes a running count of the number of records associated with each search key value.

index modification   Automatic modification of an index to reflect file maintenance or file updating.

index regeneration   Automatic generation of a totally new index to reflect file maintenance or file updating.

index searching   Matching search terms against search key values in the index, in contrast to sequential searching.

indexed field   A field whose values are used for generating the search key values in the index. See also **keyword.**

indexing, computer   Automatic generation of the index (search key values) according to categories of information designated by search keys.

indexing, intellectual   See **subject indexing, intellectual.**

indexing, intelligent computer   See **artificial intelligence.**

individual record maintenance   File maintenance that entails modifying records individually.

inferencing   Using knowledge in a knowledge base for drawing conclusions based on certain premises.

information storage and retrieval   Computerized techniques for managing (storing, maintaining, and updating) and retrieving records.

input   Information transmitted into the computer from a device operated by a person or from a medium that can be read by the computer.

input date   See **entry date.**

input device   A device, such as a keyboard or pointing device, used by a person for transmitting input to the computer.

intelligent computer indexing   See **artificial intelligence.**

intelligent computer retrieval   See **artificial intelligence.**

interactive mode   A method of operation in which the user is in direct communication with the computer and gets an immediate response from the computer after entering each message.

intermediary user   An individual who interacts with retrieval services on behalf of end-users.

intersection of search terms   A logical relationship that would result in a positive retrieval only if both search terms were successfully matched against a set of records.

inverted file   A file organized as an index according to selected search keys.

keyword   The value, usually a word or phrase, of an indexed field that becomes a search key value when the record is indexed by the computer. Keywords may originate from the content of the document or by way of intellectual subject indexing.

keyword in context (KWIC) index to controlled vocabulary   A display, sorted by words extracted from subject terms, in which an entry consists of the complete subject term. An example of a KWIC index is provided in Chapter 8.

keyword out of context (KWOC) index to controlled vocabulary   A display, sorted by words extracted from subject terms, in which an entry consists of the word as a heading followed by the complete subject terms containing that word. An example of a KWOC index is provided in Chapter 8.

knowledge base   Domain knowledge (knowledge about a subject) and inferencing rules for applying that knowledge, represented in the computer as part of a system that utilizes artificial intelligence techniques.

KWIC   Acronym for keyword in context. See **keyword in context (KWIC) index to controlled vocabulary.**

KWOC   Acronym for keyword out of context. See **keyword out of context (KWOC) index to controlled vocabulary.**

logical operator   A word or symbol that represents a logical relationship between two propositions. Used for specifying logical relationships between search terms. The basic logical operators are AND (intersection), OR (union), and NOT (complement). See also **intersection of search terms, union of search terms,** and **complement of search term.**

logoff   A procedure for terminating a session for interacting with the host computer that requires logging back on in order to initiate a new session.

logon   A procedure for initiating a session for interacting with the host computer that requires authorized identification of the user to the computer.

**mainframe   A high-speed computer having a large memory capacity. Usually used
computer**   where large volumes of information are processed, such as large corporations, universities, or government agencies.

master file   A file of permanent information that is usually updated periodically.

menu   A type of prompting message consisting of a computer-generated display of options, perhaps accompanied by explanations, which can be selected by the user to perform different functions. Options may include commands, command specifications, or search terms.

microcomputer   A small affordable computer that will satisfy an individual's personal computing needs. May be used as a terminal for retrieving information from databases provided by retrieval services.

minicomputer   A small to medium-size computer that can process several programs concurrently.

mnemonic   Easy to remember. Refers to a desirable characteristic for terms used in command languages and computer displays.

modem   A device that connects terminals with telecommunications lines for accessing host computers. Interconverts digital signals, transmitted and received by terminals and host computers, and audible signals (tones), transmitted over communications lines.

natural language query input (nonsemantic processing)
Computer processing that allows a person to enter search queries into the computer in the same language the person uses when interacting with another person. Does not involve natural language understanding based on semantics (meanings of words and relationships), but is based on treating words in the query as search terms, and applying rules for matching these terms against the index and for logically combining the search key values selected as a result of the match.

natural language query processing
Computer processing that allows a person to enter search queries into the computer in the same language the person uses when interacting with another person. Involves natural language understanding based on semantics (meanings of words and relationships), which requires accessing a knowledge base and applying rules for inferencing.

nesting of search statement
Embedding a search statement having logical operators within another search statement using parentheses to set off the embedded search statement.

network computer, telecommunications
A computer operated by a telecommunications network. A battery of network computers is able to combine messages of many users over a single circuit. See also **telecommunications network.**

noise
Retrieved items that are not relevant to the search query.

NOT logical operator
See **complement of search term.**

offline output
Hard copy output produced by a high-speed printer attached to the host computer as a result of an output instruction.

offline search
A search formulation processed as a batch process.

online public access catalog (OPAC)
A bibliographic database available for interactive computerized access to the complete bibliographic record of a library's holdings.

online search
A search formulation processed as a real time process.

OPAC
Acronym for **online public access catalog.**

optical disk   A rotating disk capable of storing massive amounts of information. Lasers are used for writing information on and reading information from the disk.

OR logical   See **union of search terms.**
operator

output   Information transmitted from the computer to a device operated by a person or to a medium that can be read by another computer.

output device   A device, such as a visual display unit or printer, used by a person for receiving output from the computer.

output   The portion of a command language a person uses for specifying the
instruction   format and degree of detail of output to be displayed or printed.

password   An authorizing unique identification code that users enter during log-on in order to access a retrieval service. Used by retrieval services for keeping track of user activity, primarily for assessing charges.

permuted index   A display sorted by words extracted from the subject terms. See also
to controlled   **keyword in context (KWIC) index to controlled vocabulary** and **key-**
subject indexing   **word out of context (KWOC) index to controlled vocabulary.**
terms

pointing device   An input device that allows users to enter commands into microcomputers using the hands or fingers but bypassing the keyboard.

positional   A word or symbol that represents the positional relationship between
operator   two search terms in a record. Includes operators for SAME-FIELD-AS, SAME-SENTENCE-AS, ADJACENT-TO, operators for specifying the maximum number of intervening words between two words, and operators for specifying a controlled indexing term/subdivider combination as a search term.

precision ratio   A measure of retrieval effectiveness expressed as follows:

$$\text{precision} = \frac{\text{number of relevant records in the retrieval set}}{\text{number of records in the retrieval set}}$$

See also **recall ratio.**

printer   An output device that converts information in character form into print on paper.

printer plotter   A printer that produces output as graphics as well as in character form.

prompting message   A message from the computer that invites the user to respond. May consist of a single word (such as USER) or symbol (such as ? or :), or a specific directive (such as ENTER AUTHOR'S LAST NAME or CONTINUE DISPLAY? (YES/NO)). See also **menu.**

proximity operator   See **positional operator.**

quick-and-dirty searching   An approach to search formulation based on employing a simple search strategy designed to easily and quickly produce a retrieval set containing records with a high degree of relevance to a query, and in which recall is knowingly sacrificed for precision, although even the degree of precision may not be great.

ranging (range searching)   Use of relational operators, such as LESS THAN, GREATER THAN, and FROM . . . TO . . . , for specifying a range of numeric values, such as dates or unique identifiers that are numeric record accession numbers.

real time process   A computer process for performing functions in immediate response to the entry of the message requesting the response.

recall ratio   A measure of retrieval effectiveness expressed as follows:

$$\text{recall} = \frac{\text{number of relevant records in the retrieval set}}{\text{number of relevant records in the database}}$$

See also **precision ratio.**

record   A collection of related information, treated as a unit. The basic unit of a file.

referral database   A database that points users to another source for complete information, in contrast to source database.

relational operator   A word or symbol that represents a mathematical relationship between two values. Includes EQUAL TO (=), LESS THAN (<), GREATER THAN (>), LESS THAN OR EQUAL TO (< =), GREATER THAN OR EQUAL TO (> =), EXCLUSIVE (not including the values) FROM . . . TO . . . , INCLUSIVE (including the values) FROM . . . TO . . . , and the complements of each of these, that is, NOT EQUAL TO(< >), NOT LESS THAN, NOT GREATER THAN, and so on.

repeat-word operator

A word or symbol that specifies intersection of a word with an identical word, or the positional relationship of a word with an identical word, but counting each word separately.

response time

The time needed by the computer for responding to messages from users.

restart

1. A user-invoked procedure that simulates logging off and immediately logging back on to the host computer for starting a new session but without requiring authorized identification of the user to the computer as is required with the actual logon procedure. 2. An option offered to users by the computer for resuming activity in a session, with the workspace having been saved, following an improper disconnect from the host computer.

retrieval

A process that includes searching a file according to one or more search statements, storage by the computer of addresses to records that match the search terms according to logical operators in the search statements, and display of records located by the stored addresses.

retrieval, intelligent computer

See **artificial intelligence.**

retrieval service

An organization that manages a number of databases in its computer (the host computer), and provides customers with the facility for retrieval from these databases.

retrieval set

The set of records selected and made available for display by the computer as a result of processing a search statement.

retrieval set result

See **search statement result.**

saved search

A search formulation stored in the computer and available for future execution. See also **execution of saved search.**

scope note

A brief statement of the intended usage of a subject term in a controlled indexing vocabulary.

scrolling

Moving text up and down or across a visual display unit for displaying text adjacent to the text on the current screen.

SDI

Acronym for **selective dissemination of information.**

SDI search	A saved search executed automatically against file updates according to saved output instructions.
search	A search statement, a search query, or a subsequent search query translation, which may be a search strategy or a search formulation.
search formulation	A translation of a search query into a set of search statements.
search key	A category of information in an index. A search key stands for information in a record.
search key value	Specific information that is an instance of a search key. Used for locating records with corresponding field values by having associated with it the addresses of the matching records.
search query	A statement of an information need that is usually not yet expressed in terms directly understood by the computer. When translated into a computer-readable format, it may correspond to any number of search statements (search formulation).
search session	See **session.**
search statement	A message to the computer entered at the terminal by the user of a retrieval system for specifying a single search term, or two or more search terms connected by logical operators.
search statement result	A count of the number of records in a retrieval set resulting from a search statement. See also **search term result.**
search strategy	An intermediate form between a search query and a search formulation, being more structured than a search query in terms of computer readability but not having the level of structure of a search formulation.
search term	A word, phrase, or other string of characters in a search statement that is matched against a set of records. May be matched against search key values in the index or directly against character strings in the record.
search term completion, automatic	Automatic completion of a search term, entered at the terminal, as soon as the computer recognizes that the portion of the term already entered is unique in the index.

search term result
A count of the number of records in a retrieval set resulting from a search statement consisting of a single search term. Counts for search terms that are search key values may be included in displays of the index to a file.

searching
A process including human entry of search statements into the computer followed by computerized matching of search terms against a file according to logical relationships in the search statements. See also **index searching, sequential searching,** and **stringsearching.**

selective dissemination of information (SDI)
A mechanism for regularly supplying a user of retrieval services with information relevant to a predefined information need. The computer stores the information need as a set of search statements (SDI search) and output instructions to be processed automatically against update files.

sequential searching
Matching search terms directly against the file, one record at a time, in contrast to index searching. See also **stringsearching.**

session
A period when a user is continuously connected to the host computer. It usually begins after logon, and ends with logoff, but there may also be a restart capability that simulates logging off and immediately logging back on to start a new session but without requiring authorized identification of the user to the computer.

sort key
1. The field or subfield by which a file or retrieval set display is sorted.
2. The search key by which an index is sorted.

source database
A database that contains complete information, in contrast to referral database.

split screen
A visual display unit screen that is divided into segments, each of which may be used for examining and interacting with a different file as displayed in the segment. See also **windowing.**

stopword
A word in textword-indexed fields that is ignored by the computer when the computer indexes the record. A stopword list includes common words that add little meaning to the subject matter being indexed.

stringsearching
Searching a set of records, usually a previous retrieval set, for a specified string of characters in a record. Stringsearching is a form of free text searching.

subdividing subject term

See **subject term, subdividing.**

subject indexing, coordinate

Assigning multiple subject terms for indexing a concept in a document. A search statement consisting of the intersection of these terms would retrieve the document.

subject indexing error, intellectual

An error involving misapplication of subject terms to documents during intellectual indexing.

subject indexing, intellectual

Assigning subject terms to a record for the purpose of augmenting the information provided directly by the item being indexed.

subject indexing policy

The official set of rules for assigning subject terms to documents.

subject term, assigned

A controlled subject term or free subject term assigned to records by intellectual subject indexing. It is entered into the record as a keyword, which then becomes a search key in the index when the record undergoes computer indexing.

subject term, subdividing

One of a relatively small set of subject terms in a controlled indexing vocabulary that qualify other subject terms according to recurring aspects of a subject.

telecommunications network

An organization whose facilities provide for the transmission of information over telecommunications lines between terminals and host computers. Networks employ special telephone lines together with a battery of small network computers that are able to combine messages of many users over a single circuit, and thereby use telephone lines more efficiently than ordinary (direct-dial) telephone communications.

terminal

A remote communications device used by a person for transmitting input to and receiving output from the computer. An output device component may include a visual display unit or printer, and an input device component may include a keyboard or pointing device.

terminal session

See **session.**

text editing

Use of an interactive computer program for creating, editing (deleting, inserting, copying, moving), displaying, and saving text in a computer file. Includes a capacity to locate individual character strings in the text.

textword   A word selected from a field as a search key value during computer indexing. Classified according to the field that is its source; for example, title textword as a textword from the title field. Searching textword search keys is a form of free text searching.

time sharing   The continuous allocation of successive slices of time to multiple simultaneous users of a computer, where switching from one user to another occurs at such high speeds that usually users cannot detect any reduction in response time.

tree classification of controlled vocabulary   See **hierarchical classification of controlled vocabulary.**

truncation of search term   A shorthand way for searching the union of search terms generated by entering a single search term whose ending characters are unspecified (right-handed truncation), or whose beginning characters are unspecified (left-handed truncation), or which has one or more unspecified middle characters (embedded truncation), where the unspecified characters are represented by a variable character symbol. See also **word stemming** and **hierarchical searching of controlled vocabulary.**

union of search terms   A logical relationship that would result in a positive retrieval if either or both search terms were successfully matched against a set of records.

universal set   A set consisting of all items in the set. The universal set may be used for representing all the records in a file.

up   Status of the computer as being in operation or of a computer program or database as being available for current use.

update file   A recently created file, reflecting new information, to be merged with a master file during file updating.

update file code A code automatically assigned each record in an update file, which identifies the record as belonging to the update file.

uploading   Electronic copying of search formulations or retrieval sets on local computer storage devices into the host computer for retrieval processing or further computer-based manipulation with possible subsequent downloading back into local storage.

user cue See **prompting message.**

user-friendly Requiring little physical or mental effort on the part of users, applied to human–computer interactions.

user profile A personal protected file established for retrieval service users for storing, displaying, and modifying the following types of information: security password; mailing address; screen or page parameters; database-specific output instruction defaults for displaying records; versions for system messages (terse vs. explanatory); aliases for system words such as command names; and option for displaying time and cost information.

validation Automatic checking of information in the computer against acceptable values, as determined by whether candidate values match authorized forms or are within specified numeric limits, or by applying rules that specify conditions for acceptable values.

variable character symbol A symbol that stands for any number of unspecified characters. The variable character symbol is used in the truncation of search terms.

VDT Acronym for **visual display terminal.**

VDU Acronym for **visual display unit.**

vendor See **retrieval service.**

Venn diagram A graphic representation of the universal set and subsets. Used for representing sets of records in a file according to how they are indexed, or for representing concepts in a search strategy.

videodisk, optical See **optical disk.**

visual display terminal (VDT) A terminal consisting of a visual display unit, with a keyboard or other input device.

visual display unit (VDU) A device for receiving output from the computer in character form and incorporating a cathode ray tube (CRT), which provides a screen on which information is displayed. May incorporate a graphics plotter for receiving output as graphics. A component of a visual display terminal when connected to a keyboard or other input device.

weighting of search term   Applying a symbol to a search term as an indicator of importance causing the search term to match against search key values qualified or categorized as representing important concepts in the documents they index.

windowing   Division of the visual display unit screen into segments, called windows, each of which may be used for examining and interacting with a different file as displayed in the window.

word completion   See **search term completion, automatic.**

word stemming   Applying a set of rules that strip words in search statements of their suffixes and substitute for each resulting root form the union of all forms of the word in the index.

workspace   A location in the computer reserved for storing information, such as search statements and addresses of records corresponding to retrieval sets, available for processing during the session; usually temporary, that is, automatically emptied when the session is terminated.

Index

Definitions are found in the Glossary (pp. 349–68), which is not indexed here. Criteria for selecting a retrieval service (in Chapter 16, pp. 227–42) are not indexed individually, but they are named in the display margin in the text.